Subnet Design for Efficient Networks

About the Author

The author is a Microsoft Certified Systems Engineer specialising in TCP/IP, IIS and SQL server. For the last 25 years he has been an independent consultant and lecturer working throughout the IT industry. As a result he has trained many thousands of industrial and commercial staff over that period. Currently, he divides his time between lecturing, consultancy and research work. He lives in the UK and travels worldwide for both business and pleasure. His client list includes many "blue-chip" companies together with government and international organisations.

Subnet Design for Efficient Networks

Keith Sutherland

OXFORD AUCKLAND BOSTON JOHANNESBURG MELBOURNE NEW DELHI

Butterworth-Heinemann
Linacre House, Jordan Hill, Oxford OX2 8DP
225 Wildwood Avenue, Woburn, MA 1801–2041
A division of Reed Educational and Professional Publishing Ltd

A member of the Reed Elsevier plc group

First published 2000

British Library Cataloguing in Publication Data
A catalogue record for this book is available from the British Library.

ISBN 07506 4465 6

Designed and typeset by ReadyText, Bath, UK
Printed and bound in Great Britain.

PLANT A TREE
BTCV
British Trust for Conservation Volunteers
FOR EVERY TITLE THAT WE PUBLISH, BUTTERWORTH-HEINEMANN WILL PAY FOR BTCV TO PLANT AND CARE FOR A TREE.

Contents

Acknowledgements

My thanks to Mike Cash for his enthusiastic support of this book and also to the staff at *Butterworth-Heinemann* for their assistance. My undying gratitude to my wife for her loyal and often bemused encouragement over the "long nights" and also to *Learning Tree International* for providing the best training courses on the planet. Graham Douglas, of *ReadyText Publishing Services*, did sterling work turning the unstructured chaos of my diagrams into clear illustrations of the principles they were meant to convey. His insightful comments assisted the clarification of some of the more difficult passages. Without his help the book would have been much less effective. The sample questions at the end of the book were inspired by the *BeachFront Quizzer* exam preparation system. If you are planning to take the MCSE exams I thoroughly recommend it.

Further information on Learning Tree and Beachfront can be obtained from

http://www.learningtree.com

and

http://www.bfq.com

respectively. Thanks to you all.

About this book

The Internet continues to grow at a very rapid rate. Together with this growth there is an accompanying growth of the technologies on which it is based. These technologies make use of TCP/IP as their networking protocols. To use TCP/IP efficiently and reliably, networks that are based on these protocols must be designed, installed and maintained in as effective a way as possible. Underpinning all of these ideas is the principle of subnet design. This book takes the principles on which subnet design is based and develops them to fully explain the fundamental design concepts on which modern TCP/IP networks depend.

This book is aimed at both the network professional and the enthusiastic network user. It explains how subnets work and the rationale behind their design and implementation. Through graded examples it guides the user from simple network issues and the associated calculation of the relevant subnet masks through to larger enterprise-level considerations for subnet designs.

1

Binary Numbers

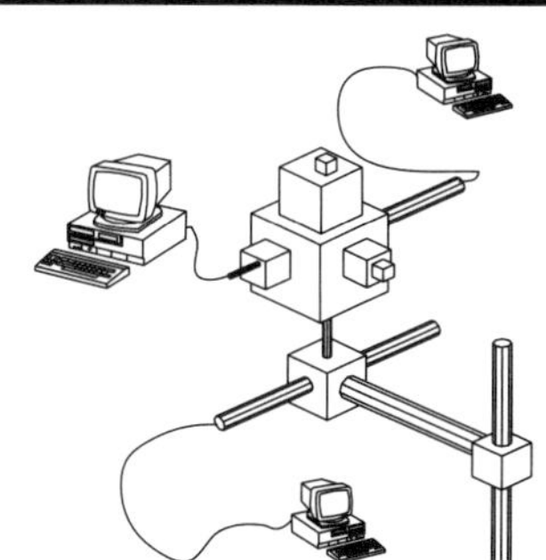

Why Learn Binary Numbers?

This book is all about creating Internet Protocol (IP) subnets. All IP networks are based on networks of computers each of which has an IP address. These IP addresses are often written in the form 10.2.4.5 or 143.123.111.122. This is referred to as "dotted decimal" notation. Unfortunately, computers do not directly recognise these numbers. What they see are the underlying binary values that these dotted decimals represent. The dotted decimal notation is an easier way for the underlying 32-bit binary addresses to be represented to the "general world". One of our initial tasks is to get a good grasp of how these two number systems relate to each other. Once we have done this many of the more advanced topics will fall into place more easily. To help us in this task we will need a reasonable working knowledge of binary numbers and the conversion between binary and decimal (base ten) numbers.

One of the problems with the computer world is that the machines themselves are based on binary switches which do not lend themselves to our "normal" or "human" calculation methods. By and large we use number systems based on ten. Let us look at what this means.

If we have three objects we have a simple representation for them, the symbol "3". If we have nine objects we have another unique representation for them, the symbol "9".

Once we have more than ten objects in our group we no longer have a unique representation. For these we use what is called "positional notation". This is familiar to most of us as our junior school "units, tens and thousands".

To represent fifteen objects we use the symbol 15 which means (one lot of ten and five lots of one). Similarly, four hundred and fifteen objects would be written 415 (four lots of one hundred, one lot of ten and five lots of one).

If we were to analyse what the positions of these numbers meant we would see something like the following:

Thousands	Hundreds	Tens	Ones
10^3	10^2	10^1	10^0

In this example 10^2 means 10 multiplied by 10 or "ten squared". So to represent "five thousand three hundred and fifty two" we would write 5352. We would interpret this as five thousands (five lots of 10^3) together with three hundreds (three lots of 10^2) together with five tens (five lots of 10^1) together with two ones (two lots of 10^0). Why does 10^0 represent 1? The answer to this is simply convention (there are actually good mathematical reasons for this as well). Put simply: any number raised to the power of 0 is taken to represent 1, so that 10^0, 4^0, 189^0 and 2^0 all represent the number 1.

So why is all this so important? The way in which we represent numbers is of fundamental importance to how we view, represent, model and deal with the world. One of the problems with many of the earlier forms of numbers was that they were limited to counting or tallying systems. This is ideal for keeping goats or sacks of corn but not too good for implementing technology or science. Some of the most fundamental principles in this area have come from various cultures throughout history. Some of the, initially, most important are those produced by Babylonians (basic time, area calculation and geometry); Hindus (additional geometry and the concept of zero) and Greeks (advanced geometry, number series). These fundamental "building blocks" were developed by subsequent generations of mathematicians, scientists and technologists who have allowed us to produce the many scientific and technological miracles of the modern world.

So here we are with a rich and diverse number system with all the associated "goodies" derived from it. After 5000 years of human development someone then invents "the computer". This has only two states as far as its number system goes. (Remember, the original computers were based on electro-mechanical switching systems in which all data were represented by these switches). Today, these switches are usually implemented in electronic form and the large "clunking" relays are a thing of the past. The principle, however, remains the same. Data are represented as a series of 1's and 0's which represent "on" (1) and "off" (0) in the older relay sense.

How can we combine the "human" number system with a computer-based number system? Of more relevance to our discussion of sub-nets and networks generally is how can we convert an IP address 10.11.12.14 into a form that the computer will use (a binary address). Remember, this binary address is all that the electronics will recognise. It will be the means whereby all data carried on the wires will be recognised by other parts of the network. All network cards, routers and other sub-systems will use this binary address to decide how to handle the associated data. Let us look at this in more detail.

Decomposition

We have the following numbers: 3, 7, 12, 23, 127 and 253 and want to represent them in binary. How can we do this? The answer lies in using positional notation. In the same way that our ordinary number systems used 10 as a basis (referred to as base 10) and we had the various "powers of ten" giving us the values of our number positions so we can do the same with binary or base 2.

Base ten

Value represented	*Actual representation*	*Power used*
Units	1	10^0
Tens	10	10^1
Hundreds	10×10	10^2
Thousands	$10 \times 10 \times 10$	10^3
Tenthousands	$10 \times 10 \times 10 \times 10$	10^4
etc.		

Binary

Value represented	*Actual representation*	*Power used*
Units	1	2^0
Two	2	2^1
Four	2×2	2^2
Eight	$2 \times 2 \times 2$	2^3
Sixteen	$2 \times 2 \times 2 \times 2$	2^4
Thirty-two	$2 \times 2 \times 2 \times 2 \times 2$	2^5
etc.		

Using the above we can create a binary table and use this to give us the binary representation of our numbers.

Figure 1.1 Diagram of binary patterns and the corresponding bit positions

Notation

There is potential for confusion when discussing numbers expressed in different bases. Does "111" represent the base 10 number "one hundred and eleven" or the bit pattern of a binary number? In the examples that follow, we'll show the base in which a particular number is expressed by the use of a subscript. For example, to distinguish between 111 in base 10 and 111 in base 2 we'll write

- 111_{10} to refer to the base 10 number "one hundred and eleven"
- 111_2 to refer to a number expressed in base 2.

By way of examples we will convert the following base 10 numbers to binary: 3_{10}, 7_{10}, 12_{10}, and 127_{10}.

Our binary (base 2) "power table" looks like this:

Power of 2	2^7	2^6	2^5	2^4	2^3	2^2	2^1	2^0
Base 10 equivalent	128	64	32	16	8	4	2	1

We will use this table to calculate the bit values representing our "ordinary" or base 10 numbers.

Examples

For example, we could represent 3_{10} as 11_2 (from the right-hand side of the table) because 3_{10} is made up from $2_{10} + 1_{10}$. This process of breaking up a larger number into smaller "fragments" or "chunks" is called *decomposition*.

7_{10} can be written as $(1 \times 4) + (1 \times 2) + (1 \times 1)$ but by using $4 = 2^2$, $2 = 2^1$ and $1 = 2^0$ we may write

$$7_{10} = (1 \times 2^2) + (1 \times 2^1) + (1 \times 2^0)$$

which gives the binary equivalent of 7_{10} as 111, i.e. $7_{10} = 111_2$.

12_{10} can be written as:

$$\begin{aligned} 12_{10} &= (1 \times 8) + (1 \times 4) + (0 \times 2) + (0 \times 1) \\ &= (1 \times 2^3) + (1 \times 2^2) + (0 \times 2^1) + (0 \times 2^0) \end{aligned}$$

which gives the binary equivalent of 12_{10} as 1100, i.e. $12_{10} = 1100_2$.

127_{10} can be written as:

$$127_{10} = (1 \times 64) + (1 \times 32) + (1 \times 16) + (1 \times 8) + (1 \times 4) + (1 \times 2) + (1 \times 1)$$
$$= (1 \times 2^6) + (1 \times 2^5) + (1 \times 2^4) + (1 \times 2^3) + (1 \times 2^2) + (1 \times 2^1) + (1 \times 2^0)$$

giving $127_{10} = 1111111_2$.

We now summarise the binary patterns for these, and a few other, numbers:

Power of 2	2^7	2^6	2^5	2^4	2^3	2^2	2^1	2^0
Decimal value	128	64	32	16	8	4	2	1
3_{10}							1	1
7_{10}						1	1	1
12_{10}					1	1	0	0
23_{10}				1	0	1	1	1
127_{10}		1	1	1	1	1	1	1
253_{10}	1	1	1	1	1	1	0	1

Our numbers — The corresponding bit patterns

As Figure 1.1 shows we can represent all of our list of numbers as binary patterns. When looking at this table remember that we have to add trailing zeroes to keep the positional notation correct so our binary representation of 12_{10} (1100_2) needs to have the zeroes at the end or it would simply represent the number 3. In all cases the binary patterns can be established by the decomposition of the original number, so 23_{10} becomes $16_{10} + 4_{10} + 2_{10} + 1_{10}$ and so on. So now we have a way or representing our ordinary (decimal or base 10) numbers as binary.

Numbers on a Network

When we come to transmit this data across a network things have to be a little more ordered than is suggested by our simple illustration. If we look back to the tables in Figure 1.1 we see that the sizes (number of bits used to represent the number) vary. So the number 7 in binary uses three bits but the number 127 uses seven bits. On a network this variably-sized block of data would cause chaos. We have to impose some order and the commonest way of doing this is to fix the number of bits in any given block of data. The typical values are 8, 16, 32 and 64 bits (other values are used but these are the most common).

To keep our data consistent with the requirement of "regular blocks" of data we will "pad" the binary with *trailing* 0's and *leading* 0's. For the sake of simplicity we will do this using an 8-bit block. This is a good choice because it will assist in the clarification of our IP address to binary conversion. Figure 1.2 summarises the principle.

Figure 1.2 Binary representation

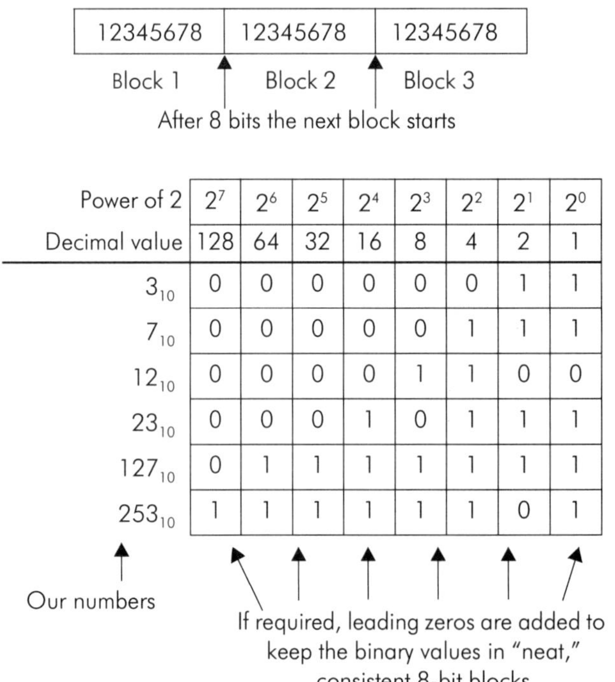

Power of 2	2^7	2^6	2^5	2^4	2^3	2^2	2^1	2^0
Decimal value	128	64	32	16	8	4	2	1
3_{10}	0	0	0	0	0	0	1	1
7_{10}	0	0	0	0	0	1	1	1
12_{10}	0	0	0	0	1	1	0	0
23_{10}	0	0	0	1	0	1	1	1
127_{10}	0	1	1	1	1	1	1	1
253_{10}	1	1	1	1	1	1	0	1

So, using this 8-bit block method what is the largest number that can be represented? Using the decomposition method this would be 128_{10} + 64_{10} + 32_{10} + 16_{10} + 8_{10} + 4_{10} + 2_{10} + 1_{10} which gives us 255_{10}! Does this look familiar? It should do! On almost all modern TCP/IP systems this value has a special predefined meaning. Using all 1's in an octet represents the value 255_{10}. Figure 1.3 shows this.

Figure 1.3 The "255" bit pattern

Power of 2	2^7	2^6	2^5	2^4	2^3	2^2	2^1	2^0
Decimal value	128	64	32	16	8	4	2	1
Number 255_{10}	1	1	1	1	1	1	1	1

255_{10} is, by decomposition, $128_{10} + 64_{10} + 32_{10} + 16_{10} + 8_{10} + 4_{10} + 2_{10} + 1_{10}$ which corresponds to a bit pattern of "all 1's".

On most network systems the value of 255_{10} (when used as the host component of an IP address) represents a broadcast address. So an address of 145.111.255.255 says that this is a broadcast address for all machines on the 145.111.0.0 network. What is a broadcast address? Put simply: it is an address that would reach all of the machines (hosts) on our local network. Broadcast addresses are used extensively in certain situations throughout the IP world. In addition to the broadcast address 255_{10} is also used to represent a subnet mask component where all eight bits of an octet are being used. There will be more on these two topics throughout the book.

We are now in a position to illustrate a number of IP addresses and their corresponding binary representations. Figure 1.4 illustrates different IP addresses and their corresponding binary representations.

Figure 1.4 Bit pattern of an IP address

IP address
10.12.13.117

Power of 2	2^7	2^6	2^5	2^4	2^3	2^2	2^1	2^0
Decimal value	128	64	32	16	8	4	2	1
10_{10}	0	0	0	0	1	0	1	0
12_{10}	0	0	0	0	1	1	0	0
13_{10}	0	0	0	0	1	1	0	1
117_{10}	0	1	1	1	0	1	0	1

In all four cases above, decomposition has been used so 10_{10} is shown as $8_{10} + 2_{10}$ and 12_{10} is $8_{10} + 4_{10}$ etc. The full binary address corresponding to 10.12.13.117 is:

00001010	00001100	00001101	01110101
10	12	13	117

Now you can see why "dotted decimal" is easier!

IP address 145.113.12.17

Power of 2	2^7	2^6	2^5	2^4	2^3	2^2	2^1	2^0
Decimal value	128	64	32	16	8	4	2	1
145_{10}	1	0	0	1	0	0	0	1
113_{10}	0	1	1	1	0	0	0	1
12_{10}	0	0	0	0	1	1	0	0
17_{10}	0	0	0	1	0	0	0	1

Again, decomposition has been used to get each of the bit patterns. The full binary address corresponding to 145.113.12.17 is

10010001	01110001	00001100	00010001
145	113	12	17

IP address 192.173.221.141

Power of 2	2^7	2^6	2^5	2^4	2^3	2^2	2^1	2^0
Decimal value	128	64	32	16	8	4	2	1
192_{10}	1	1	0	0	0	0	0	0
173_{10}	1	0	1	0	1	1	0	1
221_{10}	1	1	0	1	1	1	0	1
141_{10}	1	0	0	0	1	1	0	1

The full binary address corresponding to 192.173.221.141 is

11000000	10101101	11011101	10001101
192	173	221	141

In each case the binary patterns have been calculated in the same way as before (decomposition and positional notation).

From this last series of diagrams it should now be clear that each computer (or other equipment) that has a dotted decimal IP address actually has a 32-bit binary address attached to it. It is this 32-bit binary address that is used in all of the identification and calculations that we will look at during the following chapters. The dotted decimal notation is simply a way of making this 32-bit value more accessible for us humans!

2

Address Classes

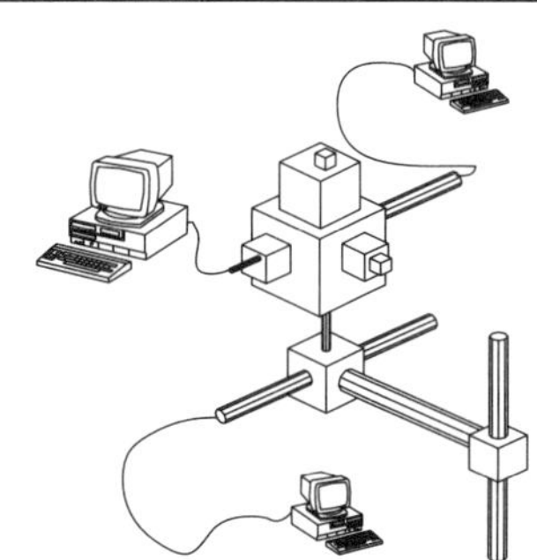

Introduction

When the Internet was in its infancy the people who were in charge of designing and implementing much of the technology wanted to ease the management of the various networks and organisations that were making use of the system. Nowadays this group is referred to as the IAB (Internet Activities Board). Their role is to look after future use, and experimentation with, new technologies and ideas.

One of the things they did to assist in the management of networks was to divide the IP addresses into various classes. This was to allow organisations that required large networks to be able to obtain a certain type of address while smaller organisations could apply for and obtain a type of address more suitable in size for their network.

With true "wisdom in hindsight" this was the wrong decision. Ten, or more, years ago no-one could have foreseen the explosive growth in the popularity of the Internet. The division of addresses into various classes has introduced some serious limitations into the way in which networks can be assigned and combined together. Various new methods of dealing with these problems have recently been introduced. We will cover some of them in later chapters.

What Exactly are our Classes?

There are five address classes defined by the IAB. They are classes A, B, C, D and E. Of these classes, D and E are not generally assigned to host computers. Class D is designated for multicast activities – which is a way of combining groups of networks together for sending data like video or audio to a large group of users. Class E is reserved for experimental purposes so as to allow the developers of Internet technologies to try out these technologies without affecting the existing systems.

We will concentrate our discussions and all of our examples to the three main classes: A, B and C. As we have seen, these address classes were introduced to assist in the management of the IP networks that were around at the time.

In Chapter 1 we saw that the IP address corresponds to a 32-bit binary address. This address is used to identify each and every computer (or other equipment) on our network. In actual fact the 32-bit address contains two pieces of information:

1. one part of the address contains information about the network that the computer is on;
2. the other part contains information to identify the actual computer on the network.

Often, this division of network identification (or NetID) and host identification (or HostID) is set on a specific 8-bit (octet) boundary. This does not have to be the case as we will see in later chapters. Figure 2.1 illustrates the basics of this principle.

In this figure we use two IP addresses to illustrate the principle of NetIDs and HostIDs. In this we use the IP addresses 11.12.13.1 and 11.100.13.27 to represent our two "machines". If we decide to use the first eight bits in any address to represent the network then the two IP addresses above both have the same value (11 in decimal or 00001011 in binary). Since the first eight bits identify the network and our two addresses have the same first eight bits we are confident that they are on the same network!

Why is this important? Simply because it is the basis upon which routing decisions are made. Using the NetID allows one computer to decide whether another computer (in a communication) is on the same network (is a local machine) or is on a remote network (and therefore the data needs to be routed).

We will study this in detail in the next chapter.

Figure 2.1 Distinguishing networks (1)

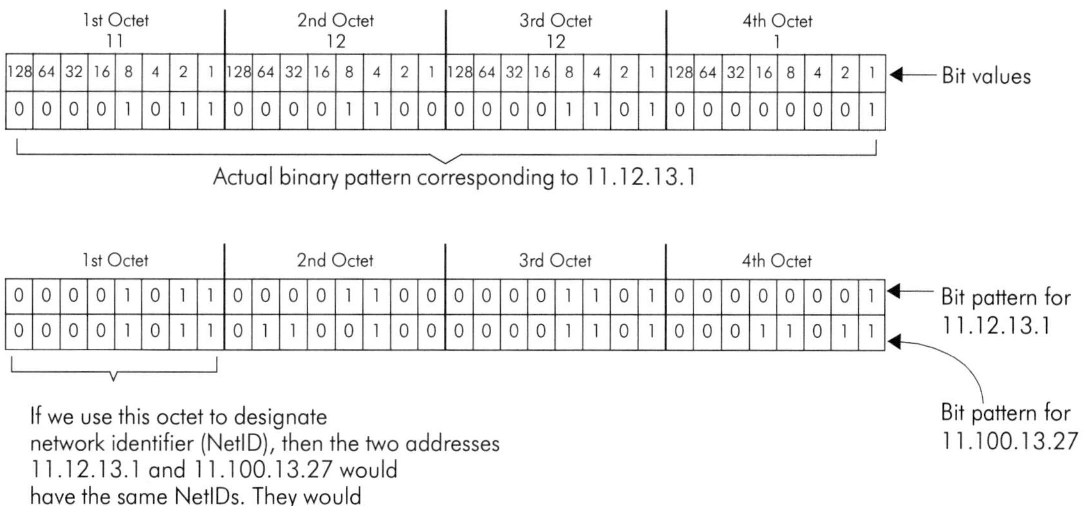

Figure 2.2 Distinguishing networks (2)

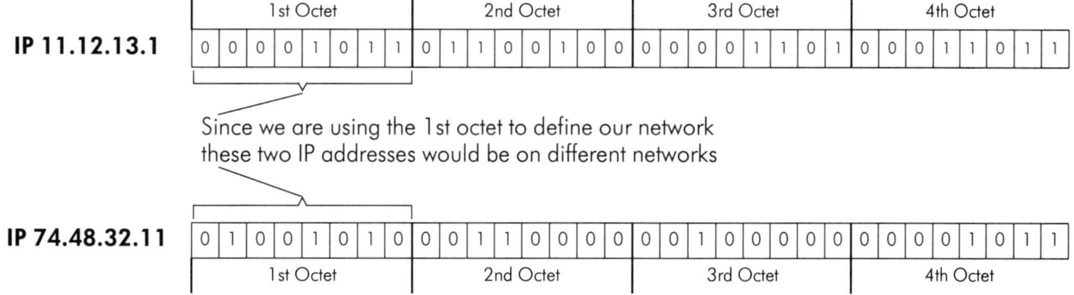

Who decides how many bits are going to be used for the NetID/HostID? The initial choice was arbitrary and was based on octet divisions. Nowadays, with variable-length subnet masks and other goodies it is left largely up to the individual network designer.

Figure 2.2 shows the same principle but with two IP addresses with different NetIDs. If we use the arbitrary rule that we are using the first octet to represent our network, how do we interpret the value of the remainder of the IP address?

Figure 2.3 shows this using four IP addresses: 11.0.0.1, 11.0.0.2, 11.0.0.27 and 11.100.0.21. The first address 11.0.0.1 would be interpreted as "machine number 1 on the 11 network". The second address would be interpreted as "machine number 2 on the 11 network" and the third address 11.0.0.27 would be "machine 27 on the 11 network". The last address is there for you to work out!

Figure 2.3 Machine identification

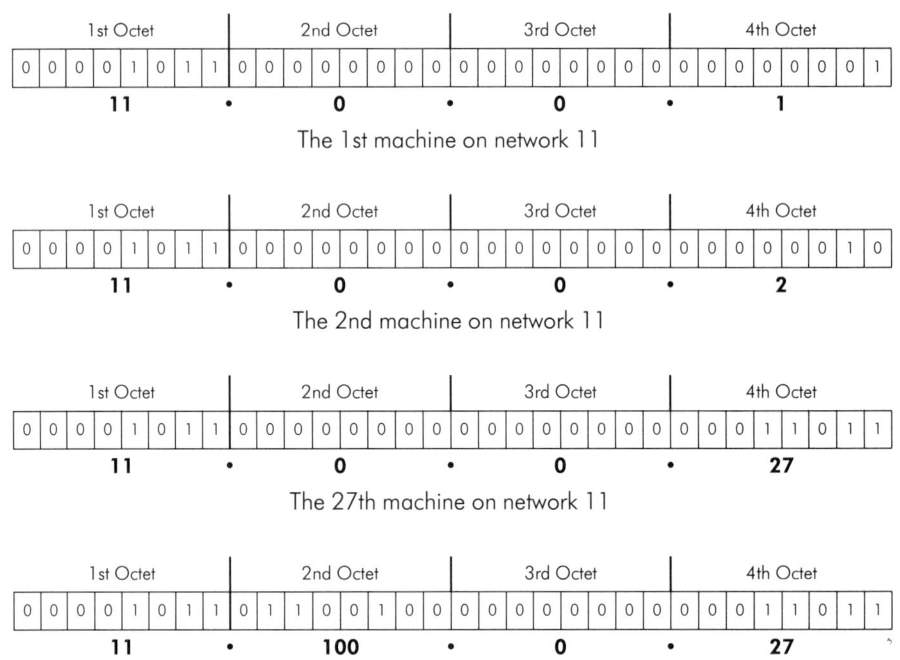

Which machine is this? Answer...count from the right! It is a very large number.

So what decisions were taken to divide-up the NetID and HostID boundaries? They are illustrated in Figure 2.4.

Host Boundaries

When looking at the figure note that (roughly) class A addresses use the first octet for the NetID. Class B addresses use the first two octets for the NetID and class C addresses use the first three octets for the NetID. This is not the whole story since certain initial bits are defined for each of the classes as shown in Figure 2.4.

Figure 2.4 Initial bit patterns

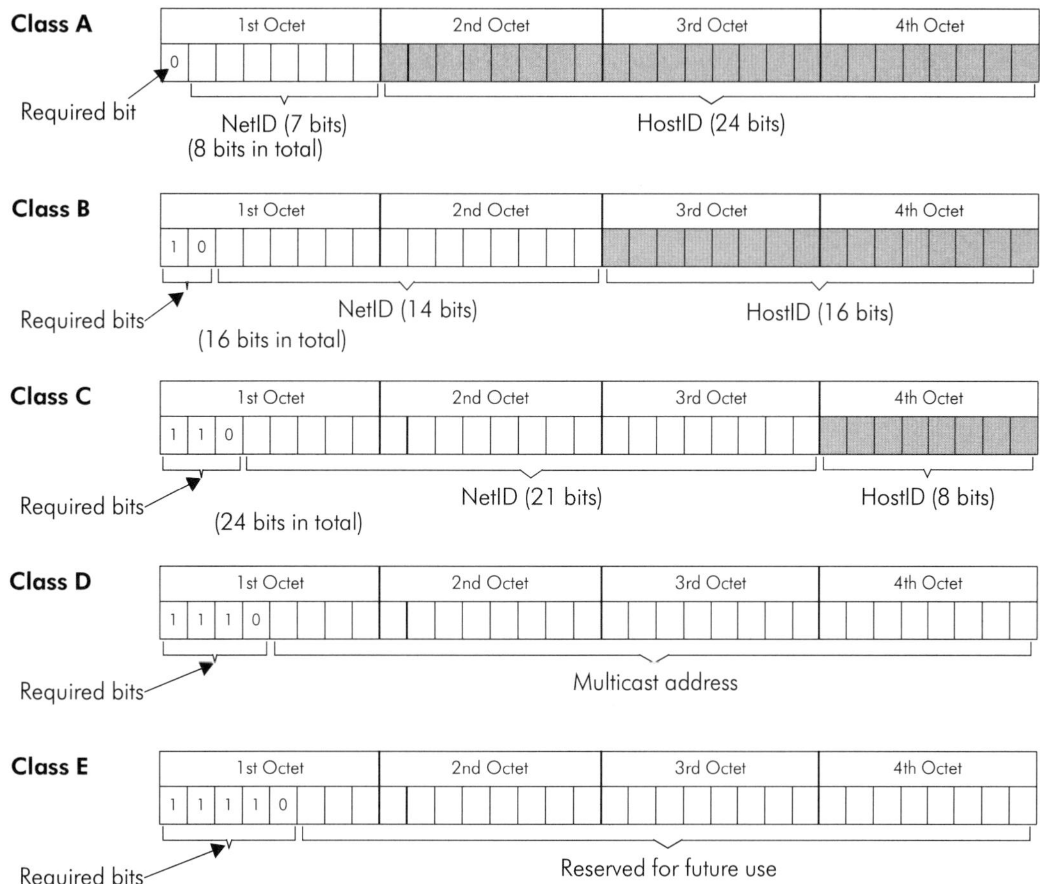

With these initial bit patterns set for each of the address ranges it means that there are strict limits on the IP addresses for each of the machines in each of the ranges. As an example, a machine with an address starting with 10.x.y.z can only be a class A address since the value 10 has the binary value 00001010 in the first octet. This corresponds to the rule that class A addresses must start with a 0 as the first bit and this rules out networks starting with 10 as belonging to any of the other classes.

Similarly, with class B addresses having (by definition) to start with the bit pattern 10 this restricts the class B addresses to the range 128 through to 191. By the same argument class C addresses start with the pattern 110 and have a range of addresses commencing with 192 through to 223.

Figure 2.4 also shows that with class A networks there are seven bits (excluding the compulsory first bit) which can be used to identify networks. This gives a total network identification of eight bits. The remaining 24 bits can all be used to identify hosts on each of the networks. As such, there tend to be few class A networks but each network can have many millions of hosts.

Class B networks have 14 bits uniquely identifying the network identifier (NetID). Including the initial 2 fixed bits gives 16 bits in total. They have 16 bits identifying the hosts on each of these networks. Class C networks have 21 bits uniquely identifying the NetID. Including the initial 3 fixed bits makes a total of 24 bits to define the network and 8 bits identifying the hosts on each of these networks. There are many class C networks but only 254 hosts on each one.

Before we go into this in detail let us consider the rules that govern the allocation of network addresses:

1. All class A addresses start with a 0 as the leftmost bit.
2. For class A addresses the value 127 is defined as the loopback address and cannot, therefore, be used as a network address.
3. All class B addresses start with the bit pattern 10.
4. All class C addresses start with the bit pattern 110.
5. All class D (multicast addresses) start with the bit pattern 1110.
6. All class E (reserved addresses) start with the bit pattern 11110.
7. You cannot have all 1's in the host component of an address since this is defined as a "broadcast to all hosts on a network" address.
8. You cannot have all 0's in the host component of an address since this is defined as "the current network".

Most of these rules are straightforward. One or two need some clarification. Rule 2 defines the loopback address as 127. Any data written to a network that starts with the number 127 will not actually be sent out on the wire but will be written to the output buffer of the network card and then read in from the input buffer of the same card. In this way different network tests may be carried out to check the integrity of any programs that are being developed without compromising the network itself.

At first glance the above rules seem OK. If we look at it more closely we will see that under these rules a whole class A network has been utilised for the testing of development software. We will look at the implications of this a little later.

Rule 7 defines a broadcast address. If we have a class A network (say it starts with 10) then a broadcast on that network would be 10.255.255.255. In bit terms this would be the network identifier followed by all 1's. Similarly, by definition of rule 8, the network identifier is 10.0.0.0. We will discuss these in more detail when we consider routing.

With our rules and our initial bit patterns for each of our classes we are in a position to look at the types of networks and the ranges we can have in each of our different classes. Figure 2.5 shows this in detail.

Figure 2.5 Address ranges

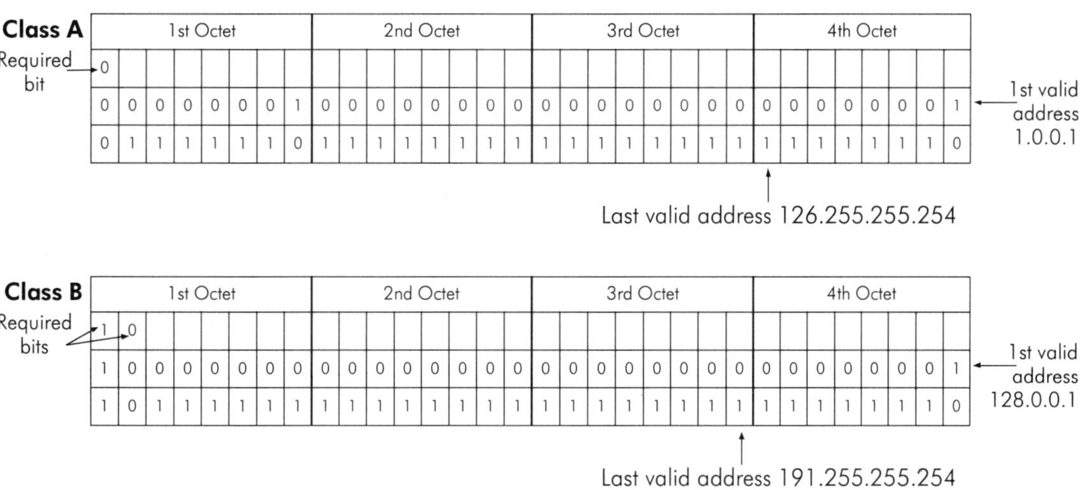

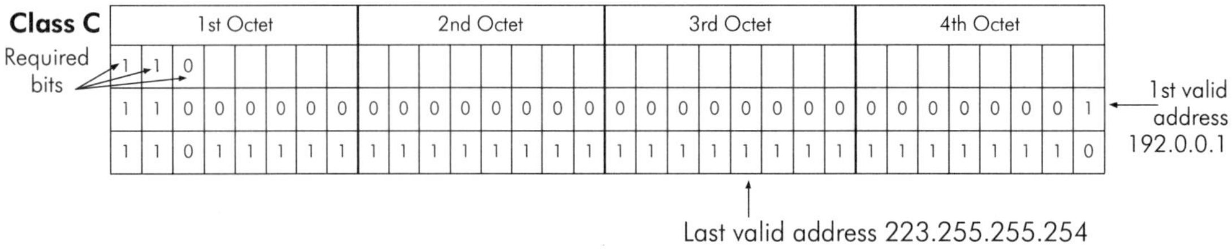

Class C

	1st Octet	2nd Octet	3rd Octet	4th Octet	
Required bits	1 1 0				
	1 1 0 0 0 0 0 0	0 0 0 0 0 0 0 0	0 0 0 0 0 0 0 0	0 0 0 0 0 0 0 1	1st valid address 192.0.0.1
	1 1 0 1 1 1 1 1	1 1 1 1 1 1 1 1	1 1 1 1 1 1 1 1	1 1 1 1 1 1 1 0	

Last valid address 223.255.255.254

With Figure 2.5 we can see that the following address ranges apply:

Class	First	Last
A	1.0.0.1	126.255.255.254
B	128.0.0.1	191.255.255.254
C	192.0.0.1	223.255.255.254

Following on from this argument we can see that the class D address range starts with 224 and class E address ranges starts at 240.

How do we get the above numbers? This frequently causes some confusion. Let us take a couple of examples to illustrate the principle.

Class A, First Address

We have as a starting point the fact that the network component cannot be all 0's and cannot be all 1's. Similarly for the host component. Also, any class A address has to begin with a 0 as the first bit.

We can use the remaining seven bits in the first octet as our network designator. The first acceptable bit pattern is 00000001 since this meets all of the above requirements. If we were to use 1.0.0.0 this would designate a network address *not* a host address since all 0's in the host component constitute a network identifier (NetID). So the first available host address is 1.0.0.1 which meets all of our requirements:

1. Bit pattern must start with a 0 (class A).
2. HostID cannot be all 1's or all 0's.
3. NetID cannot be all 0's or all 1's.

Using our set of rules for the last address in the class A range we see that we could use 01111111 as our network identifier (NetID). This meets the class A requirements (must start with a 0) and the requirement that the network identifier cannot contain all 1's or all 0's. *However*, the bit pattern 01111111 represents the value 127 and this is predefined as the loopback address and so cannot be used! The next lowest value is the bit pattern 01111110 (126) which is the first octet value of the last valid IP address in the range.

So our last valid class A address is 126.255.255.254 – why 254 at the final octet? Simply because if we had all 1's in the final part this would constitute a broadcast on a class A network and would be unacceptable. So the address 126.255.255.255 represents a broadcast to all IP addresses in the 126.0.0.0 network. As such it cannot be used for a host machine on the network. Coming down one value from that gives us the last valid HostID of 126.255.255.254.

Due to the slightly vague way in which the RFC[1] is worded some authors/implementations may interpret these ranges slightly differently. The rule here is that if you are interested in "squeezing out" the absolutely last machine into each network then make sure your implementation will let you do what you want to do!

Network Sizes

Looking at Figure 2.5 we can see that there are some major consequences with our choice of "class-based" networks. Many of these consequences come about because the class-based system depends on some rules. These rules were put into place in order to make sense of some network configurations as well as allowing for certain things such as "broadcasts" to be clarified. An unfortunate side effect of these rules is that we loose a whole class A address for our loopback test (usually only done on one machine!) and also we have to choose from class B or class C addresses when deciding on a network address. Class B addresses give us networks with 65,534 machines on each one whereas class C networks have only 254 machines on each! A finer degree of selection would have been more useful to most organisations.

1. Request For Comments: the principle way in which Internet standards or "guidelines" are published.

The following table shows the number of networks and machines associated with each of the address classes:

Class	Maximum number of networks	Maximum number of hosts per network
A	126	16,777,214
B	16,384	65,534
C	2,097,152	254

How are these worked out? We are back to our positional notation calculations again. With class A addresses we have seven bits that can be used to identify the networks. As before with two bits we get 2^2 (4) networks. With three bits we have 2^3 (8) networks and with seven bits we get 2^7 (128) networks. The *numerical* maximum number of networks is therefore 128; however, we can't have all 0's in the network component, and 127 is predefined so the maximum permissible number of networks is 126.

There are 24 bits for the hosts on each of the class A networks which gives us 2^{24} (16,777,216) hosts on each of the networks. These hosts cannot have all 0's or all 1's so we must remove two from this value giving us a total of 16,777,214 maximum hosts on each of the class A networks.

With class B networks we have 14 bits for the network component; 2^{14} gives us 16,384 networks and since all class B networks start with bit patterns 10 our rules about not having all 1's or all 0's apply automatically. So with class B networks we can have 16,384 networks and each network can have 2^{16} hosts on them. 2^{16} gives us 65,536 but again we cannot have all 1's or all 0's so the actual value is 65,534 hosts on each network.

Class C networks have 21 bits designating the network component and this gives 2^{21} (2,097,152) maximum networks. Once more, with a compulsory initial bit pattern of 110 our rule (can't have all 1's or all 0's) applies automatically. So we can have 2,097,152 networks each with 2^8 (256) hosts on them. The value of 256 contains all 1's and all 0's so we must remove 2 from that value giving us 2,097,152 networks each with a maximum of 254 hosts for our class C networks.

With commendable foresight the IAB have designated some address ranges as "private" or "non-allocated" addresses. These are intended for use on private networks and will not be allocated to any Internet networks. Their specific use will be discussed during the chapters on network design. Here are the reserved addresses for each class:

Class A	10.0.0.0 through to 10.255.255.255
Class B	172.16.0.0 through to 172.31.255.255
Class C	192.168.0.0 through to 192.168.255.255

So if we wanted to install a private (internal) IP network using a class B address we could use 172.16.0.0 or 172.17.0.0 or 172.18.0.0 etc. In this way it is possible to create a completely internal IP network without having to connect to the Internet. More on this at the end of the book.

3

Names, Addresses and Name Resolution

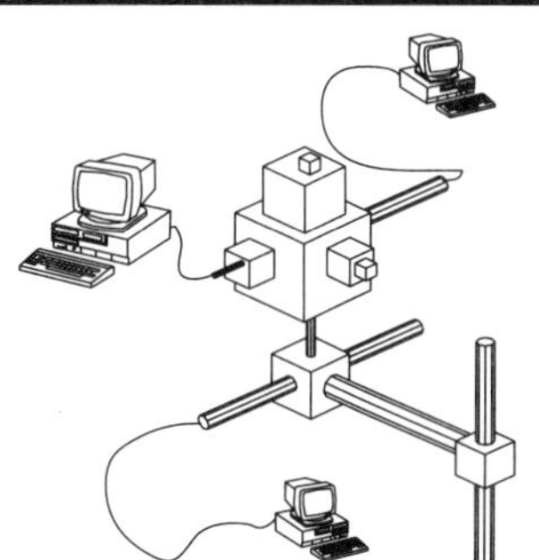

Introduction

So far we have talked about IP addresses. In an ideal world there would only be one method of identifying computers on a network. Unfortunately for us history has a way of starting with a number of options and allowing them all to continue until a clear "victor" emerges. So it is with computer identification on most networks.

Historically, many different methods were tried for computer identification. So far, four methods have emerged as the most common and one of these is nearing the end of its days. In a few years' time it is likely that all computer users will be aware of their fully qualified domain name and little else. Before that day arrives we have to consider all the current possibilities.

To enable communication to take place between computers on a network we need to be able to identify *individual* computers and also do this by the use of *names*. In this context our definition of a network is two or more computers linked by a cable (or cables) that share data and communicate with each other.

Why do we Need Names for our Computers?

The simple reason is that at the lowest level the method by which computers communicate is pretty tedious for humans to remember. What is this method? On almost all networked computer systems the network card (the piece of equipment that prepares the data and messages for transmission across the cables) is identified by a unique number. This means that each and every card in the world has a distinct identification number. This does not change and is assigned jointly by the card manufacturer and a centralised "steering" committee. What does this number look like? Here are a few examples:

00 40 95 05 D3 8A
00 3C 00 03 A3 3D
00 10 4B 27 51 92
00 60 08 9A AD 05

These addresses are often referred to as hardware addresses or MAC (media access control) addresses. This MAC address is used by computers to identify each other on a local network. By local network we mean all the computers on the same piece of cable or all computers in the same immediate locality. Normally this means a small number of computers in one room, floor or small building (there are other considerations which we will discuss later).

These are not the easiest of number patterns to try and remember. If we were to use these numbers to communicate between computers the average user would get very confused and almost certainly give up. Unfortunately for us a number of computer manufacturers and computer-user organisations came up with a variety of solutions to these problems. Two of the commonest that are now in use are outlined below.

Solution 1 – NETBIOS

Microsoft came up with a simplified method of identifying computers on a network. This method was called NETBIOS (network basic input/output system). This method was simple, unsophisticated, relatively inefficient and quite noisy (more on this later). NETBIOS has recently come in for a considerable degree of criticism but when it was developed it represented an ideal solution to the problem of computers communicating on small networks. What do we mean by small networks? The original specification said that NETBIOS was suitable for computer systems linking 2 to 20 computers.

Why do we say NETBIOS is noisy? Figure 3.1 shows some data captured from a network as one machine is switched on. The constant, initial, NETBIOS broadcasts could saturate a larger network.

Figure 3.1 NETBIOS broadcast traffic on a small network

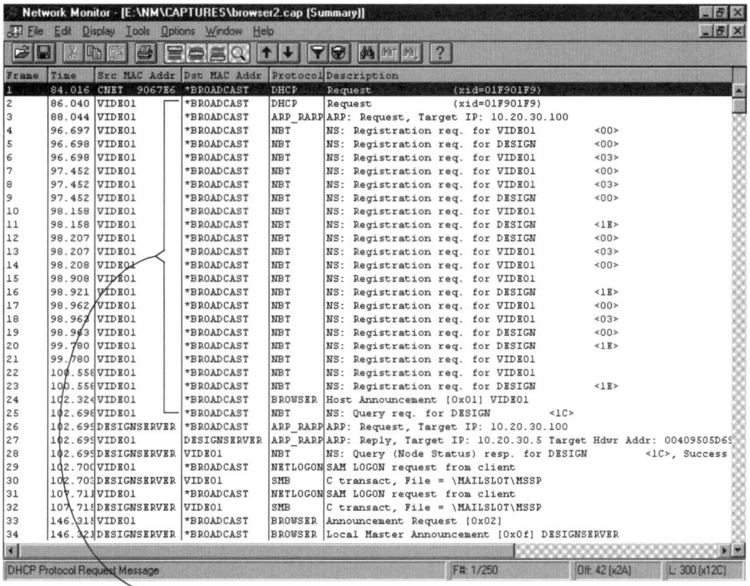

Network Monitor - [E:\NM\CAPTURES\browser2.cap (Summary)]

File Edit Display Tools Options Window Help

Frame	Time	Src MAC Addr	Dst MAC Addr	Protocol	Description
1	84.016	CNET 9067E6	*BROADCAST	DHCP	Request (xid=01F901F9)
2	86.040	VIDEO1	*BROADCAST	DHCP	Request (xid=01F901F9)
3	88.044	VIDEO1	*BROADCAST	ARP_RARP	ARP: Request, Target IP: 10.20.30.100
4	96.697	VIDEO1	*BROADCAST	NBT	NS: Registration req. for VIDEO1 <00>
5	96.698	VIDEO1	*BROADCAST	NBT	NS: Registration req. for DESIGN <00>
6	96.698	VIDEO1	*BROADCAST	NBT	NS: Registration req. for VIDEO1 <03>
7	97.452	VIDEO1	*BROADCAST	NBT	NS: Registration req. for VIDEO1 <00>
8	97.452	VIDEO1	*BROADCAST	NBT	NS: Registration req. for VIDEO1 <03>
9	97.452	VIDEO1	*BROADCAST	NBT	NS: Registration req. for DESIGN <00>
10	98.158	VIDEO1	*BROADCAST	NBT	NS: Registration req. for VIDEO1
11	98.158	VIDEO1	*BROADCAST	NBT	NS: Registration req. for DESIGN <1E>
12	98.207	VIDEO1	*BROADCAST	NBT	NS: Registration req. for DESIGN <00>
13	98.207	VIDEO1	*BROADCAST	NBT	NS: Registration req. for VIDEO1 <03>
14	98.208	VIDEO1	*BROADCAST	NBT	NS: Registration req. for VIDEO1 <00>
15	98.908	VIDEO1	*BROADCAST	NBT	NS: Registration req. for VIDEO1
16	98.921	VIDEO1	*BROADCAST	NBT	NS: Registration req. for DESIGN <1E>
17	98.962	VIDEO1	*BROADCAST	NBT	NS: Registration req. for VIDEO1 <00>
18	98.963	VIDEO1	*BROADCAST	NBT	NS: Registration req. for VIDEO1 <03>
19	98.963	VIDEO1	*BROADCAST	NBT	NS: Registration req. for DESIGN <00>
20	99.780	VIDEO1	*BROADCAST	NBT	NS: Registration req. for DESIGN <1E>
21	99.780	VIDEO1	*BROADCAST	NBT	NS: Registration req. for VIDEO1
22	100.556	VIDEO1	*BROADCAST	NBT	NS: Registration req. for VIDEO1
23	100.556	VIDEO1	*BROADCAST	NBT	NS: Registration req. for DESIGN <1E>
24	102.324	VIDEO1	*BROADCAST	BROWSER	Host Announcement [0x01] VIDEO1
25	102.698	VIDEO1	*BROADCAST	NBT	NS: Query req. for DESIGN <1C>
26	102.699	DESIGNSERVER	*BROADCAST	ARP_RARP	ARP: Request, Target IP: 10.20.30.100
27	102.699	VIDEO1	DESIGNSERVER	ARP_RARP	ARP: Reply, Target IP: 10.20.30.5 Target Hdwr Addr: 00409505D69
28	102.699	DESIGNSERVER	VIDEO1	NBT	NS: Query (Node Status) resp. for DESIGN <1C>, Success
29	102.700	VIDEO1	*BROADCAST	NETLOGON	SAM LOGON request from client
30	102.703	DESIGNSERVER	VIDEO1	SMB	C transact, File = \MAILSLOT\MSSP
31	107.711	VIDEO1	*BROADCAST	NETLOGON	SAM LOGON request from client
32	107.715	DESIGNSERVER	VIDEO1	SMB	C transact, File = \MAILSLOT\MSSP
33	146.315	VIDEO1	*BROADCAST	BROWSER	Announcement Request [0x02]
34	146.321	DESIGNSERVER	*BROADCAST	BROWSER	Local Master Announcement [0x0f] DESIGNSERVER

DHCP Protocol Request Message F#: 1/250 Off: 42 (x2A) L: 300 (x12C)

All this broadcast traffic is *one* machine coming onto the network. Imagine what 100 machines would do to your network!

The use of computers on even small networks has outgrown the modest plans of the developers of NETBIOS. Unfortunately, however relevant and well planned the design may be, the ever-increasing demands of industry almost guarantee that shortcomings will be found at some point as the system is used in larger and larger networks.

Even using the simplified NETBIOS naming system the underlying identification of computers is through their hardware or MAC address. The software that is used is hidden from the user but converts requests to contact a particular computer into a MAC address and communication continues at the lower level.

What is a computer name? Quite simply it can be any "suitable" name up to 15 characters long. Some examples could be Mypc, Workpc, Gamews or Finance1. In all cases the software will convert these machine names into the associated (unique) MAC address that is on the hardware card.

Figure 3.2 Computer name to MAC address translation plus MAC-to-MAC delivery

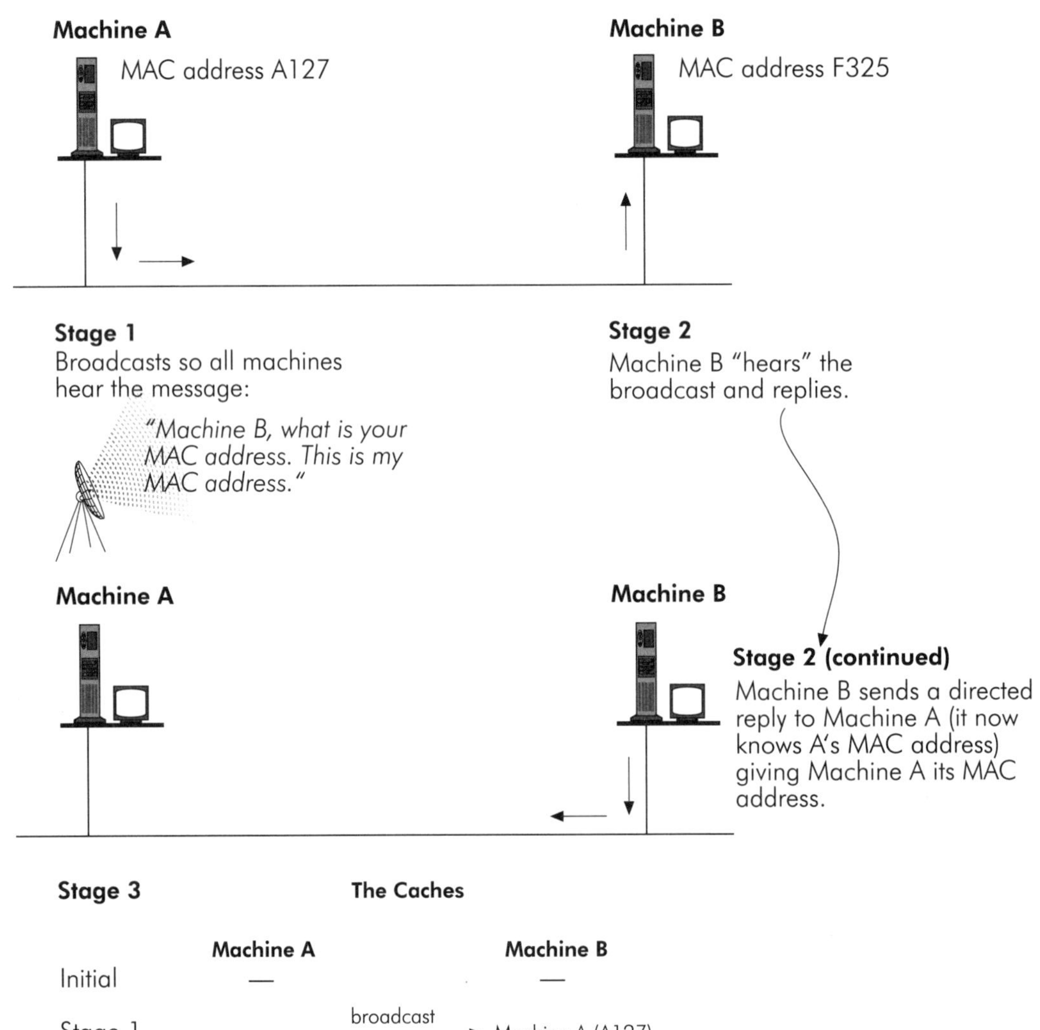

Stage 3 **The Caches**

	Machine A		Machine B
Initial	—		—
Stage 1	—	broadcast →	Machine A (A127)
Stage 2	Machine B (F325)	← directed	Machine A (A127)

Solution 2 – IP Addresses and Fully Qualified Domain Names

In the same way that NETBIOS names represent an improvement over MAC addresses, the designers of the Internet came up with both a numbering system and a naming convention which were intended to simplify the identification of computers on the Internet. Unfortunately, the Internet's structure and their wish to provide an expandable system meant that they faced problems considerably more complex than those faced by the designers of the NETBIOS naming system.

The address of each computer on the Internet is unique. This address is also quite separate from the MAC address. Remember MAC addresses are used to identify computers on a local network (all computers on the same network cable or in the same immediate location). This is no good for the Internet which has computers spread over many hundreds (and thousands) of miles.

As we have seen, an Internet computer address is made up from four numbers arranged in what is referred to as "dotted decimal" notation. Here are some more examples: 132.19.73.4, 145.122.111.23 and 111.111.123.144.

Again, each of these numbers identify a particular computer on the Internet but like the underlying MAC addresses they are not, for most people, very easy to remember. The Internet's designers came up with a naming convention that helps. This naming convention seems cumbersome at first but it has a structure that allows for expansion, flexibility and a reliable means of marrying-up the computer name with the underlying IP address.

Here is an example of a computer name from the Internet:

```
mypc.xyzcompany.com
```

which is the computer `mypc` in an organisation called `xyzcompany` and is part of a larger organisational structure called `com` (commercial). Here is another example:

```
newpc.physics.londonuniversity.ac.uk
```

This says that the computer `newpc` is part of the `physics` department in the `londonuniversity` organisation (or domain) which is in the academic group of computer systems in the UK.

The naming convention, as stated above, can be expanded and provides a reliable means of identifying computers on the Internet.

Summary so far

1. On a local network computers use a MAC address to identify each other and to transfer data between themselves.
2. These MAC addresses are cumbersome, so NETBIOS names are used on smaller systems to simplify (humanise) the process. Humans use the NETBIOS names and the computer software translates these into MAC addresses.
3. On a much larger network these MAC addresses are inefficient and cannot be used. A more sophisticated address system has to be employed – the IP (Internet Protocol) address which is usually expressed in "dotted decimal" notation. e.g., 144.19.72.4.
4. This address structure is confusing for humans so a structured naming convention is used for computers on the Internet. These names are called *fully qualified domain names* and are of the form `mypc.finance.company.com`.
5. Both NETBIOS names and IP, or fully qualified domain names, exist and can often both be present on one computer.

The following points are important. A computer can be identified on a network by:

1. Its MAC address.
2. Its NETBIOS name.
3. Its IP address.
4. Its Fully Qualified Domain Name.

Depending on which method is used some form of name resolution needs to occur. Why is this? Because at the local level only MAC addresses are used for data delivery and at the remote level only IP addresses are used. The NETBIOS and FQDN (Fully Qualified Domain Name) methods are used to "simplify" or "humanise" the process.

Name Resolution

If we were to be content with quoting IP addresses or MAC addresses at each other the system could have remained a lot simpler. Unfortunately the introduction of the "humanised" names makes matters a lot more complex. With these "humanised" names we have to convert between the names and their corresponding addresses. These conversion processes take time, resources and introduce the potential for some serious problems. Why do we have to convert between the different types? Quite simply because at one level the computer uses the hardware address and at another level the user of the computer uses the more friendly name. The computer programs between these two extremes are busy converting from one form to another in order to maintain consistency and to give the user the appearance of "seamless" connectivity.

The process of converting from a "humanised" name to a computer address is called *name resolution*. Before we discuss the stages just remember:

1. All local delivery is via the MAC address.
2. All long distance delivery is via the IP address.
3. There is no simple relationship between the two addressing schemes *or* between the computer names and their corresponding addresses.

The stages in the process are as follows:

1. **For local delivery**
   The computer converts from the NETBIOS name or the IP address (they can both be present on a computer and used by different programs) to the MAC address and delivers the data locally.

2. **For long distance delivery**
   The computer converts from the domain name (`mypc.work.com`) or the NETBIOS name to the IP address (111.123.121.11) and delivers the data to the remote network. At the local network the final router uses the MAC address for the final stage in the process – that of delivering the data locally. When delivering the data to the remote network a number of stages might well

be present. These stages or "hops" are how the data can move round the world.

How does the system determine if the destination address is local or remote? It does this by using a technique referred to as an *adjacency test*. To understand how this works we need to have a basic understanding of how the subnet mask works.

For our current discussion the subnet mask can be thought of as a way of determining which part of the IP address represents the network identifier (NetID) and which part represents the HostID. Before we look at this let us consider an aspect of computer programming called a bitwise AND.

In the bitwise AND operation we have two sets of binary numbers. For the current discussion we will call one set the address and the other set the mask. A simple set of rules dictate what will happen if the mask bit is a 1 or if the mask bit is a 0.

Rule 1. Any bit ANDed with a 1 is copied to the result.
Rule 2. Any bit ANDed with a 0 produces a 0 in the result.

- **Example 1**

Address bits 1001
Mask bits 1100
Result bits 1000

Here the first two (leftmost) bits are copied down to the results part since the two mask bits are 1's. The rightmost bits are set to 0 since the two mask bits are themselves 0.

- **Example 2**

Address bits 110011
Mask bits 111100
Result bits 110000

Here the first four bits of the address are copied down since the first four mask bits are 1's. The rightmost address bits are set to 0 since the rightmost mask bits are 0.

- **Example 3**

Address bits 110011001110
Mask bits 111111000000
Result bits 110011000000

Here the left six bits of the address pattern are copied down and the rightmost six bits are all set to 0 since the mask bits are themselves 0.

Let us apply the above ideas to the issue of IP addresses and subnet masks. The aim of our exercise is to take an IP address and split it into two parts: the network identifier (NetID) and the HostID. Our address will be 10.10.10.1 (a simple one!) and we will use the first 16 bits to represent the NetID. Since the address is simple and the NetID is represented by the first 16 bits we can see that our NetID is 10.10.0.0 and the HostID is 0.0.10.1. How can we create this using a subnet mask?

The binary pattern for the IP address 10.10.10.1 is

00001010000010100000101000000001

To use the first 16 bits of this address as our NetID we must copy these 16 bits into our "result" section. To do this we use a mask of sixteen 1's and then AND this with the above binary address:

	10 : 10 : 10 : 1
Address	00001010000010100000101000000001
Mask	11111111111111110000000000000000
Result	00001010000010100000000000000000
	10 : 10 : 0 : 0

Hence the NetID is 10.10.0.0 and the HostID is the remainder value 0.0.10.1.

What does a mask of all 16 bits correspond to? If we apply our method of positional notation to each of the two octets (16 bits means 2 octets) we see that the 16-bit subnet mask corresponds to 255.255.0.0. Using a similar approach, an 8-bit subnet mask is 255.0.0.0 and a 24-bit mask is 255.255.255.0. How does this assist us in the determination of the local or remote delivery problem?

The adjacency test that we mentioned earlier works as follows:

1. The software that requires the test (it could be part of the TCP/IP stack or the application software itself) carries out a test on both the source and destination IP addresses and determines if they have the same network identifier (NetID).
2. If they do, then the two computers in question are on the same subnet (or physical network segment) and the actual delivery will be carried out using the MAC address.
3. Should the two NetIDs be deemed to be on different network segments then the data will be sent to the default router (or gateway). The router will then forward the packet to another router or to a locally connected network. The router decides what to do by a process very similar to the adjacency test described above.

Here are a couple of examples.

- **Example 1**

Source IP address	10.10.10.1
Subnet mask	255.255.0.0
NetID	10.10.0.0
Destination IP address	10.10.27.33
Subnet mask	255.255.0.0
NetID	10.10.0.0

The conclusion is that both machines are on the same network and so delivery will be made using the MAC addresses of the two machines.

- **Example 2**

Source IP address	10.15.170.1
Subnet mask	255.255.0.0
NetID	10.15.0.0
Destination IP address	10.15.27.63
Subnet mask	255.255.0.0
NetID	10.15.0.0

The conclusion is that both machines are on the same network and so delivery will be made using the MAC addresses of the two machines.

- **Example** 3

Source IP address	10.15.174.1
Subnet mask	255.255.255.0
NetID	10.15.174.0
Destination IP address	10.15.27.63
Subnet mask	255.255.255.0
NetID	10.15.27.0

The conclusion is that both machines are on different networks and so the data will be sent to the default gateway or router. In all of the above cases (and in general) the subnet mask that is used is the subnet mask of the source computer.

This illustrates the fact that if the subnet mask is set up incorrectly then the conclusion reached by the adjacency test will be incorrect and the two computers will fail to communicate. This failure will occur because the data will be routed remotely when it should be delivered locally or vice versa, where the source machine attempts to deliver the data locally but no machine responds. This is where the "destination network unreachable" and the "request timeout" problems come from.

The human analogy would be that the domain name and IP address allow mail to move from sorting office to sorting office, or from railway station to railway station. The MAC addresses function like the local postman: they get the data to the target address on the local system.

Some explanations of these addressing schemes have used the concept of a house number to represent the MAC address and the name of the family to represent the NETBIOS, or DNS, name. This suggests that the house number cannot change but the name of the family occupying the house may change over time. In the same way the MAC or hardware address rarely changes but the NETBIOS or DNS name might change in time. This may occur when a computer has new software installed or is moved from one company site to another.

Why is the system so complex and awkward? Quite simply we have three or four different technologies, developed at different times, to handle different tasks and all evolving at different rates that have now all been "made" to work together. The result is far from perfect. If we could stop the world and the development of electronics and computers for five years, say, then during that time it would be possible to put together a more comprehensive and cohesive system but I do not think that this will happen!

The situation that we now have is that there are methods of naming computers and two different methods of identifying them by address. MAC addresses are used for local delivery and IP (Internet Protocol) addresses are used for long distance delivery. In almost all cases the MAC address is hidden from users although they may be required to enter the NETBIOS or DNS name as they copy data, use printers or "surf" the Internet.

Broadcasts and Other Issues

In the previous figures we have seen that, at the local level, the MAC address is used to deliver data. If one computer does not have the MAC address of the destination computer in a data delivery process it broadcasts (transmits to all machines on the local network) to find out the correct MAC address. This is a fundamental aspect of how these network systems work and cannot be changed. Why, therefore, is NETBIOS considered so "noisy". The answer is, quite simply, that in addition to the underlying broadcast aspects of the network almost all NETBIOS-based systems will initiate a broadcast – almost whenever they wish – to communicate for whatever reason. The machines broadcast when they start up and at regular intervals thereafter. The machines broadcast when browsing the network, they broadcast when transferring data etc. It is possible to reduce this information by using a WINS server and by preloading caches but this simply reduces NETBIOS's dependence on broadcast traffic to perform the simplest of tasks.

IP-based traffic tends to broadcast only at the local level and only when the ARP cache (the cache that holds IP addresses and their corresponding MAC addresses) is empty. From Figure 3.1 it can be seen that even on a simple network the network-generated traffic can be considerable. In general, NETBIOS-based systems will generate 10 to 30 times more broadcasts than purely TCP/IP-based networks.

4

Subnetted Class B Addresses

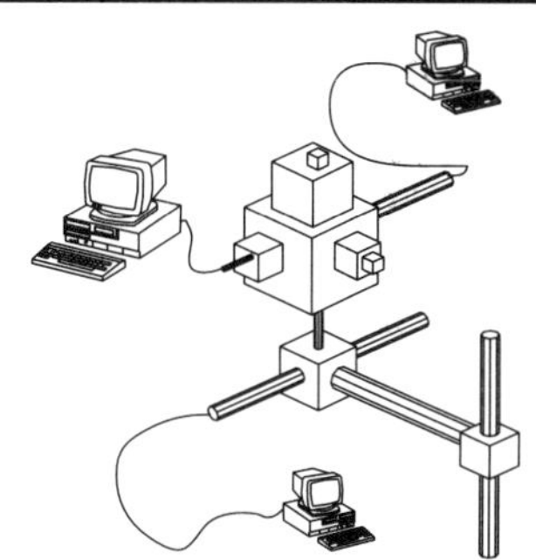

Class B Addresses

We have seen how class B addresses use the first two octets to define the network component and the second two octets to define the host component of any IP address. These ideas are summarised in Figure 4.1.

Figure 4.1 Class B octet boundaries

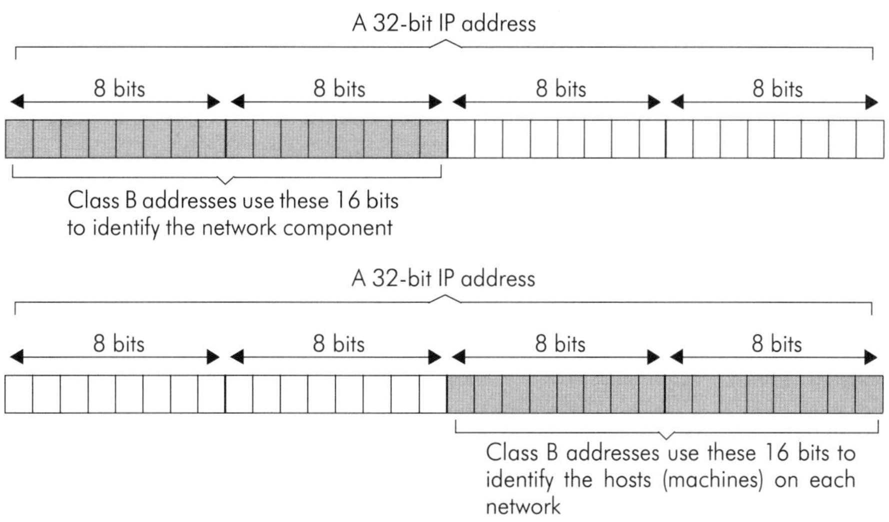

Using the above structure our class B addresses can support 16,384 networks and each network can have 65,534 hosts on it. This gives us the scope for a very large internal network using a class B address but our problems start if we wish to subdivide the single large network so that we can manage and administrate it more easily.

Here is an illustration of the problem. We have an IP network address 154.132.0.0 with a default subnet mask of 255.255.0.0. The network can use all of the last 16 bits to identify hosts so the following IP addresses are all suitable for hosts on this network:

154.132.10.1
154.132.10.19
154.132.110.123
154.132.254.254

In each case, with a subnet mask of 255.255.0.0 any adjacency test between these hosts on this network would result in the decision "all on the same network" (154.132.0.0). What we want to do is to subdivide the network into more "manageable" chunks as illustrated in Figure 4.2.

Figure 4.2 Bridged or routed networks?

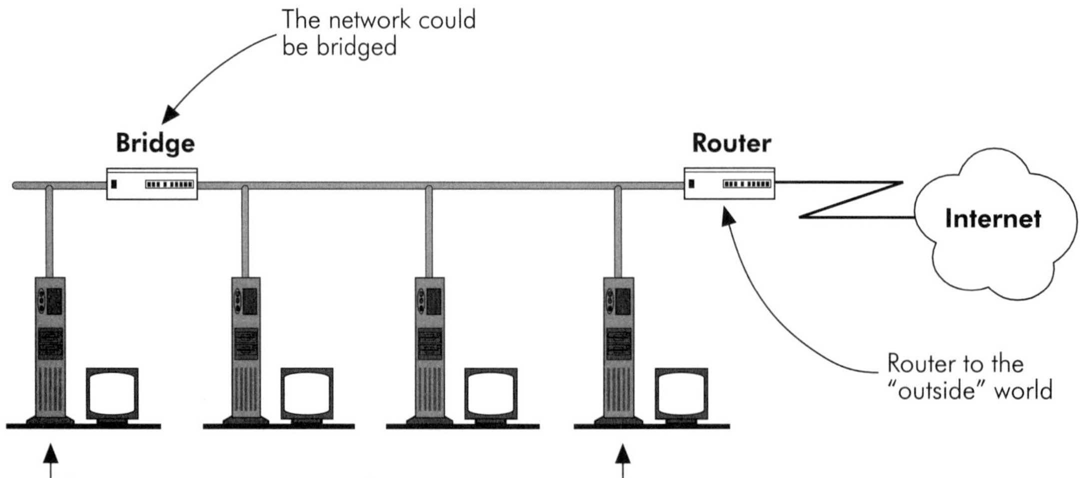
The network could be bridged
Bridge
Router
Internet
Router to the "outside" world
All 65,534 hosts on one physical network. This could be bridged but would be very prone to broadcast storms, since bridges will pass *all* broadcast traffic on a network.

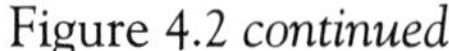

Figure 4.2 *continued*

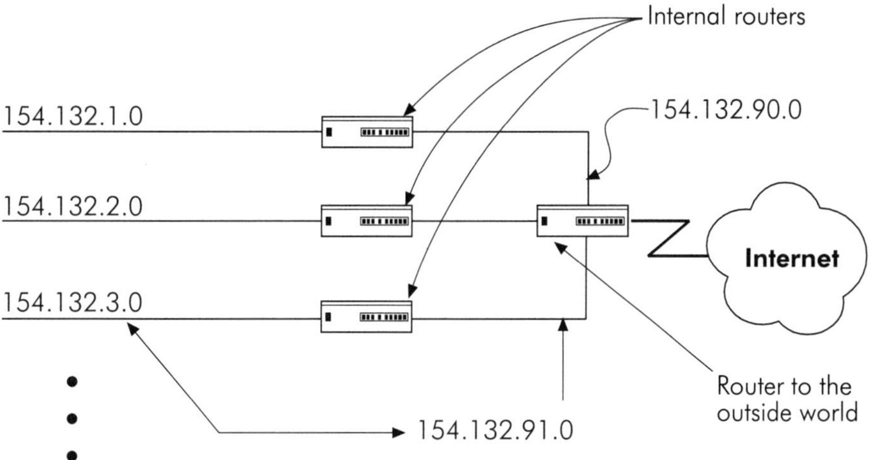

How can we do this? Each subdivision of our network is effectively a network in its own right so the routers will have to forward datagrams across the relevant sections. We cannot use the default subnet mask since this gives the appearance to all network segments that they are all on the same physical network. The answer is to extend the default subnet mask so that the mask covers the third octet and in this way allows us to subdivide or "subnet" the network.

Subnetted Networks

We will now use the following subnet mask 255.255.255.0. Since we are now using three octets for the subnet mask our mask could be written /24 (3 times 8 bits) so our network address together with the relevant subnet mask could be written 154.132.0.0 /24 whereas the original network address, using only the first 16 bits (two octets) would have been written 154.132.0.0 /16. Both the /24 and 255.255.255.0 methods of identifying subnets are currently in use and are interchangeable.

Using the /24 subnet means that the following addresses on our network would be interpreted as being on different networks:

154.132.10.1 /24
154.132.20.1 /24

The bit maps for these are illustrated in Figure 4.3.

Figure 4.3 Sample /24-bit subnets

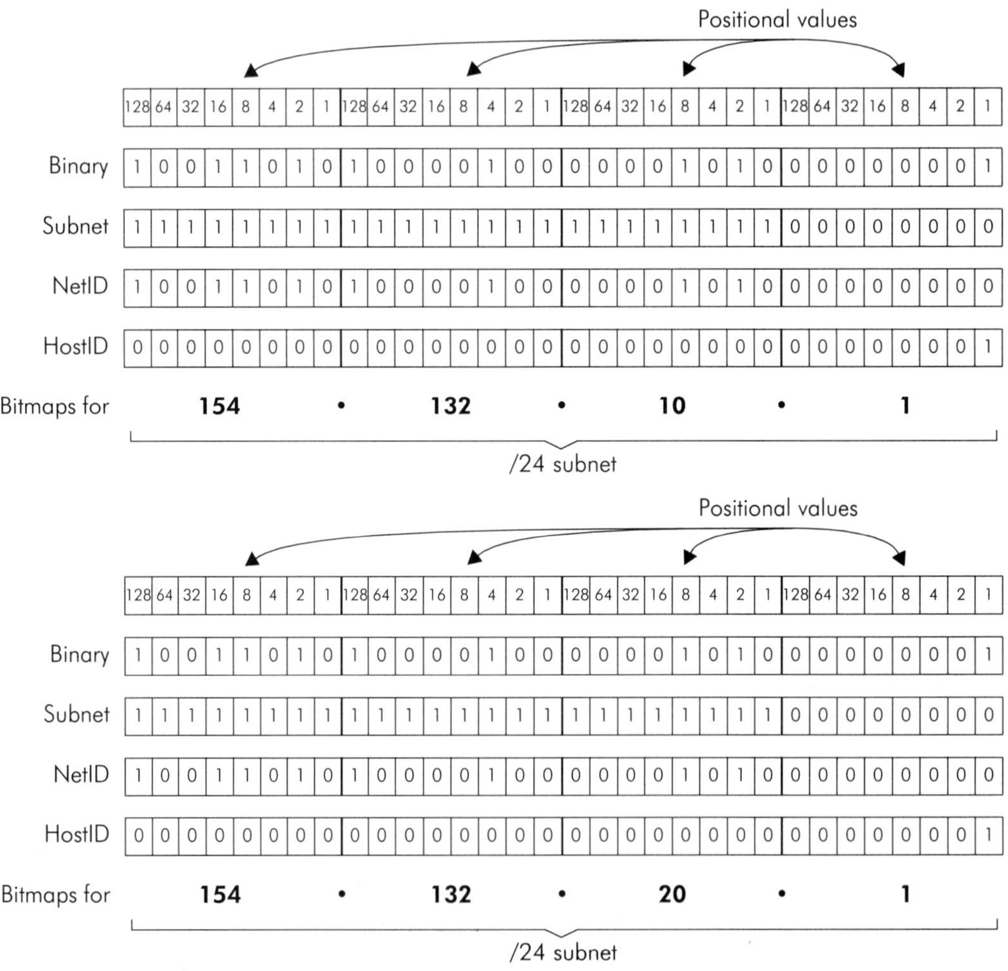

In the first instance the network address is 154.132.10.0 and in the second the network address is 154.132.20.0 so any adjacency test using these two would decide that they are on separate networks and pass the datagrams to the router.

Using the machine addresses shown above we can now see that almost all of them would be interpreted as being on different networks. With the first two addresses the machines (hosts) would be machine numbers 1 and 19 on network 154.132.10.0 and the last one would be machine number 254 on network 154.132.254.0.

IP Address	Subnet Mask	NetID	HostID
154.132.10.1	255.255.255.0	154.132.10.0	0.0.0.1
154.132.10.19	255.255.255.0	154.132.10.0	0.0.0.19
154.132.110.123	255.255.255.0	154.132.110.0	0.0.0.123
154.132.254.254	255.255.255.0	154.132.254.0	0.0.0.254

How useful is this? Using a /24 subnet mask on a class B network means that we can subdivide the network into a number of sections or subnets. These provide us with considerably greater administrative control and a far more flexible means of arranging the network layout. As usual, whenever a great improvement is offered there is a cost.

Dividing up the Class B Network

With a "standard", or non-subnetted, class B network we had support for 65,534 hosts on our single network.With a subnetted class B network we have scope for 254 networks with only 254 hosts on each. One of the rules outlined in the RFCs is that no subnetwork can have all 1's or all 0's in it. Some modern routers are capable of ignoring this but they are currently far from common. This gives us the following first and last network layouts in our subnetted class B network:

First and last valid network	First valid host	Last valid host
154.132.1.0	154.132.1.1	154.132.1.254
154.132.254.0	154.132.254.1	154.132.254.254

The bit map diagrams are illustrated in Figure 4.4.

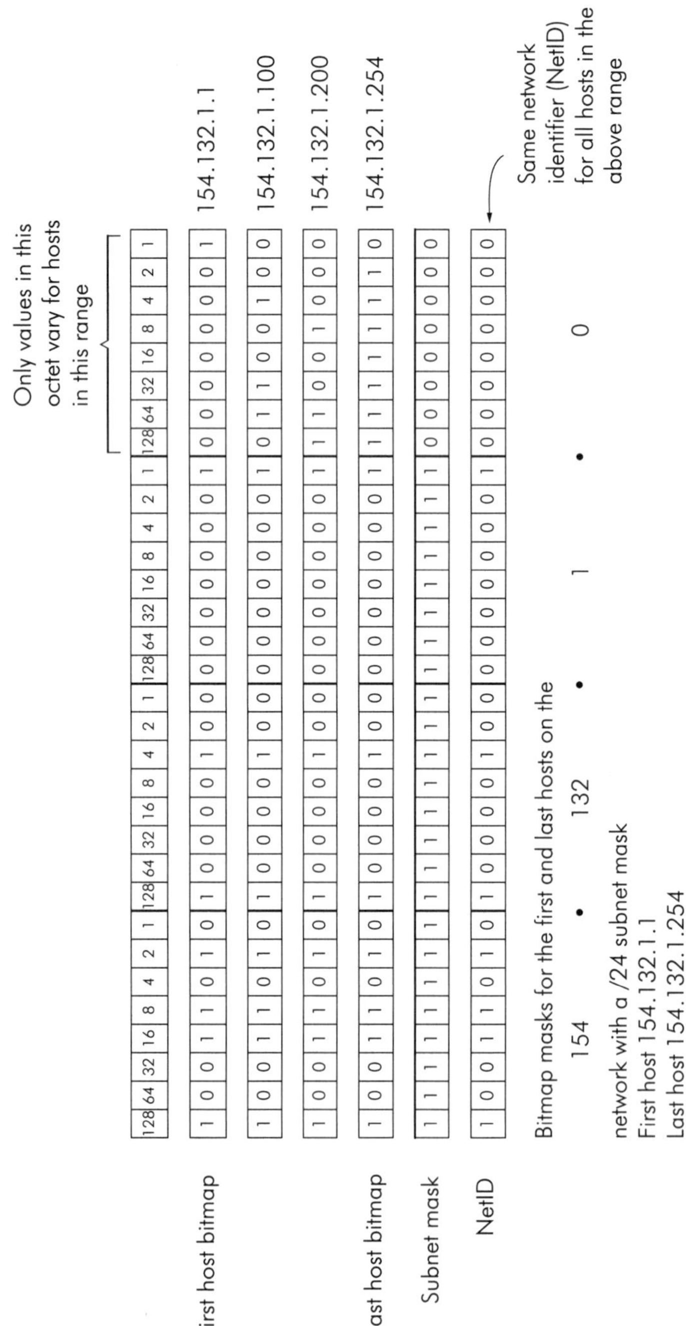

Figure 4.4 Valid host ranges on first and last valid networks

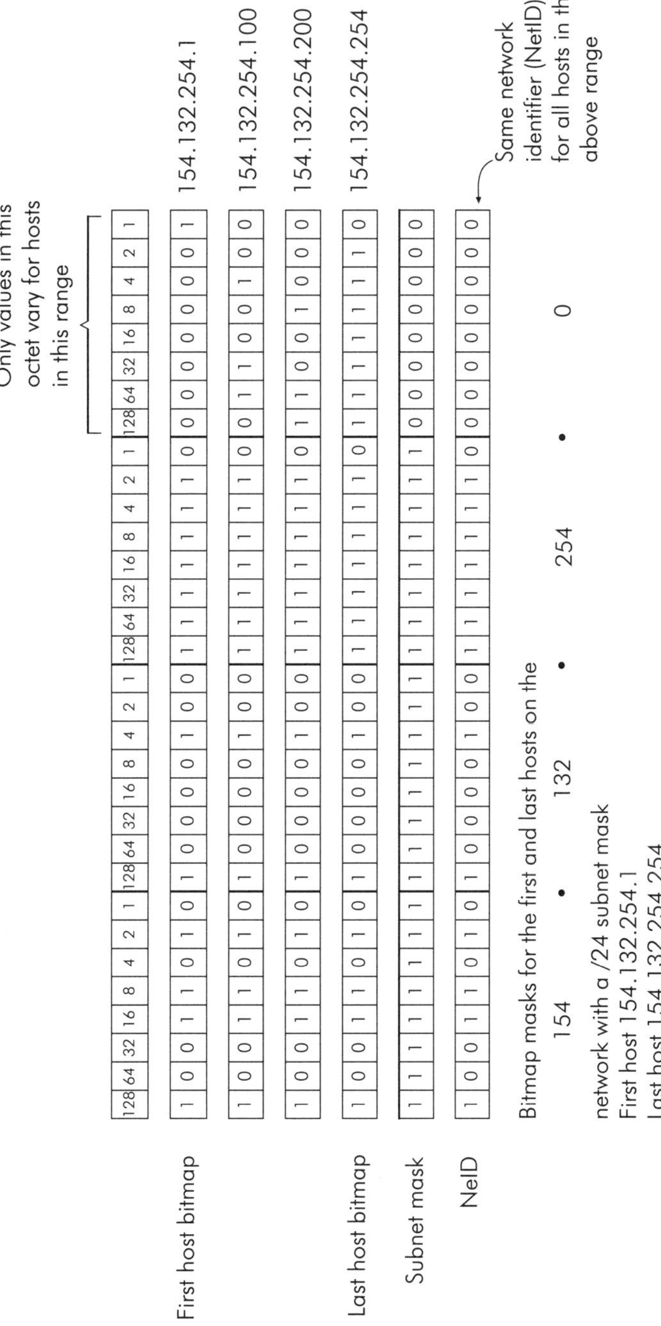

Figure 4.4 (continued) Valid host ranges on first and last valid networks

Let us imagine a scenario where the above information will be used. A company has decided to use one of the non-assigned class B addresses 172.16.0.0 for their network. They have applied for one valid IP address to allow them to connect to the Internet and they have decided to use a subnet mask of 24 bits (/24 or 255.255.255.0). Figure 4.5 shows a possible design using this setup in conjunction with a proxy server. There are many different ways of both cabling this network and assigning the address ranges. Typical considerations are throughput requirements, router specifications and overall access requirements for the different divisions. Only a detailed examination of the specific requirements in each installation can answer these questions and produce a relevant network layout.

Figure 4.5 Subnetted class B layout

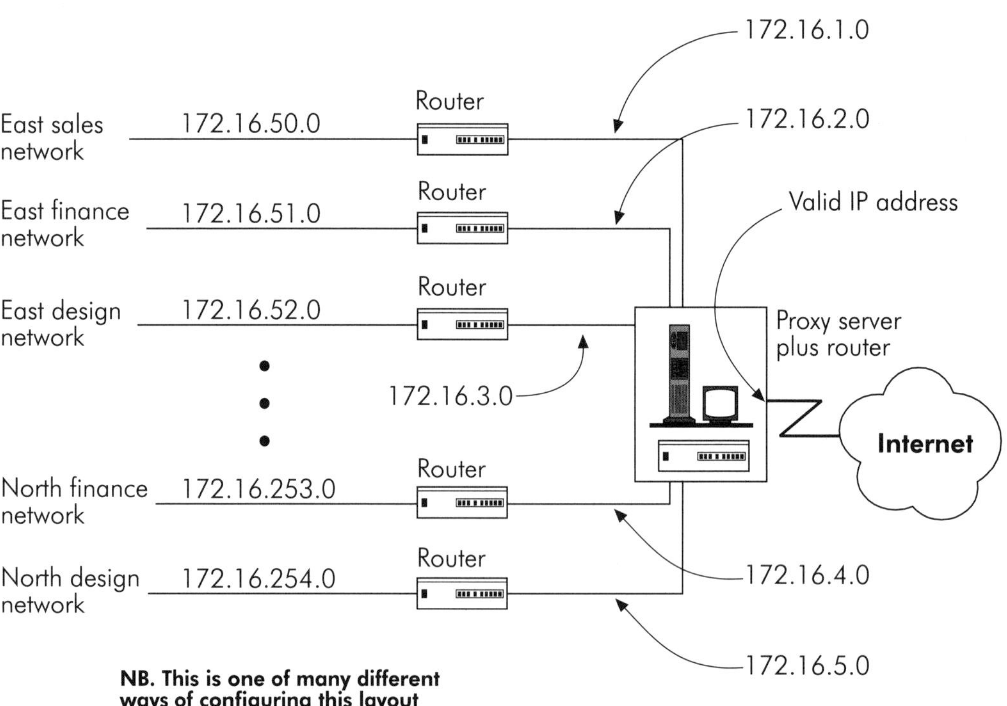

What happens if the above company does not want 254 networks each with 254 hosts? Perhaps they only want 10 networks but with up to 600 hosts on each. Or they may want six networks each with 2000 hosts. To do this, the rather rigid approach of using all of the third octet as the subnet mask is too inflexible. What we want to do is to use some, or all of the third octet to subdivide our networks. This is called *variable-length subnet masking* and is covered in the next chapter.

5

Variable-length Subnet Masks

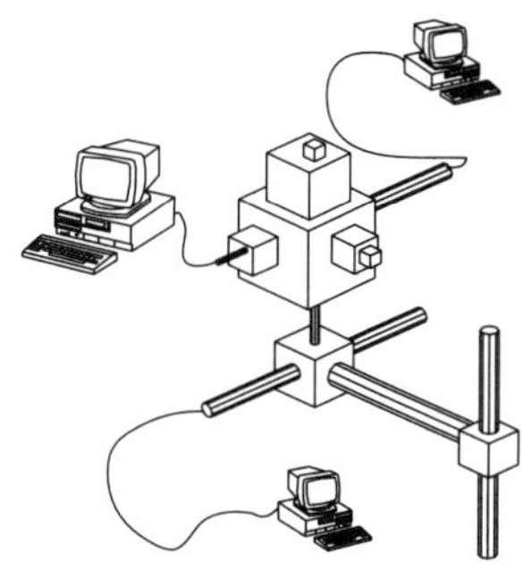

Introduction

The primary purpose of the subnet mask is to allow the source computer, in an exchange of data, to determine if the destination computer is on the same network segment or subnet. If it is then the data is delivered using the hardware address of the network card. If it is not then almost certainly the data has to be sent to a router – often referred to as the default gateway. The use of the subnet mask to determine whether two communicating machines are on the same subnet is called an adjacency test.

By using suitable subnet masks it is possible to divide our network into smaller segments or subnets. Apart from the adjacency test this division of the network into more manageable "chunks" also has a beneficial effect in an administrative sense. The standard masks determine both the number of networks possible and the number of machines that can occur on each of the networks.

Review of Standard Rules

The range of network and machine combinations using the standard subnet masks is shown below. The basic rules for the different address classes must be remembered when looking at the diagrams. Here are the rules from Chapter 2:

1. All class A addresses start with a 0 as the leftmost bit.
2. For class A addresses the value 127 is defined as the loopback address and cannot, therefore, be used as a network address.

3. All class B addresses start with the bit pattern 10.
4. All class C addresses start with the bit pattern 110.
5. All class D (multicast addresses) start with the bit pattern 1110.
6. All class E (reserved addresses) start with the bit pattern 11110.
7. You cannot have all 1's in the host component of an address since this is defined as a "broadcast to all hosts on a network" address.
8. You cannot have all 0's in the host component of an address since this is defined as "the current network".

Figure 5.1 shows the IP ranges and the subnets for each of the different address classes.

Figure 5.1

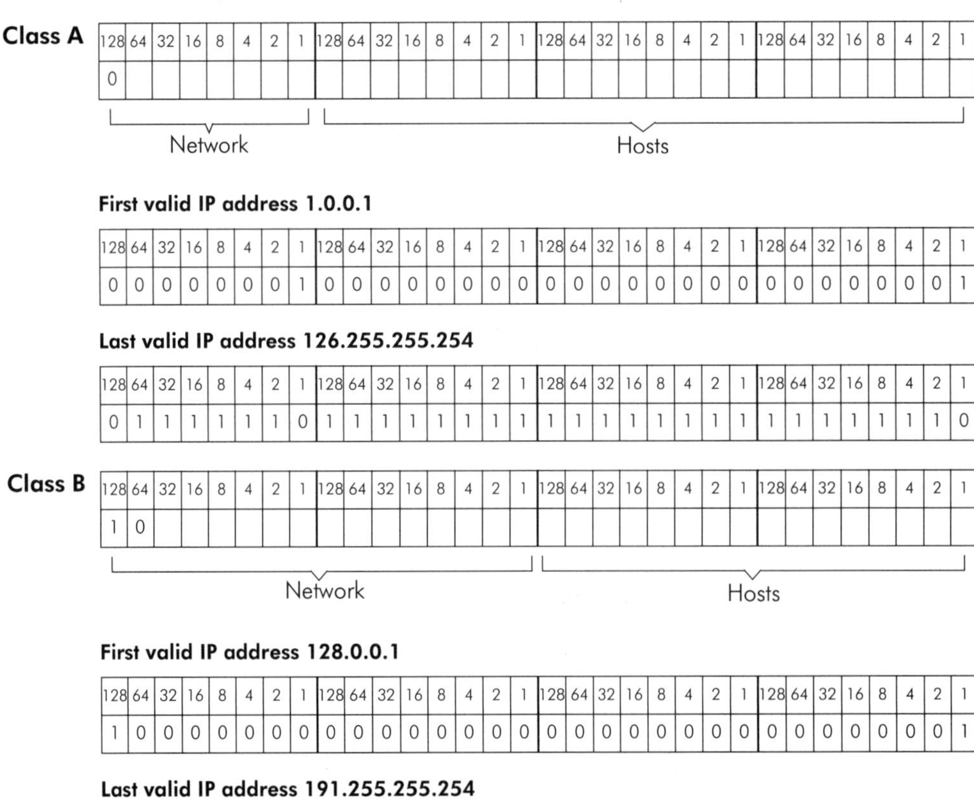

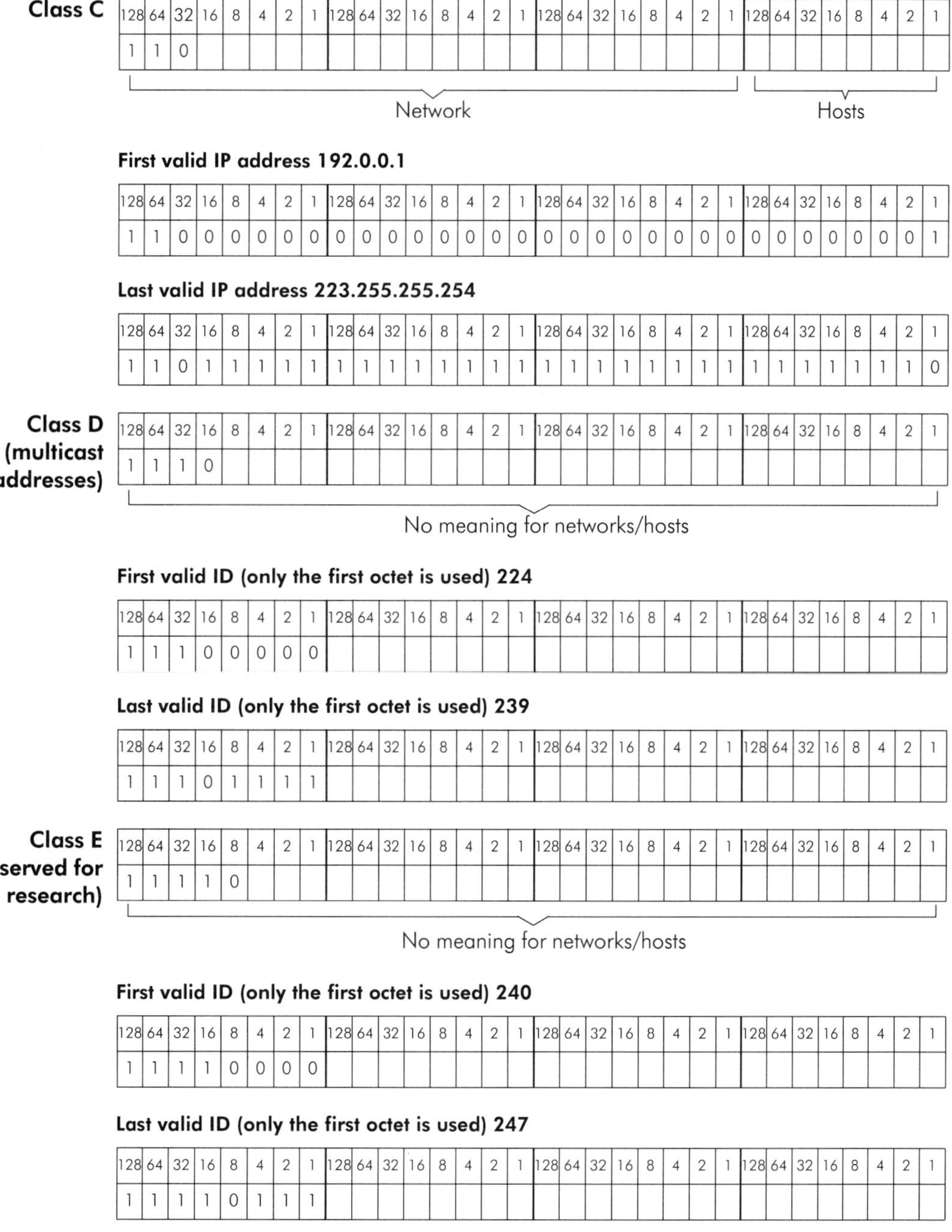
Class C
128 64 32 16 8 4 2 1 128 64 32 16 8 4 2 1 128 64 32 16 8 4 2 1 128 64 32 16 8 4 2 1
1 1 0
Network
Hosts
First valid IP address 192.0.0.1
128 64 32 16 8 4 2 1 128 64 32 16 8 4 2 1 128 64 32 16 8 4 2 1 128 64 32 16 8 4 2 1
1 1 0 0 0 0 0 0 0 0 0 0 0 0 0 0 0 0 0 0 0 0 0 0 0 0 0 0 0 0 0 1
Last valid IP address 223.255.255.254
128 64 32 16 8 4 2 1 128 64 32 16 8 4 2 1 128 64 32 16 8 4 2 1 128 64 32 16 8 4 2 1
1 1 0 1 1 1 1 1 1 1 1 1 1 1 1 1 1 1 1 1 1 1 1 1 1 1 1 1 1 1 1 0
Class D (multicast addresses)
128 64 32 16 8 4 2 1 128 64 32 16 8 4 2 1 128 64 32 16 8 4 2 1 128 64 32 16 8 4 2 1
1 1 1 0
No meaning for networks/hosts
First valid ID (only the first octet is used) 224
128 64 32 16 8 4 2 1 128 64 32 16 8 4 2 1 128 64 32 16 8 4 2 1 128 64 32 16 8 4 2 1
1 1 1 0 0 0 0 0
Last valid ID (only the first octet is used) 239
128 64 32 16 8 4 2 1 128 64 32 16 8 4 2 1 128 64 32 16 8 4 2 1 128 64 32 16 8 4 2 1
1 1 1 0 1 1 1 1
Class E (reserved for research)
128 64 32 16 8 4 2 1 128 64 32 16 8 4 2 1 128 64 32 16 8 4 2 1 128 64 32 16 8 4 2 1
1 1 1 1 0
No meaning for networks/hosts
First valid ID (only the first octet is used) 240
128 64 32 16 8 4 2 1 128 64 32 16 8 4 2 1 128 64 32 16 8 4 2 1 128 64 32 16 8 4 2 1
1 1 1 1 0 0 0 0
Last valid ID (only the first octet is used) 247
128 64 32 16 8 4 2 1 128 64 32 16 8 4 2 1 128 64 32 16 8 4 2 1 128 64 32 16 8 4 2 1
1 1 1 1 0 1 1 1

To further illustrate points 7 and 8 above, if we imagine a network ID of 172.16.0.0 (a reserved class B address) we can see that the first valid address should be 172.16.0.1 since address 172.16.0.0 would refer to the network itself (according to the definition above). Similarly, the address 172.16.255.254 is the last address since the address 172.16.255.255 would represent a broadcast on network 172.16.0.0.

A Quick Refresher on Address Classes

Since we are using only seven bits to define the network component of a class A address we can create only 126 networks. (We have seven bits since the first bit-value is fixed in our definition of a class A address). By using the first octet to define our network value this leaves the remaining three octets (24 bits) free to define the hosts on each of our 126 networks. This gives us 16,777,214 hosts on each of the networks. Due to the size of each of the class A networks it is common to find them allocated to very large organisations or nation states.

Class B networks use 16 bits for both the network component and the host component. This means that we can have 16,384 networks each of which has up to 65,534 hosts on it. Why the discrepancy between the two figures? Surely if we have 16 bits available for each the two numbers should be the same? The answer lies in the fact that the initial bit pattern that corresponds to a class B address is 10. This effectively rules out a whole block of network addresses from being used and so the total number of networks available for class B addresses drops to 16,384.

Class C networks have 24 bits available for the network component and eight bits available for the hosts. As such we can have 2,097,152 different networks and each network can have 254 hosts on it. Why only 254 and not 256? This is because the address corresponding to all 1's in the last octet would meet our definition of a broadcast on a class C network. As such it cannot be used for a host address. Similarly, with all 0's in the last octet this would correspond to the network identity and, again, cannot be used.

As an initial example, let us imagine that we are setting up a class B network and we are now considering the choices available for the subnet mask.

What happens if we do not want to use the default class B network range with its associated division of some 65,000 hosts on each network? We have decided to use one of the non-assigned class B addresses on our internal network and we want to have available approximately 60 networks with as many hosts as possible on each network.

To do this our default class B subnet mask of 255.255.0.0 will not work. This defines one network with 65,535 hosts on it. What we need to be able to do is to use part of the third octet for the purposes of defining the networks themselves. This means not just using the initial two octets but using some part of the third octet to give us more flexible network definitions.

Here is an illustration of what is possible. Imagine that we are using just two bits to distinguish our network range. With these two bits we have the following possibilities: 00, 01, 10 and 11.

By using only two bits in the third octet to designate our network component we will be using those bits corresponding to a place value of 192 (made up from 128 + 64). With such an arrangement and using both of the first octets in addition to the first two bits of the third octet our subnet mask will be 255.255.192.0. This assumes we are using the standard convention of leftmost contiguous bits in our mask.

This gives us four possible network combinations if all of these bit patterns were valid network addresses. If we use three bits the patterns are as follows: 000, 001, 010, 011, 100, 101, 110 and 111.

Our mask will then be (using 128 + 64 + 32) 224. This, together with the initial two octets, gives us a complete mask of 255.255.224.0.

With three bits we have eight possible network combinations. If we used four bits we would have 16 (2^4) network combinations. Continuing this argument with five bits we have 32 networks, six bits give us 64 networks and so on.

Figure 5.2 Subnet mask sizes and bit patterns

2 bits subnet mask 192

128	64
0	0
0	1
1	0
1	1

3 bits subnet mask 224

128	64	32
0	0	0
0	0	1
0	1	0
0	1	1
1	0	0
1	0	1
1	1	0
1	1	1

4 bits subnet mask 240

128	64	32	16
0	0	0	0
0	0	0	1
0	0	1	0
0	0	1	1
0	1	0	0
0	1	0	1
0	1	1	0
0	1	1	1
1	0	0	0
1	0	0	1
1	0	1	0
1	0	1	1
1	1	0	0
1	1	0	1
1	1	1	0
1	1	1	1

5 bits subnet mask 248

128	64	32	16	8
0	0	0	0	0
0	0	0	0	1
0	0	0	1	0
0	0	0	1	1
0	0	1	0	0
0	0	1	0	1
0	0	1	1	0
0	0	1	1	1
0	1	0	0	0
0	1	0	0	1
0	1	0	1	0
0	1	0	1	1
0	1	1	0	0
0	1	1	0	1
0	1	1	1	0
0	1	1	1	1

5 bits subnet mask 248

128	64	32	16	8
1	0	0	0	0
1	0	0	0	1
1	0	0	1	0
1	0	0	1	1
1	0	1	0	0
1	0	1	0	1
1	0	1	1	0
1	0	1	1	1
1	1	0	0	0
1	1	0	0	1
1	1	0	1	0
1	1	0	1	1
1	1	1	0	0
1	1	1	0	1
1	1	1	1	0
1	1	1	1	1

Figure 5.2 illustrates the bit patterns for two, three, four and five bits when used in the third octet. In all cases the initial two octets would be used giving us the corresponding actual subnet masks of:

255.255.192.0 (two bits used in the third octet)
255.255.224.0 (three bits used in the third octet)
255.255.240.0 (four bits used in the third octet)
255.255.248.0 (five bits used in the third octet)

We now hit two more of the rules for network identifiers. These rules were set up in the early days of network design and, as usual, made sense then. Now they look a little archaic since much of the hardware has improved in both its capabilities and its "intelligence". We will use the standard rules throughout this discussion but bear in mind that many newer routers can take advantage of some or all of the "banned" network identifiers (NetIDs). We will discuss this in more detail in the chapter on classless routing.

Rules for subnets:

1. No subnet can have all 0's as its identifier.
2. No subnet can have all 1's as its identifier.

The relevance to the examples above is that in each case we have to remove two values from the list of possible network identifiers:

- using two bits these values are 00 and 11
- using three bits the values are 000 and 111
- using four bits the values are 0000 and 1111

and so on.

Let us look at some of the relevant bit patterns that correspond with each of the above statements. Remember, we are using a class B network address and are planning to use the third octet to give our network address.

Network Identification

How does the adjacency test manage to sort out the different combinations of bit patterns in the third octet? To understand this we must examine in more detail the implications of using part of the third octet as our network address.

Figure 5.3 shows the eight possible bit patterns that we get when we use 224 (three bits) in the third octet. Two of these combinations (000 and 111) are not allowable under the rules above but the remaining patterns would all be calculated as separate networks.

This means that the value of the IP address in the third octet represents two things. Up until now the third octet of the IP value has always represented either a network or a host. Using part of this octet to represent the network identifier (NetID) means that part of the IP value also represents the NetID, the remaining part represents the host component of the given network.

Figure 5.3 A class B address subnetted on the third octet

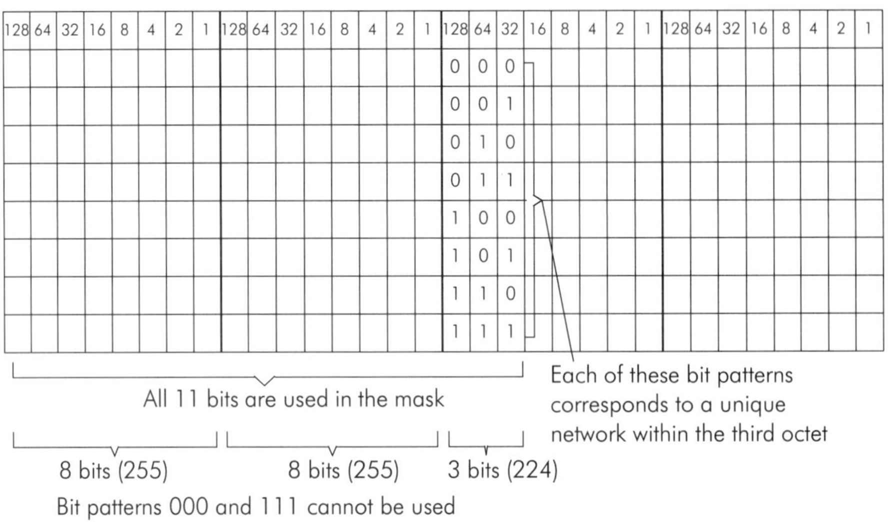

Figure 5.4 illustrates this point. Here we have five IP addresses: 172.16.32.0, 172.16.33.0, 172.16.34.0, 172.16.35.0 and 172.16.36.0. In all cases the subnet mask is 255.255.224.0 and the bit patterns for the third octet are clearly shown.

Figure 5.4 Example IP address with a third octet NetID

IP address	172								• 16								• 32								• 0							
	128	64	32	16	8	4	2	1	128	64	32	16	8	4	2	1	128	64	32	16	8	4	2	1	128	64	32	16	8	4	2	1
	1	0	1	0	1	1	0	0	0	0	0	1	0	0	0	0	0	0	1	0	0	0	0	0	0	0	0	0	0	0	0	0
mask	1	1	1	1	1	1	1	1	1	1	1	1	1	1	1	1	1	1	1	0	0	0	0	0	0	0	0	0	0	0	0	0

IP address	172								• 16								• 33								• 0							
	128	64	32	16	8	4	2	1	128	64	32	16	8	4	2	1	128	64	32	16	8	4	2	1	128	64	32	16	8	4	2	1
	1	0	1	0	1	1	0	0	0	0	0	1	0	0	0	0	0	0	1	0	0	0	0	1	0	0	0	0	0	0	0	0
mask	1	1	1	1	1	1	1	1	1	1	1	1	1	1	1	1	1	1	1	0	0	0	0	0	0	0	0	0	0	0	0	0

IP address	172							•	16							•	34							•	0							
	128	64	32	16	8	4	2	1	128	64	32	16	8	4	2	1	128	64	32	16	8	4	2	1	128	64	32	16	8	4	2	1
	1	0	1	0	1	1	0	0	0	0	0	1	0	0	0	0	0	0	1	0	0	0	1	0	0	0	0	0	0	0	0	0
mask	1	1	1	1	1	1	1	1	1	1	1	1	1	1	1	1	1	1	1	0	0	0	0	0	0	0	0	0	0	0	0	0

IP address	172							•	16							•	35							•	0							
	128	64	32	16	8	4	2	1	128	64	32	16	8	4	2	1	128	64	32	16	8	4	2	1	128	64	32	16	8	4	2	1
	1	0	1	0	1	1	0	0	0	0	0	1	0	0	0	0	0	0	1	0	0	0	1	1	0	0	0	0	0	0	0	0
mask	1	1	1	1	1	1	1	1	1	1	1	1	1	1	1	1	1	1	1	0	0	0	0	0	0	0	0	0	0	0	0	0

IP address	172							•	16							•	36							•	0							
	128	64	32	16	8	4	2	1	128	64	32	16	8	4	2	1	128	64	32	16	8	4	2	1	128	64	32	16	8	4	2	1
	1	0	1	0	1	1	0	0	0	0	0	1	0	0	0	0	0	0	1	0	0	1	0	0	0	0	0	0	0	0	0	0
mask	1	1	1	1	1	1	1	1	1	1	1	1	1	1	1	1	1	1	1	0	0	0	0	0	0	0	0	0	0	0	0	0

The mask is in all cases: **255 • 255 • 224 • 0**

When the adjacency test compares the network components to determine if the source and destination computers are on the same network it does so by comparing the first 19 bits of the IP address (8 + 8 + 3 bits). In all five cases (above) the network bit patterns are identical and would, therefore, satisfy the adjacency test's requirements of "on the same network".

In the first example of Figure 5.4 (172.16.32.0) we can see that the bit patterns for the host component of the IP address is "all 0's". This is not allowable under our earlier rules and so this address corresponds to a network address. It could not be assigned to an individual host under our standard rules.

The second example of Figure 5.4 172.16.33.0 shows that the host component of the IP address is not all zeros (we have the bit pattern of 00100001 in the third octet) and this could be used as a valid host address on the network in question. The same analysis could be applied to the remaining three addresses in Figure 5.4.

What about our rule that the host addresses cannot be all 1's or all 0's? In the IP addresses shown in Figure 5.4 the host addresses are made up from the last 13 bits of the IP address. In the last four examples in Figure 5.4 none of these are "all zero" and as such are valid.

In each of the last four cases in Figure 5.4 the third octet value in the IP address can be interpreted as a machine on network number 32.

Figure 5.5 shows how we can interpret the addresses of the first, middle and last machines on this network. In all cases the bit patterns for the first three bits of the third octet in the IP address are the same. The adjacency test would therefore decide that all of the machines within the range 172.16.32.1 through 172.16.63.254 are on the same network.

Figure 5.5 A sample of valid IP addresses

IP address	172								16								32								1							
	128	64	32	16	8	4	2	1	128	64	32	16	8	4	2	1	128	64	32	16	8	4	2	1	128	64	32	16	8	4	2	1
First machine on network "32"	1	0	1	0	1	1	0	0	0	0	0	1	0	0	0	0	0	0	1	0	0	0	0	0	0	0	0	0	0	0	0	1
	1	1	1	1	1	1	1	1	1	1	1	1	1	1	1	1	1	1	1	0	0	0	0	0	0	0	0	0	0	0	0	0
IP address	172								16								35								255							
A "middle" machine on network "32"	128	64	32	16	8	4	2	1	128	64	32	16	8	4	2	1	128	64	32	16	8	4	2	1	128	64	32	16	8	4	2	1
	1	0	1	0	1	1	0	0	0	0	0	1	0	0	0	0	0	0	1	0	0	0	1	1	1	1	1	1	1	1	1	1
	1	1	1	1	1	1	1	1	1	1	1	1	1	1	1	1	1	1	1	0	0	0	0	0	0	0	0	0	0	0	0	0
IP address	172								16								63								254							
	128	64	32	16	8	4	2	1	128	64	32	16	8	4	2	1	128	64	32	16	8	4	2	1	128	64	32	16	8	4	2	1
The last machine on network "32"	1	0	1	0	1	1	0	0	0	0	0	1	0	0	0	0	0	0	1	1	1	1	1	1	1	1	1	1	1	1	1	0
	1	1	1	1	1	1	1	1	1	1	1	1	1	1	1	1	1	1	1	0	0	0	0	0	0	0	0	0	0	0	0	0
The mask is in all cases:	255								255								224								0							

Address Boundaries

Things get a little more interesting when we examine the bit patterns at the end of the address range for the 32 network and the bit patterns at the start of the next network in the range – the 64 network.

This is illustrated in Figure 5.6 where the final address of the 32 network is shown together with the broadcast address for the 32 network. Note how all of the host part of the IP address is set to 1's. Finally, the address of the first host on the 64 network is shown for comparison. When comparing the bit patterns of the first three bits of the third octet in networks 32 and 64 note how the 001 (network 32) has now been replaced by 010 (network 64) and that as a result the adjacency test would determine that these two are on different networks.

Figure 5.6 Bit patterns as NetID changes

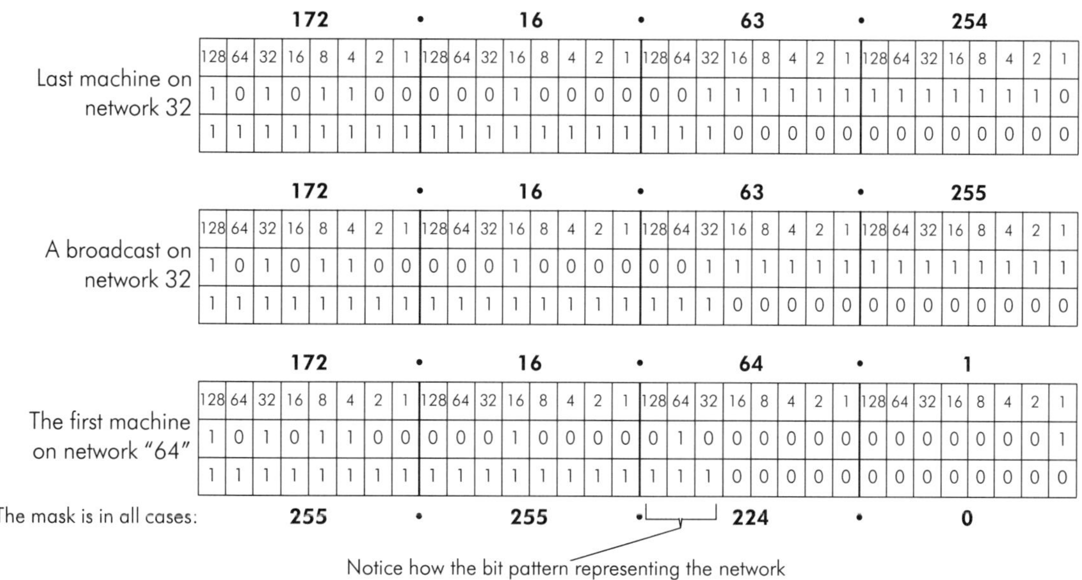

	172								• 16								• 63								• 254							
	128	64	32	16	8	4	2	1	128	64	32	16	8	4	2	1	128	64	32	16	8	4	2	1	128	64	32	16	8	4	2	1
Last machine on network 32	1	0	1	0	1	1	0	0	0	0	0	1	0	0	0	0	0	0	1	1	1	1	1	1	1	1	1	1	1	1	1	0
	1	1	1	1	1	1	1	1	1	1	1	1	1	1	1	1	1	1	1	0	0	0	0	0	0	0	0	0	0	0	0	0

	172								• 16								• 63								• 255							
	128	64	32	16	8	4	2	1	128	64	32	16	8	4	2	1	128	64	32	16	8	4	2	1	128	64	32	16	8	4	2	1
A broadcast on network 32	1	0	1	0	1	1	0	0	0	0	0	1	0	0	0	0	0	0	1	1	1	1	1	1	1	1	1	1	1	1	1	1
	1	1	1	1	1	1	1	1	1	1	1	1	1	1	1	1	1	1	1	0	0	0	0	0	0	0	0	0	0	0	0	0

	172								• 16								• 64								• 1							
	128	64	32	16	8	4	2	1	128	64	32	16	8	4	2	1	128	64	32	16	8	4	2	1	128	64	32	16	8	4	2	1
The first machine on network "64"	1	0	1	0	1	1	0	0	0	0	0	1	0	0	0	0	0	1	0	0	0	0	0	0	0	0	0	0	0	0	0	1
	1	1	1	1	1	1	1	1	1	1	1	1	1	1	1	1	1	1	1	0	0	0	0	0	0	0	0	0	0	0	0	0
The mask is in all cases:	255								• 255								• 224								• 0							

Notice how the bit pattern representing the network component has changed from the above two networks

Figure 5.7 shows the bit patterns for some additional hosts on the 32 network. In all cases the final octet is all 0's but this does not contradict our rule of "hosts cannot have all 0's in their address" since the preceding five bits that are also part of the host address are not all 0.

How the adjacency test interprets two IP addresses (one for the source computer and one for the destination computer) is shown in Figure 5.8. Here we use IP address 172.16.33.17 to represent our source computer and 172.16.63.99 as our destination computer. In the bit patterns shown in Figure 5.8 we can see that the network component is the same in both cases. The adjacency test would therefore decide that the two machines were on the same network segment and use the hardware address to deliver the data.

Figure 5.7 Further bit patterns on the "32" network

The network component is the same for all these networks

IP address	172								• 16								• 33								• 0							
	128	64	32	16	8	4	2	1	128	64	32	16	8	4	2	1	128	64	32	16	8	4	2	1	128	64	32	16	8	4	2	1
	1	0	1	0	1	1	0	0	0	0	0	1	0	0	0	0	0	0	1	0	0	0	0	1	0	0	0	0	0	0	0	1
	1	1	1	1	1	1	1	1	1	1	1	1	1	1	1	1	1	1	1	0	0	0	0	0	0	0	0	0	0	0	0	0
mask	255								• 255								• 224								• 0							

IP address	172								• 16								• 40								• 0							
	128	64	32	16	8	4	2	1	128	64	32	16	8	4	2	1	128	64	32	16	8	4	2	1	128	64	32	16	8	4	2	1
	1	0	1	0	1	1	0	0	0	0	0	1	0	0	0	0	0	0	1	0	1	0	0	0	0	0	0	0	0	0	0	0
	1	1	1	1	1	1	1	1	1	1	1	1	1	1	1	1	1	1	1	0	0	0	0	0	0	0	0	0	0	0	0	0
mask	255								• 255								• 224								• 0							

IP address	172								• 16								• 63								• 0							
	128	64	32	16	8	4	2	1	128	64	32	16	8	4	2	1	128	64	32	16	8	4	2	1	128	64	32	16	8	4	2	1
	1	0	1	0	1	1	0	0	0	0	0	1	0	0	0	0	0	0	1	1	1	1	1	1	0	0	0	0	0	0	0	0
	1	1	1	1	1	1	1	1	1	1	1	1	1	1	1	1	1	1	1	0	0	0	0	0	0	0	0	0	0	0	0	0
mask	255								• 255								• 224								• 0							

The host component varies for each network only; "all 1's" and "all 0's" are not allowed

Figure 5.8 Comparison of source and destination IP addresses

Adjacency test bit patterns for source computer 172.16.33.17 and destination computer 172.16.63.99. In both cases the subnet mask is 255.255.224.0.

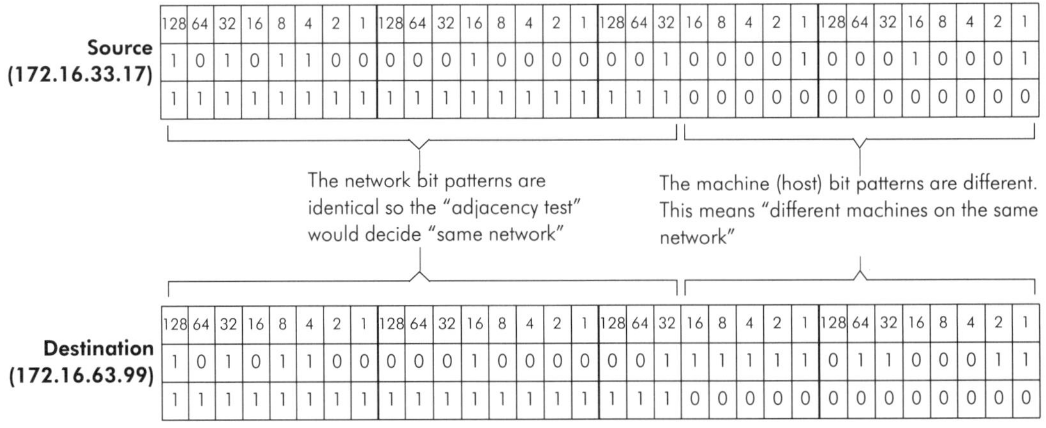

We are now in a position to examine the relationship between the network numbers and the equivalent host numbers on each network.

With a standard class B network we can have 65,535 hosts on each class B network. By using some of the bits in the third octet as our network designator we reduce the number of bits that are available for host use. This is illustrated in Figure 5.9. Here we can see that by using the rightmost bits for our host addresses we have, effectively, the same combinations that we used when we calculated the networks.

Figure 5.9 Host bit combinations

128	64	32	16	8	4	2	1	128	64	32	16	8	4	2	1
														0	0
														0	1
														1	0
														1	1

Two bits used for hosts gives us 4 (2^2) possible combinations

128	64	32	16	8	4	2	1	128	64	32	16	8	4	2	1
													0	0	0
													0	0	1
													0	1	0
													0	1	1
													1	0	0
													1	0	1
													1	1	0
													1	1	1

Three bits used for hosts gives us 8 (2^3) possible combinations

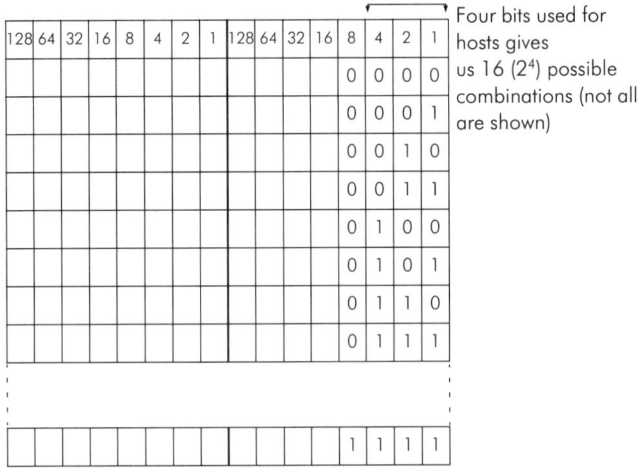

128	64	32	16	8	4	2	1	128	64	32	16	8	4	2	1
												0	0	0	0
												0	0	0	1
												0	0	1	0
												0	0	1	1
												0	1	0	0
												0	1	0	1
												0	1	1	0
												0	1	1	1
												1	1	1	1

Four bits used for hosts gives us 16 (2^4) possible combinations (not all are shown)

For two host bits we get 4 (2^2) possible combinations; three host bits provides 8 (2^3) combinations and four bits gives us 16 (2^4) combinations. In each case we have two values that contradict our rules. These are "all 1's" and "all 0's". As with the network values we must subtract these two from each of our possible combinations. This leads to the following sets of figures for our hosts:

Number of bits	Formula	Total combinations†
2	$2^2 - 2$	$4 - 2 = 2$
3	$2^3 - 2$	$8 - 2 = 6$
4	$2^4 - 2$	$16 - 2 = 14$
5	$2^5 - 2$	$32 - 2 = 30$
6	$2^6 - 2$	$64 - 2 = 62$
7	$2^7 - 2$	$128 - 2 = 126$
8	$2^8 - 2$	$256 - 2 = 254$

†. i.e., the number of hosts on each network.

This is how we arrive at the calculation of 254 hosts on a class C network (one in which we use only the last octet to distinguish the hosts on a network). The actual value is 256 but we cannot use all 1's and we cannot use all 0's so we end up with 254 hosts on each network.

If we continue the above argument (so that we continue to use the rightmost bits in the third octet) we see that we can steadily increase the number of hosts as we use each of the additional bits. This argument is illustrated in Figure 5.10 and enables us to prepare the table (in Figure 5.10.) which summarises the various network and host combinations for each of the different bit patterns.

Figure 5.10 Adjustment of host numbers as part of the 3rd octet is used for subnetting

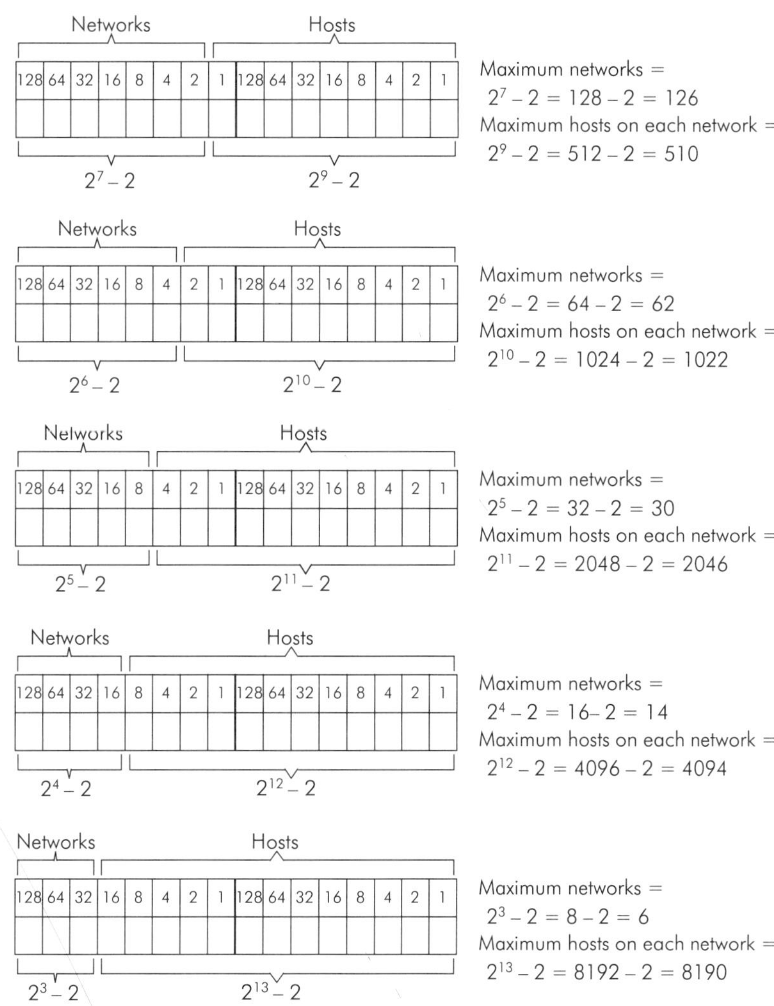

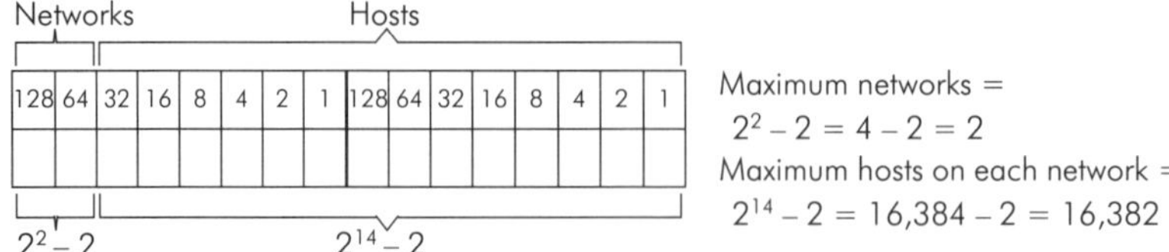

Bits used for the network	Subnet mask	Maximum number of networks	Maximum number of hosts per network
2	192	2	16,382
3	224	6	8,190
4	240	14	4,094
5	248	30	2,046
6	252	62	1,022
7	254	126	510
8	255	254	254

Using Subnets in Network Design

We are now in a position to discuss our original requirements. We wanted to use a class B address with around 60 networks and the maximum number of machines on each network. We will be using the unassigned class B address of 172.16.0.0. To meet these requirements we will use a subnet mask of 252. This uses six of the available eight bits of the third octet for network use and allows us to have 1022 hosts on each of the 62 networks.

Figure 5.11 illustrates some of the various network combinations using the above scheme. In each case the first and last machine addresses for each network are shown. Figure 5.12 (page 63) shows a possible network design using the above scheme.

This addressing scheme raises a few questions and some aspects of the interpretation of these addresses that we will discuss in later chapters.

Figure 5.11 Class B networks using a 22-bit subnet mask

First machine on network 172.16.4.0

	128	64	32	16	8	4	2	1	128	64	32	16	8	4	2	1	128	64	32	16	8	4	2	1	128	64	32	16	8	4	2	1
IP address: 172.16.4.1	1	0	1	0	1	1	0	0	0	0	0	1	0	0	0	0	0	0	0	0	0	1	0	0	0	0	0	0	0	0	0	1
subnet mask: 255.255.252.0	1	1	1	1	1	1	1	1	1	1	1	1	1	1	1	1	1	1	1	1	1	1	0	0	0	0	0	0	0	0	0	0

Last machine on network 172.16.4.0

	128	64	32	16	8	4	2	1	128	64	32	16	8	4	2	1	128	64	32	16	8	4	2	1	128	64	32	16	8	4	2	1
IP address: 172.16.7.254	1	0	1	0	1	1	0	0	0	0	0	1	0	0	0	0	0	0	0	0	0	1	1	1	1	1	1	1	1	1	1	0
subnet mask: 255.255.252.0	1	1	1	1	1	1	1	1	1	1	1	1	1	1	1	1	1	1	1	1	1	1	0	0	0	0	0	0	0	0	0	0

Broadcast on network 172.16.4.0

	128	64	32	16	8	4	2	1	128	64	32	16	8	4	2	1	128	64	32	16	8	4	2	1	128	64	32	16	8	4	2	1
IP address: 172.16.7.255	1	0	1	0	1	1	0	0	0	0	0	1	0	0	0	0	0	0	0	0	0	1	1	1	1	1	1	1	1	1	1	1
subnet mask: 255.255.252.0	1	1	1	1	1	1	1	1	1	1	1	1	1	1	1	1	1	1	1	1	1	1	0	0	0	0	0	0	0	0	0	0

First machine on network 172.16.128.0

	128	64	32	16	8	4	2	1	128	64	32	16	8	4	2	1	128	64	32	16	8	4	2	1	128	64	32	16	8	4	2	1
IP address: 172.16.128.1	1	0	1	0	1	1	0	0	0	0	0	1	0	0	0	0	1	0	0	0	0	0	0	0	0	0	0	0	0	0	0	1
subnet mask: 255.255.252.0	1	1	1	1	1	1	1	1	1	1	1	1	1	1	1	1	1	1	1	1	1	1	0	0	0	0	0	0	0	0	0	0

Last machine on network 172.16.128.0

	128	64	32	16	8	4	2	1	128	64	32	16	8	4	2	1	128	64	32	16	8	4	2	1	128	64	32	16	8	4	2	1
IP address: 172.16.131.254	1	0	1	0	1	1	0	0	0	0	0	1	0	0	0	0	1	0	0	0	0	0	1	1	1	1	1	1	1	1	1	0
subnet mask: 255.255.252.0	1	1	1	1	1	1	1	1	1	1	1	1	1	1	1	1	1	1	1	1	1	1	0	0	0	0	0	0	0	0	0	0

Broadcast on network 172.16.128.0

	128	64	32	16	8	4	2	1	128	64	32	16	8	4	2	1	128	64	32	16	8	4	2	1	128	64	32	16	8	4	2	1
IP address: 172.16.131.255	1	0	1	0	1	1	0	0	0	0	0	1	0	0	0	0	1	0	0	0	0	0	1	1	1	1	1	1	1	1	1	1
subnet mask: 255.255.252.0	1	1	1	1	1	1	1	1	1	1	1	1	1	1	1	1	1	1	1	1	1	1	0	0	0	0	0	0	0	0	0	0

First machine on network 172.16.160.0

	128	64	32	16	8	4	2	1	128	64	32	16	8	4	2	1	128	64	32	16	8	4	2	1	128	64	32	16	8	4	2	1
IP address: 172.16.160.1	1	0	1	0	1	1	0	0	0	0	0	1	0	0	0	0	1	0	1	0	0	0	0	0	0	0	0	0	0	0	0	1
subnet mask: 255.255.252.0	1	1	1	1	1	1	1	1	1	1	1	1	1	1	1	1	1	1	1	1	1	1	0	0	0	0	0	0	0	0	0	0

Last machine on network 172.16.160.0

	128	64	32	16	8	4	2	1	128	64	32	16	8	4	2	1	128	64	32	16	8	4	2	1	128	64	32	16	8	4	2	1
IP address: 172.16.163.254	1	0	1	0	1	1	0	0	0	0	0	1	0	0	0	0	1	0	1	0	0	0	1	1	1	1	1	1	1	1	1	0
subnet mask: 255.255.252.0	1	1	1	1	1	1	1	1	1	1	1	1	1	1	1	1	1	1	1	1	1	1	0	0	0	0	0	0	0	0	0	0

Broadcast on network 172.16.160.0

	128	64	32	16	8	4	2	1	128	64	32	16	8	4	2	1	128	64	32	16	8	4	2	1	128	64	32	16	8	4	2	1
IP address: 172.16.163.255	1	0	1	0	1	1	0	0	0	0	0	1	0	0	0	0	1	0	1	0	0	0	1	1	1	1	1	1	1	1	1	1
subnet mask: 255.255.252.0	1	1	1	1	1	1	1	1	1	1	1	1	1	1	1	1	1	1	1	1	1	1	0	0	0	0	0	0	0	0	0	0

First machine on network 172.16.216.0

	128	64	32	16	8	4	2	1	128	64	32	16	8	4	2	1	128	64	32	16	8	4	2	1	128	64	32	16	8	4	2	1
IP address: 172.16.216.1	1	0	1	0	1	1	0	0	0	0	0	1	0	0	0	0	1	1	0	1	1	0	0	0	0	0	0	0	0	0	0	1
subnet mask: 255.255.252.0	1	1	1	1	1	1	1	1	1	1	1	1	1	1	1	1	1	1	1	1	1	1	0	0	0	0	0	0	0	0	0	0

Last machine on network 172.16.216.0

	128	64	32	16	8	4	2	1	128	64	32	16	8	4	2	1	128	64	32	16	8	4	2	1	128	64	32	16	8	4	2	1
IP address: 172.16.219.254	1	0	1	0	1	1	0	0	0	0	0	1	0	0	0	0	1	1	0	1	1	0	1	1	1	1	1	1	1	1	1	0
subnet mask: 255.255.252.0	1	1	1	1	1	1	1	1	1	1	1	1	1	1	1	1	1	1	1	1	1	1	0	0	0	0	0	0	0	0	0	0

Broadcast on network 172.16.216.0

	128	64	32	16	8	4	2	1	128	64	32	16	8	4	2	1	128	64	32	16	8	4	2	1	128	64	32	16	8	4	2	1
IP address: 172.16.219.255	1	0	1	0	1	1	0	0	0	0	0	1	0	0	0	0	1	1	0	1	1	0	1	1	1	1	1	1	1	1	1	1
subnet mask: 255.255.252.0	1	1	1	1	1	1	1	1	1	1	1	1	1	1	1	1	1	1	1	1	1	1	0	0	0	0	0	0	0	0	0	0

Figure 5.12 Sample network layout

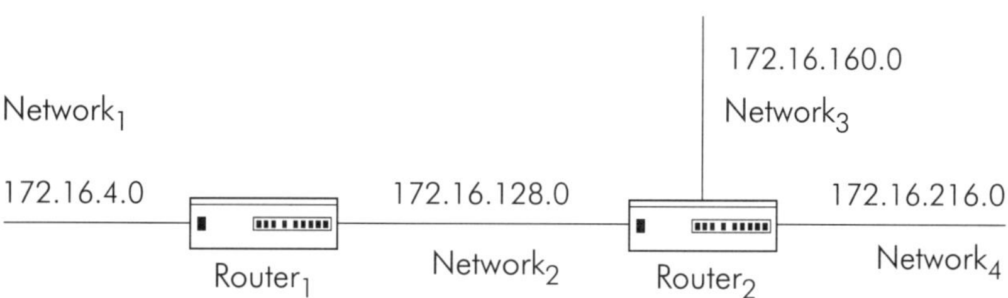

All networks use a mask of 255.255.252.0
Other possible networks are (not an exhaustive list): 172.16.8.0
.12.0
.16.0
.20.0
•
•
•
.220.0
.224.0
•
•
•
.248.0

6

Subnetted Class C Addresses

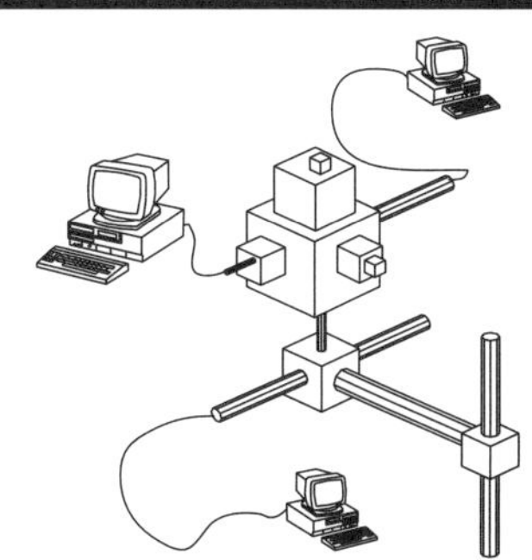

Overview of Class C Networks

We have seen that it is possible to subnet class B addresses so that the default 16 bits are utilised to give us some additional networking flexibility. Is it possible to use the class C network addresses in the same way? The answer is most certainly yes. This area of subnetting is very common since many smaller companies and organisations will have use of a class C network address.

Let us recap on what this means. A class C network address is one in the range 192.0.0.1 through to 223.255.255.254. As our network example we will use the non-assigned or "private" class C address of 192.168.10.0. The first three octets define the network component and the last octet defines the host component.

Our default subnet mask for this network is 255.255.255.0. This means that the entire first 24 bits are used to define the network component and all 254 hosts will be on the single network 192.168.10.0. Is this what we want? It might well be that it suits us to have all of our machines on one physical network. However, in many instances it would be better to think about the organisation of the network and to subnet according to the site's requirements.

Let us continue the previous chapter's discussion on variable-length masks for a class B network into the current network. In a class C network we have one octet (the last) that can be used for subnetting. We have eight bits to play around with. Let us consider some of the possibilities. Figure 6.1 illustrates the first three sets of possibilities.

Figure 6.1 Initial options for subnetting class C networks

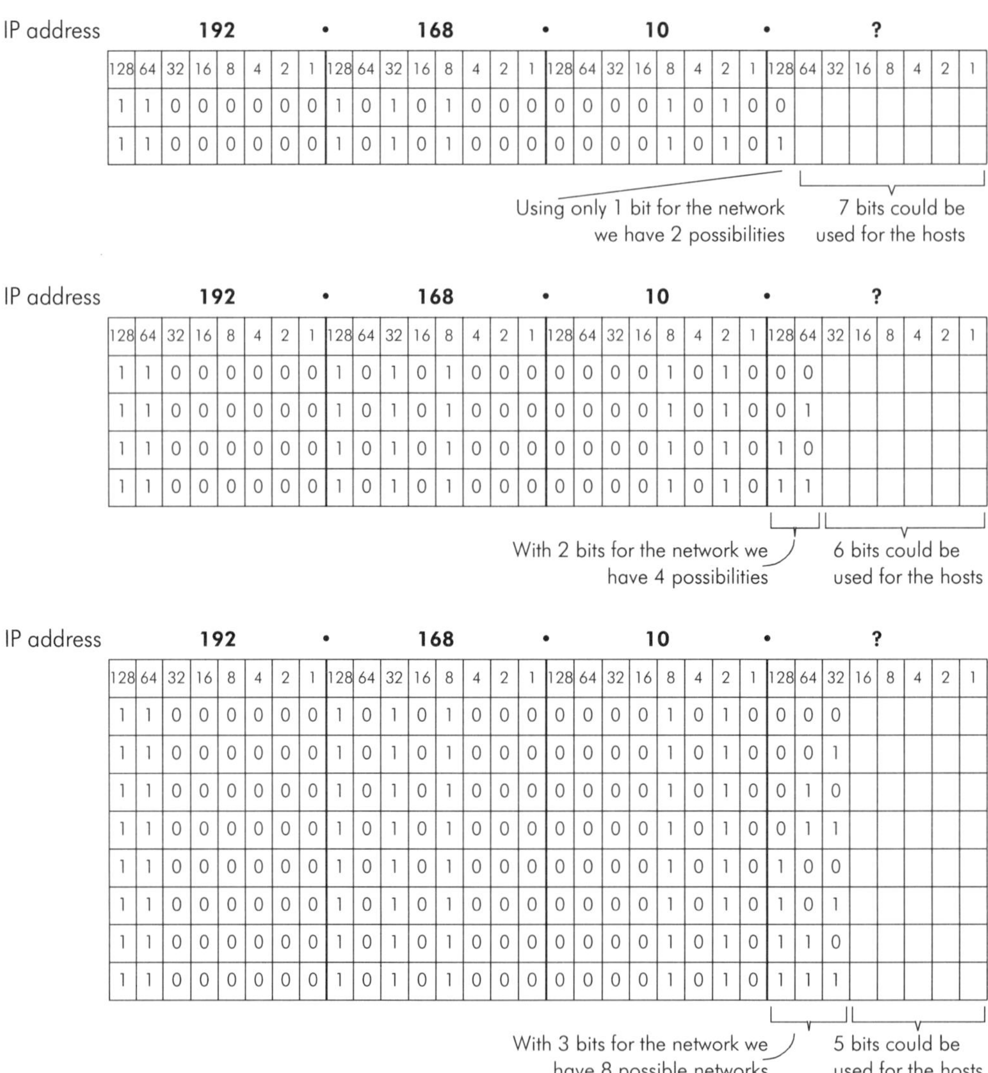

In the first example of Figure 6.1 we have used one bit in our last octet as our network component. This gives us two options for the network. The network designator, in the final octet component, is either a 0 or a 1. These are our two network possibilities and each network has seven bits of the remaining octet that can be used for hosts. These seven bits give us 2^7 (128) hosts on each of the networks – so our networks can have 128 hosts on them. Or can they? According to our previous set of rules we cannot have all 1's or all 0's as our host designators on any given network. So our maximum of 128 hosts gets reduced by two (126 actual hosts). Of more importance is the fact that according to the standard definitions we cannot have subnets of all 0's or all 1's either. Our "one bit" subnet division allows only 1 or 0 and therefore, according to the standard definitions these are unacceptable.

"Side Effects" of Rule Enforcement

The effect of enforcing these rules is to "wipe out" a considerable number of network possibilities from subnetted class C designs. More recent RFC proposals have offered alternative ways of looking at this problem and have proposed ways in which routers could copy with a subnet of 1 or 0. This would enable the utilisation of far more networks in a subnetted class C network design. Unfortunately, these "extensions" are not at all common and we will stick to the "standard" methods of calculating the possibilities.

With the second option shown in Figure 6.1 we start to see the real possibilities of class C subnetting. Here we are using two bits of the final octet as our subnet designator. Here we have four possibilities but two of them are, as above, illegal on standard networks. This leaves us with two networks 01 and 10 which are valid. On each of these there are 2^6 (64) possibilities for the hosts. The "all 1's" and the "all 0's" are, again, not valid for host addresses; so, using two bits for our class C subnets we can have two networks each of which can have 64 –2 = 62 hosts on them.

Here we can see the price we pay for the flexibility of our network design. We started out with a standard class C network and using a standard subnet mask we had one network with 254 machines on it. Now we have the flexibility of two networks but we can only have 62 machines on each. The difference is due to the fact that each of our two "illegal" networks could have had 62 machines on them and we have effectively "lost" these options from our network. This is why many TCP/IP vendors are implementing the more modern interpretation to allow subnets of all 1's or all 0's. It is this reduction in effective numbers of machines that has provided the pressure to try and change the underlying technological rules.

Figure 6.2 A valid class C subnet

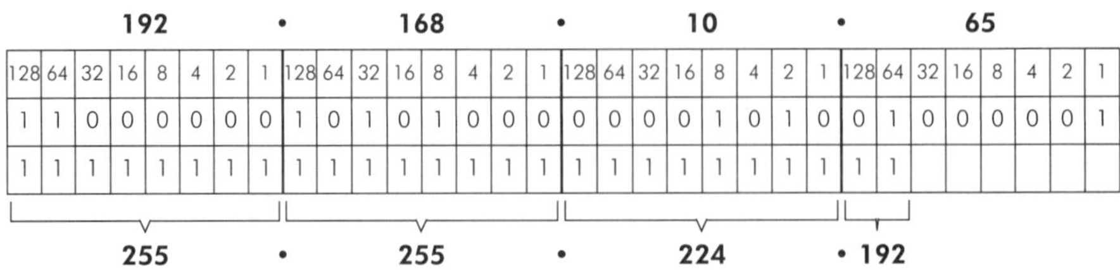

Figure 6.3 Network values for the "64" subnet

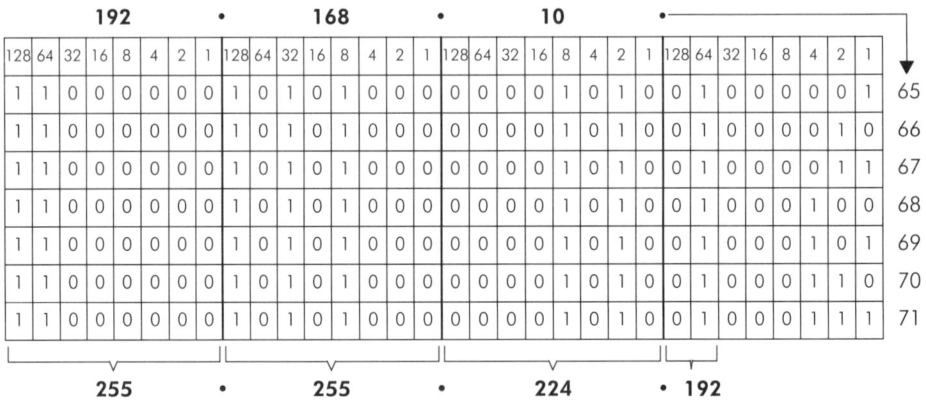

If we use the two bits for the network designation then what is our subnet mask? Figure 6.2 illustrates the position for a 2-bit subnet mask. Here we can see that the subnet mask for our network is 255.255.255.192. This states that we are using two bits in the final octet to subdivide our network. What are the available host ranges for these networks? Figure 6.3 shows us some of the initial bit patterns for some of the first machines in this range. From Figure 6.3 we can see that the first machine on the first acceptable network[1] corresponds to network 64. The bit values of all 0's in the host part would represent a network address so IP address 192.168.10.64 with a subnet mask of 255.255.255.192 is actually a network address. The first allowable host address on network 64 is the one with bit pattern

1. 01 in the initial bit positions – remember that the very first network 00 was not allowed under our standard rules.

01000001. This corresponds to 65 in base 10 so IP address 192.168.10.65 with subnet mask 255.255.255.192 is the first machine on the 64 network in our subnetted class C network.

The other valid network using two bits is the 10 network. This is again because the 11 and 00 networks are not allowed. The two valid networks are 01 or 64 and 10 or 128. Let us look at the bit patterns that correspond to the final machines in the 64 network as we start to approach the 128 network boundary. Figure 6.4 illustrates these bit patterns.

Figure 6.4 Approaching the "128" network boundary on the "64" network

192								168								10																
128	64	32	16	8	4	2	1	128	64	32	16	8	4	2	1	128	64	32	16	8	4	2	1	128	64	32	16	8	4	2	1	
1	1	0	0	0	0	0	0	1	0	1	0	1	0	0	0	0	0	0	0	1	0	1	0	0	1	1	1	0	1	0	0	116
1	1	0	0	0	0	0	0	1	0	1	0	1	0	0	0	0	0	0	0	1	0	1	0	0	1	1	1	0	1	0	1	117
1	1	0	0	0	0	0	0	1	0	1	0	1	0	0	0	0	0	0	0	1	0	1	0	0	1	1	1	0	1	1	0	118
1	1	0	0	0	0	0	0	1	0	1	0	1	0	0	0	0	0	0	0	1	0	1	0	0	1	1	1	0	1	1	1	119
1	1	0	0	0	0	0	0	1	0	1	0	1	0	0	0	0	0	0	0	1	0	1	0	0	1	1	1	1	0	0	0	120
1	1	0	0	0	0	0	0	1	0	1	0	1	0	0	0	0	0	0	0	1	0	1	0	0	1	1	1	1	0	0	1	121
1	1	0	0	0	0	0	0	1	0	1	0	1	0	0	0	0	0	0	0	1	0	1	0	0	1	1	1	1	0	1	0	122
1	1	0	0	0	0	0	0	1	0	1	0	1	0	0	0	0	0	0	0	1	0	1	0	0	1	1	1	1	0	1	1	123
1	1	0	0	0	0	0	0	1	0	1	0	1	0	0	0	0	0	0	0	1	0	1	0	0	1	1	1	1	1	0	0	124
1	1	0	0	0	0	0	0	1	0	1	0	1	0	0	0	0	0	0	0	1	0	1	0	0	1	1	1	1	1	0	1	125
1	1	0	0	0	0	0	0	1	0	1	0	1	0	0	0	0	0	0	0	1	0	1	0	0	1	1	1	1	1	1	0	126†
1	1	0	0	0	0	0	0	1	0	1	0	1	0	0	0	0	0	0	0	1	0	1	0	0	1	1	1	1	1	1	1	127‡
1	1	0	0	0	0	0	0	1	0	1	0	1	0	0	0	0	0	0	0	1	0	1	0	1	0	0	0	0	0	0	0	128*
1	1	0	0	0	0	0	0	1	0	1	0	1	0	0	0	0	0	0	0	1	0	1	0	1	0	0	0	0	0	0	1	129
1	1	0	0	0	0	0	0	1	0	1	0	1	0	0	0	0	0	0	0	1	0	1	0	1	0	0	0	0	0	1	0	130

†. 192.168.10.126 is the last valid host on the 64 network
‡. 192.168.10.127 is the broadcast address on the 64 network
*. 192.168.10.128 is the network address of the 128 network

These are the first 2 valid host addresses on the 128 network

As can be seen from Figure 6.4 the bit patterns become more interesting as we approach the boundary between the "64" network and the "128" network. The following addresses are important (in all cases the subnet mask is 255.255.255.192). This is because they illustrate the bit patterns as the NetID changes from "64" to "128", to the illegal network "11".

- 192.128.10.64 Network address for first valid subnet the "64" network
- 192.128.10.65 First valid host on the "64" network
- 192.128.10.126 Last valid host on the "64" subnet
- 192.128.10.127 Broadcast address on the "64" subnet
- 192.128.10.128 Network address for the second valid subnet the "128" network
- 192.128.10.129 First valid host on the "128" subnet
- 192.128.10.190 Last valid host on the "128" subnet
- 192.128.10.191 Broadcast address on the "128" subnet
- 192.128.10.192 Start of the non-valid "11" network

The last three sets of bit patterns are illustrated in Figure 6.5.

Figure 6.5 Final bit patterns on the "128" network

192								168								10																
128	64	32	16	8	4	2	1	128	64	32	16	8	4	2	1	128	64	32	16	8	4	2	1	128	64	32	16	8	4	2	1	
1	1	0	0	0	0	0	0	1	0	1	0	1	0	0	0	0	0	0	0	1	0	1	0	1	0	1	1	1	1	1	0	190†
1	1	0	0	0	0	0	0	1	0	1	0	1	0	0	0	0	0	0	0	1	0	1	0	1	0	1	1	1	1	1	1	191‡
1	1	0	0	0	0	0	0	1	0	1	0	1	0	0	0	0	0	0	0	1	0	1	0	1	1	0	0	0	0	0	0	192

Invalid network address since 11 is not permissible

†. Last valid host address on the "128" network
‡. Broadcast address on the 128 network

Extending our Options

Continuing the above discussion on class C subnets we can see the effect of using three bits for the subnets. This gives us 2^3 (8) theoretical networks of which two (000 and 111) are not permissible. This leaves us with six possible networks each of which can have 2^5 (32) hosts on them. Again, our rules state that "all 1's" is the broadcast address and "all 0's" is the network address so three bits gives us 6 networks each of which can have 30 hosts on them. The subnet mask would use three bits and is 224 (128 + 64 + 32). So our overall subnet mask would be 255.255.255.224.

The table below summarises the bits used, the subnet mask required and the number of networks and hosts for each bit combination.

Bits used	Mask	Power	Networks	Power	Hosts
2	192	2^2	4 (2 actual)	2^6	64 (62 actual)
3	224	2^3	8 (6 actual)	2^5	32 (30 actual)
4	240	2^4	16 (14 actual)	2^4	16 (14 actual)
5	248	2^5	32 (30 actual)	2^3	8 (6 actual)
6	252	2^6	64 (62 actual)	2^2	4 (2 actual)

From the above table we can see that by choosing a mask of 240 (255.255.255.240) in the final octet we can have 14 networks each with 14 hosts on them in our class C subnet. In the same way using a subnet mask of 255.255.255.224 we could have 6 networks each with 30 machines on them. With a final octet mask of 224, what network addresses could we have? The answer to this is illustrated in Figure 6.6.

Figure 6.6 Valid networks with a 27-bit mask

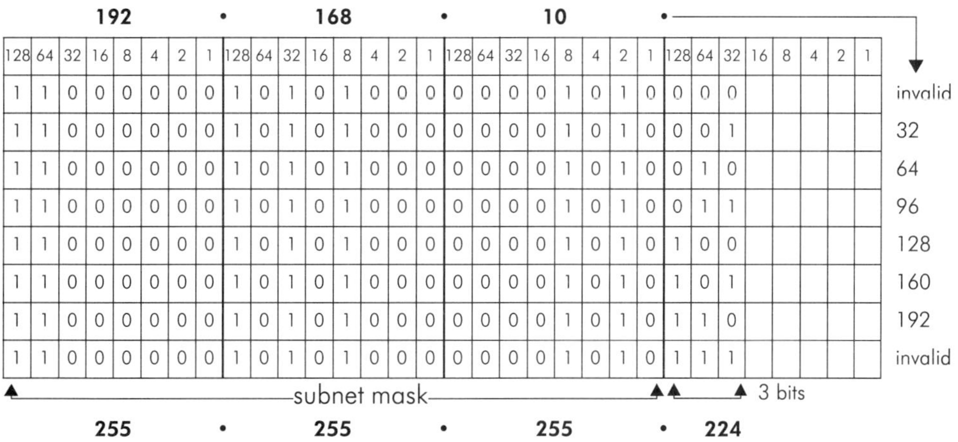

Using a "3-bit" mask–i.e., 255.255.255.224 – we can use the following valid networks:

192.168.10.32	192.168.10.128
192.168.10.64	192.168.10.160
192.168.10.96	192.168.10.192

Each of these networks can have 30 valid host addresses on them. The range of addresses for two of these networks is shown in Figure 6.7. Only the last octet bit patterns are shown in each case.

Figure 6.7 Range of valid addresses (final octet) for 2 class C addresses

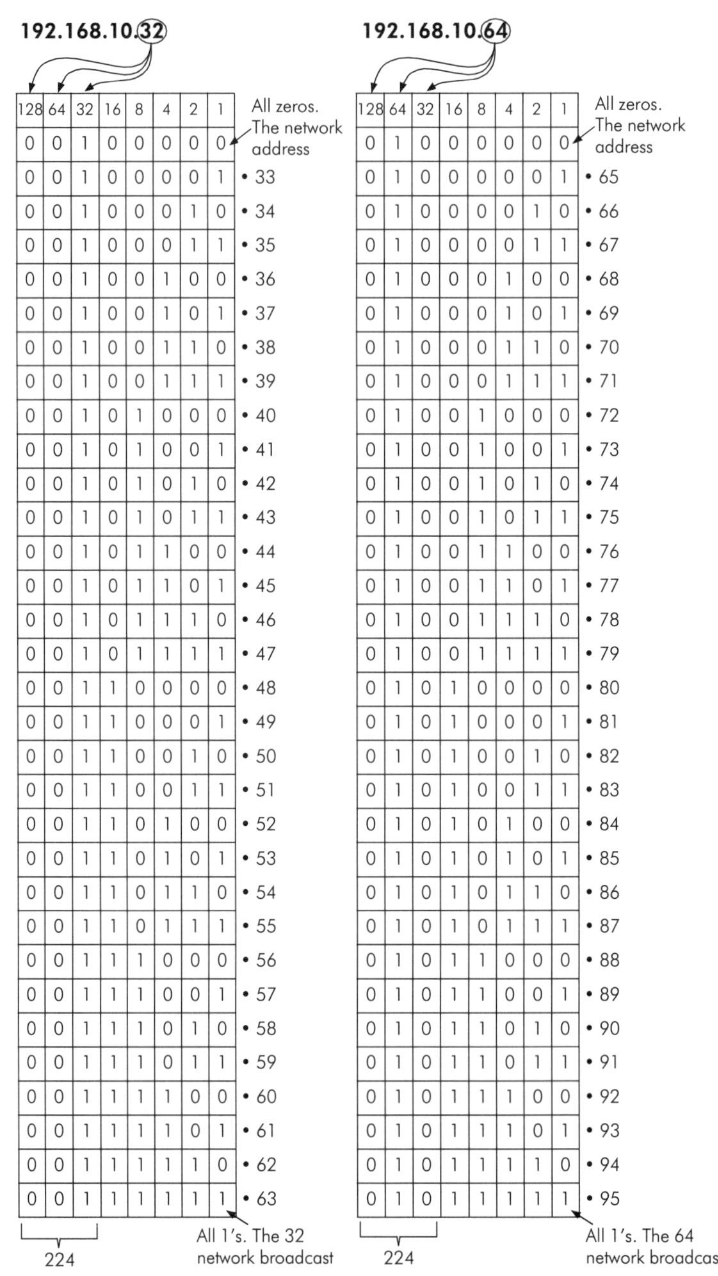

192.168.10.32

128	64	32	16	8	4	2	1	
0	0	1	0	0	0	0	0	All zeros. The network address
0	0	1	0	0	0	0	1	• 33
0	0	1	0	0	0	1	0	• 34
0	0	1	0	0	0	1	1	• 35
0	0	1	0	0	1	0	0	• 36
0	0	1	0	0	1	0	1	• 37
0	0	1	0	0	1	1	0	• 38
0	0	1	0	0	1	1	1	• 39
0	0	1	0	1	0	0	0	• 40
0	0	1	0	1	0	0	1	• 41
0	0	1	0	1	0	1	0	• 42
0	0	1	0	1	0	1	1	• 43
0	0	1	0	1	1	0	0	• 44
0	0	1	0	1	1	0	1	• 45
0	0	1	0	1	1	1	0	• 46
0	0	1	0	1	1	1	1	• 47
0	0	1	1	0	0	0	0	• 48
0	0	1	1	0	0	0	1	• 49
0	0	1	1	0	0	1	0	• 50
0	0	1	1	0	0	1	1	• 51
0	0	1	1	0	1	0	0	• 52
0	0	1	1	0	1	0	1	• 53
0	0	1	1	0	1	1	0	• 54
0	0	1	1	0	1	1	1	• 55
0	0	1	1	1	0	0	0	• 56
0	0	1	1	1	0	0	1	• 57
0	0	1	1	1	0	1	0	• 58
0	0	1	1	1	0	1	1	• 59
0	0	1	1	1	1	0	0	• 60
0	0	1	1	1	1	0	1	• 61
0	0	1	1	1	1	1	0	• 62
0	0	1	1	1	1	1	1	• 63 All 1's. The 32 network broadcast

224

192.168.10.64

128	64	32	16	8	4	2	1	
0	1	0	0	0	0	0	0	All zeros. The network address
0	1	0	0	0	0	0	1	• 65
0	1	0	0	0	0	1	0	• 66
0	1	0	0	0	0	1	1	• 67
0	1	0	0	0	1	0	0	• 68
0	1	0	0	0	1	0	1	• 69
0	1	0	0	0	1	1	0	• 70
0	1	0	0	0	1	1	1	• 71
0	1	0	0	1	0	0	0	• 72
0	1	0	0	1	0	0	1	• 73
0	1	0	0	1	0	1	0	• 74
0	1	0	0	1	0	1	1	• 75
0	1	0	0	1	1	0	0	• 76
0	1	0	0	1	1	0	1	• 77
0	1	0	0	1	1	1	0	• 78
0	1	0	0	1	1	1	1	• 79
0	1	0	1	0	0	0	0	• 80
0	1	0	1	0	0	0	1	• 81
0	1	0	1	0	0	1	0	• 82
0	1	0	1	0	0	1	1	• 83
0	1	0	1	0	1	0	0	• 84
0	1	0	1	0	1	0	1	• 85
0	1	0	1	0	1	1	0	• 86
0	1	0	1	0	1	1	1	• 87
0	1	0	1	1	0	0	0	• 88
0	1	0	1	1	0	0	1	• 89
0	1	0	1	1	0	1	0	• 90
0	1	0	1	1	0	1	1	• 91
0	1	0	1	1	1	0	0	• 92
0	1	0	1	1	1	0	1	• 93
0	1	0	1	1	1	1	0	• 94
0	1	0	1	1	1	1	1	• 95 All 1's. The 64 network broadcast

224

When looking at Figure 6.7 note how the addresses all increment and then the broadcast address of one network "rolls over" to become the network address of the next network in the series.

These final octet bit patterns allow us to see how the role of the final octet changes as the subnet mask is modified. Consider the IP address 192.168.10.37. If we apply the subnet mask 255.255.255.0 to this it represents a host machine on the 192.168.10.0 class C network. If we apply the subnet mask 255.255.255.224 to the same IP address we get machine number 5 on the 192.168.10.32 subnetted class C network. The implication of the differences in the interpretation of this address affects most aspects of network behaviour and performance.

We will investigate the use of these techniques in network design in the final chapters.

7

CIDR (Classless Inter Domain Routing)

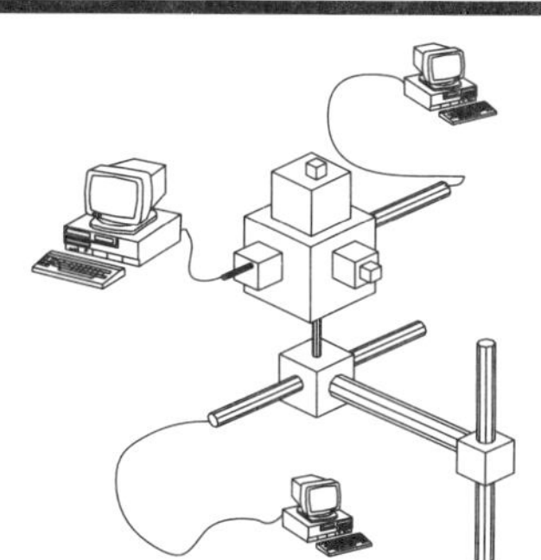

Combining Networks

In previous chapters we have seen how it is possible to subnet, or divide, a particular Internet address into a number of smaller subnets. The main reason for this is that the typical class B address, giving some 65,000 computers on one network, is too large and unwieldy for most organisations. By subnetting we are able to adjust the "balance" between the number of networks and the number of machines on each of the networks.

When looking, particularly at the class C networks, you may have noticed that with certain combinations of network groups the bit patterns in the octet being used for the subnets often contain almost identical bit patterns in the initial (leftmost) positions of the octet. Might it be possible to combine these groups together to give us, say, multiple class C addresses and therefore provide another way of meeting an organisation's networking needs, using multiple class C addresses instead of a divided class B address? The answer to this is yes and the technique used to provide this is CIDR (pronounced "si-der"). This technique is often referred to as *supernetting*.

In addition to CIDR offering the capability of combining class C addresses together, the RFC (request for comment) that deals with supernetting (RFC 1518) and CIDR also clarifies some of the more confusing aspects of network design.

In the "early" days of TCP/IP networks the standards that dealt with subnet masks were, intentionally, a little vague. The aim was to provide flexibility rather than a set of rigid standards and so it was possible to have non-contiguous subnet masks. What exactly is a non-contiguous subnet mask? This term refers to the use of subnet masks that consist of a mixture of 1's and 0's. Instead of using 11111111 in the first octet a mask of 10011111 (159) would be possible. This aim of having "flexible" masks was soon realised to be unworkable, unless extreme care was used when applying them, and they rapidly dropped out of fashion. One of the other rules associated with these guidelines was that it was not possible to have subnets of all 0's or all 1's. This is why in our earlier examples we did not allow these subnet values in our calculations.

By using a CIDR-compliant router (or TCP/IP implementation) we cannot have non-contiguous masks (no great loss) but we can have subnets of all 0's or all 1's. This is a major improvement – especially if we are on a smaller network (typically a class C).

Let us look at a simple example and explore the differences that CIDR makes to the division that we can apply to a class C address:

- address 201.144.13.0
- standard subnet mask 255.255.255.0

Imagine that we want to create four networks out of this. Previously we have tried to use a subnet mask of 192. This uses two bits in the third octet and this gives us four networks each with 64 machines (hosts). The bit patterns for the four network combinations are as follows: 00, 01, 10 and 11.

Using the standard rules the bit patterns of 00 and 11 are not allowable. This excludes two networks, each capable of holding 64 machines from our design. To say the least, losing 50% of our possible networks seems a little excessive if not downright wasteful. The other implication is that this restriction means that we would need to use a subnet mask of 224 (three bits) and this will reduce the number of available machines on each network to 32. Perhaps this is not what we want.

By using a CIDR-compliant TCP/IP stack (program) we would be able to use these two subnets of 00 and 11. This would mean that our original requirement for four networks could be met quite simply by using a subnet mask of 192. So with a CIDR-compliant system we are able to utilise the two additional networks and in general can use subnets of all 0's or all 1's.

Figures 7.1 and 7.2 show the relevant bit patterns for a "with and without CIDR" scenario.

Figure 7.1 Network options without CIDR

201 • **144** • **13** • **0** ← NetID

128	64	32	16	8	4	2	1	128	64	32	16	8	4	2	1	128	64	32	16	8	4	2	1	128	64	32	16	8	4	2	1	
1	1	0	0	1	0	0	1	1	0	0	1	0	0	0	0	0	0	0	0	1	1	0	1	0	0	0	0	0	0	0	0	← NetID
																																Addresses
1	1	0	0	1	0	0	1	1	0	0	1	0	0	0	0	0	0	0	0	1	1	0	1	0	0	0	0	0	0	0	1	❶ First
1	1	0	0	1	0	0	1	1	0	0	1	0	0	0	0	0	0	0	0	1	1	0	1	0	0	1	1	1	1	1	0	❷ Last
1	1	0	0	1	0	0	1	1	0	0	1	0	0	0	0	0	0	0	0	1	1	0	1	0	1	0	0	0	0	0	1	❸ First
1	1	0	0	1	0	0	1	1	0	0	1	0	0	0	0	0	0	0	0	1	1	0	1	0	1	1	1	1	1	1	0	❹ Last
1	1	0	0	1	0	0	1	1	0	0	1	0	0	0	0	0	0	0	0	1	1	0	1	1	0	0	0	0	0	0	1	❺ First
1	1	0	0	1	0	0	1	1	0	0	1	0	0	0	0	0	0	0	0	1	1	0	1	1	0	1	1	1	1	1	0	❻ Last
1	1	0	0	1	0	0	1	1	0	0	1	0	0	0	0	0	0	0	0	1	1	0	1	1	1	0	0	0	0	0	1	❼ First
1	1	0	0	1	0	0	1	1	0	0	1	0	0	0	0	0	0	0	0	1	1	0	1	1	1	1	1	1	1	1	0	❽ Last

255 • **255** • **255** • **192**

We can see that 4 possible networks 00 (❶ + ❷) and 11 (❼ + ❽) are invalid with a non-CIDR network. 01 (❸ + ❹) and 10 (❺ + ❻) are valid.

So without CIDR we lose the networks and hosts:

201.144.13.1	through	201.144.13.62	*and*
201.144.13.193	through	201.144.13.254	

The only valid networks and hosts are:

201.144.13.65	through	201.144.13.126	*and*
201.144.13.129	through	201.144.13.190	

Clearly, this is very wasteful of network space. (❶ + ❷) represents the zero (0) subnet, (❸ + ❹) represent the 64 subnet, (❺ + ❻) represent the 128 subnet and (❼ + ❽) represent the 192 subnet.

Figure 7.2 Network options with CIDR

201 • 144 • 13 • 0 ← NetID

128	64	32	16	8	4	2	1	128	64	32	16	8	4	2	1	128	64	32	16	8	4	2	1	128	64	32	16	8	4	2	1	
1	1	0	0	1	0	0	1	1	0	0	1	0	0	0	0	0	0	0	0	1	1	0	1	0	0	0	0	0	0	0	0	← NetID
																																Addresses
1	1	0	0	1	0	0	1	1	0	0	1	0	0	0	0	0	0	0	0	1	1	0	1	0	0	0	0	0	0	0	1	❶ First
1	1	0	0	1	0	0	1	1	0	0	1	0	0	0	0	0	0	0	0	1	1	0	1	0	0	1	1	1	1	1	0	❷ Last
1	1	0	0	1	0	0	1	1	0	0	1	0	0	0	0	0	0	0	0	1	1	0	1	0	1	0	0	0	0	0	1	❸ First
1	1	0	0	1	0	0	1	1	0	0	1	0	0	0	0	0	0	0	0	1	1	0	1	0	1	1	1	1	1	1	0	❹ Last
1	1	0	0	1	0	0	1	1	0	0	1	0	0	0	0	0	0	0	0	1	1	0	1	1	0	0	0	0	0	0	1	❺ First
1	1	0	0	1	0	0	1	1	0	0	1	0	0	0	0	0	0	0	0	1	1	0	1	1	0	1	1	1	1	1	0	❻ Last
1	1	0	0	1	0	0	1	1	0	0	1	0	0	0	0	0	0	0	0	1	1	0	1	1	1	0	0	0	0	0	1	❼ First
1	1	0	0	1	0	0	1	1	0	0	1	0	0	0	0	0	0	0	0	1	1	0	1	1	1	1	1	1	1	1	0	❽ Last

255 • 255 • 255 • 192

With a CIDR-based network, all subnetwork identifiers (00, 01, 10, 11) are valid. With CIDR all subnets are valid so we have the following network choices with a subnet mask of 192:

(❶ + ❷) networks and hosts on the zero subnet:

201.144.13.1 through 201.144.13.63

(❸ + ❹) networks and hosts on the 64 subnet:

201.144.13.65 through 201.144.13.126

(❺ + ❻) networks and hosts on the 128 subnet:

201.144.13.129 through 201.144.13.190

(❼ + ❽) networks and hosts on the 192 subnet:

201.144.13.193 through 201.144.13.254

A much more efficient way of allocating networks.

So CIDR gives us the capability of using subnets of all 0's or all 1's. This is often referred to as a "subnet zero" network. This is a major improvement over earlier designs but it doesn't stop there. Included in the standard are the possibilities of combining together groups of addresses. Most often this is applied to class C address groups and we will use a similar approach in this illustration.

Imagine that we have a requirement to produce an "Internet Valid" network and that we need to have at least 600 machines on this network. Clearly, with a class C network we are not going to be able to achieve this since a class C network can only hold 254 machines. A valid class B network, were one available, would give us in the region of 65,000 computers – a considerable waste of resources. What we would like to do is combine, say, three or four class C networks to give us something suitable.

CIDR allows us to do this by manipulating the subnet mask to include a range of addresses. The technique is essentially the same as subnet masking except that it works by masking the similarities of the networks rather than the differences.

Figures 7.3 and 7.4 show some suitable class C addresses. Note that these have identical bit patterns in the first two octets as well as the first initial bits of the third octet.

Figure 7.3 Example supernets

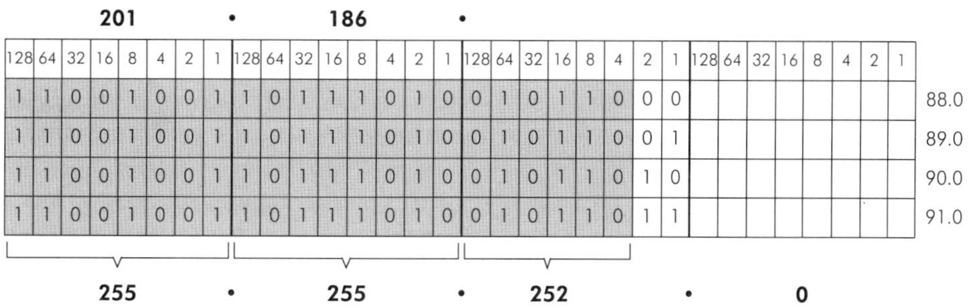

The four networks:

201.186.88.0
201.186.89.0
201.186.90.0
201.186.91.0

together with the subnet mask of 255.255.252.0 (/22) would appear to the outside world as one network since the relevant subnet bits (all 22 of them) appear to be the same.

Figure 7.4 Extension of supernet example

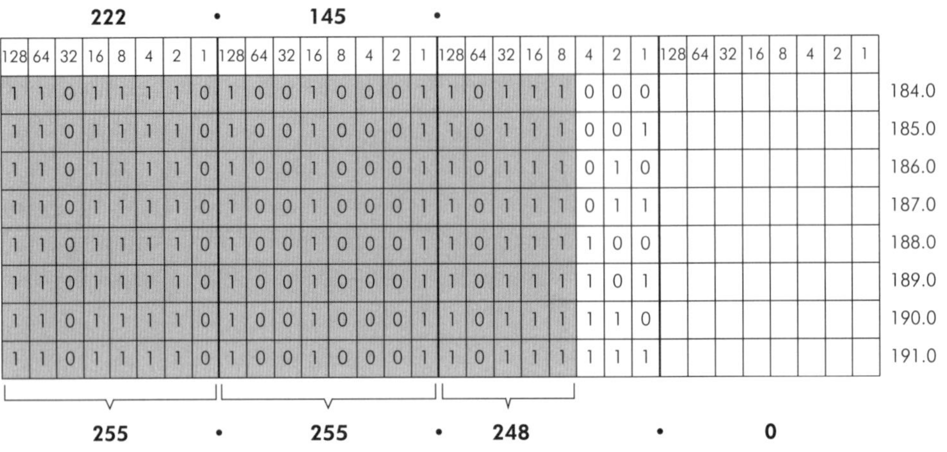

222 • 145 •

128	64	32	16	8	4	2	1	128	64	32	16	8	4	2	1	128	64	32	16	8	4	2	1	128	64	32	16	8	4	2	1	
1	1	0	1	1	1	1	0	1	0	0	1	0	0	0	1	1	0	1	1	1	0	0	0									184.0
1	1	0	1	1	1	1	0	1	0	0	1	0	0	0	1	1	0	1	1	1	0	0	1									185.0
1	1	0	1	1	1	1	0	1	0	0	1	0	0	0	1	1	0	1	1	1	0	1	0									186.0
1	1	0	1	1	1	1	0	1	0	0	1	0	0	0	1	1	0	1	1	1	0	1	1									187.0
1	1	0	1	1	1	1	0	1	0	0	1	0	0	0	1	1	0	1	1	1	1	0	0									188.0
1	1	0	1	1	1	1	0	1	0	0	1	0	0	0	1	1	0	1	1	1	1	0	1									189.0
1	1	0	1	1	1	1	0	1	0	0	1	0	0	0	1	1	0	1	1	1	1	1	0									190.0
1	1	0	1	1	1	1	0	1	0	0	1	0	0	0	1	1	0	1	1	1	1	1	1									191.0

255 • 255 • 248 • 0

Here we have eight networks:

222.145.184.0	222.145.188.0
222.145.185.0	222.145.189.0
222.145.186.0	222.145.190.0
222.145.187.0	222.145.191.0

with an associated mask of 255.255.248.0 (/21). To the outside world all networks appear to be the same since they have identical bit patterns in their first 21 bits.

Figure 7.5 Invalid supernets

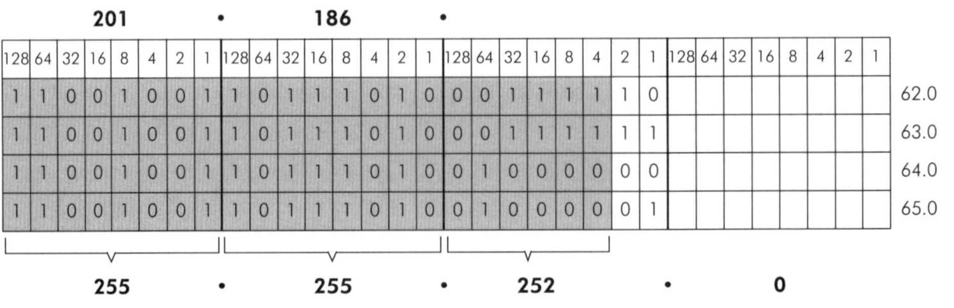

201 • 186 •

128	64	32	16	8	4	2	1	128	64	32	16	8	4	2	1	128	64	32	16	8	4	2	1	128	64	32	16	8	4	2	1	
1	1	0	0	1	0	0	1	1	0	1	1	1	0	1	0	0	0	1	1	1	1	1	0									62.0
1	1	0	0	1	0	0	1	1	0	1	1	1	0	1	0	0	0	1	1	1	1	1	1									63.0
1	1	0	0	1	0	0	1	1	0	1	1	1	0	1	0	0	1	0	0	0	0	0	0									64.0
1	1	0	0	1	0	0	1	1	0	1	1	1	0	1	0	0	1	0	0	0	0	0	1									65.0

255 • 255 • 252 • 0

The four networks:

201.186.62.0
201.186.63.0
201.186.64.0
201.186.65.0

with a mask of 255.255.252.0 (/22) do not have identical bit patterns throughout the 22 bits of the subnet component. Therefore, they are not suitable for use as a CIDR address range.

It is not possible for all address groups to be used as CIDR aggregates. Some ranges cause the preceding bit patterns to change so these ranges cannot be used. Figure 7.5 illustrates one such example.

Additional Requirements for Supernetting

In all of the CIDR examples the bit patterns corresponding to the subnets are all identical. This is the first and most often quoted requirement of CIDR. The second and equally important rule is that all of the remaining bit patterns in the non-identical part of the relevant octet must be used up in the supernetted range. As an example consider Figure 7.6 where we have supernetted using a 21-bit mask. This gives us three bits in the third octet that we can use for our supernetted networks. Three bits give us eight possible networks, as seen in Figure 7.4. What happens if we only use five of these available networks? Figure 7.6 illustrates the problem.

Figure 7.6 Non-complete CIDR network

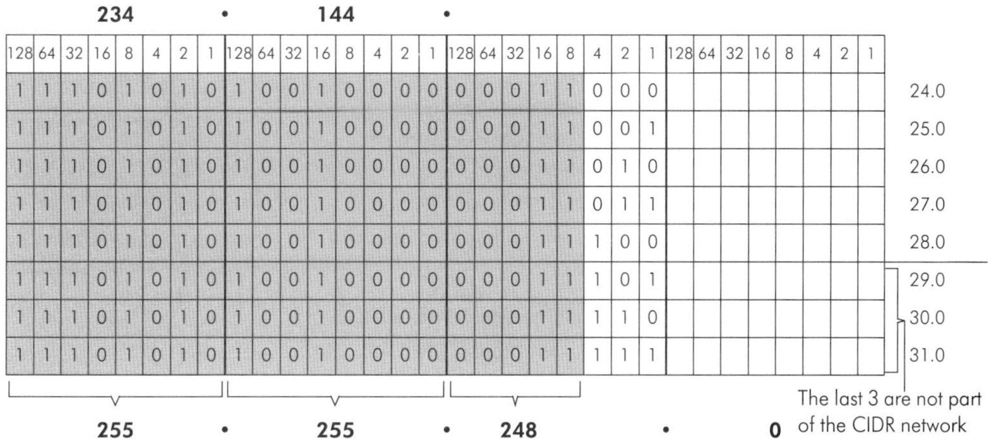

Here we have 8 possible supernetted networks but only 5 of these have been used. The remaining 3 if put onto another separate external network would cause routing-table chaos if there were two distinct separate networks that could both be addressed by 234.144.24.0 /21.

To further illustrate the way in which the outside world and the internal network see the various supernetted networks Figure 7.7 shows how a correctly assigned CIDR network operates. Figure 7.8 shows how the incorrect example from Figure 7.6 would cause problems.

Figure 7.7 Correct CIDR implementation

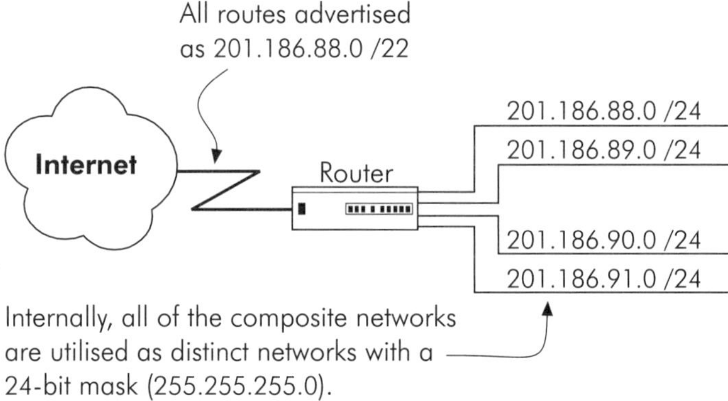
The 4 supernetted networks 201.186.88.0, 201.186.89.0, 201.186.90.0 and 201.186.91.0 (from Figure 7.3) are supernetted with a 22-bit mask (255.255.252.0).
All routes advertised as 201.186.88.0 /22
Internet
Router
201.186.88.0 /24
201.186.89.0 /24
201.186.90.0 /24
201.186.91.0 /24
Internally, all of the composite networks are utilised as distinct networks with a 24-bit mask (255.255.255.0).

Figure 7.8 Incorrect CIDR implementation

From Figure 7.6 only 5 of the available 8 supernets have been used. This will cause router chaos as shown below.

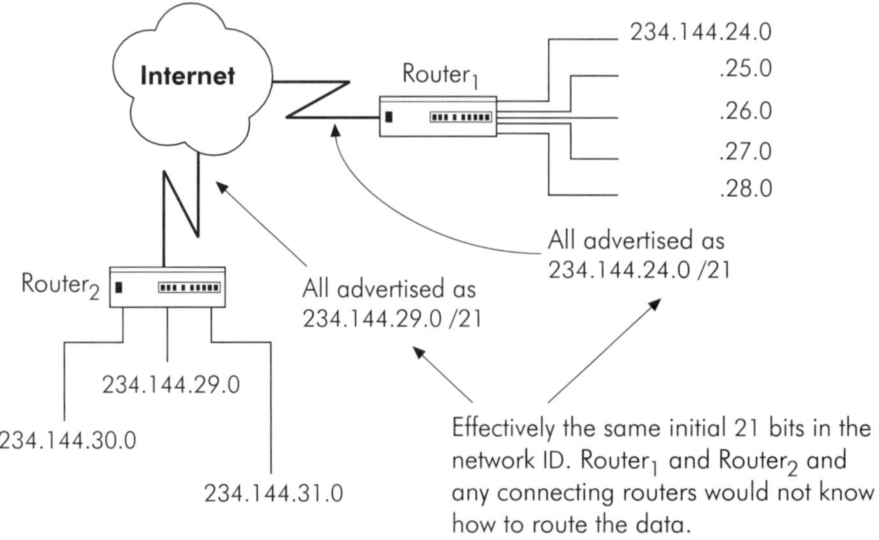
Internet
Router1
234.144.24.0
.25.0
.26.0
.27.0
.28.0
All advertised as 234.144.24.0 /21
Router2
All advertised as 234.144.29.0 /21
234.144.29.0
234.144.30.0
234.144.31.0
Effectively the same initial 21 bits in the network ID. Router1 and Router2 and any connecting routers would not know how to route the data.

From the above two diagrams we can see that the internal arrangement of 4 networks appears to the outside world as one single network. To support CIDR all relevant routers have to conform to the standards set out in RFCs 1518 and 1519.

8

DHCP

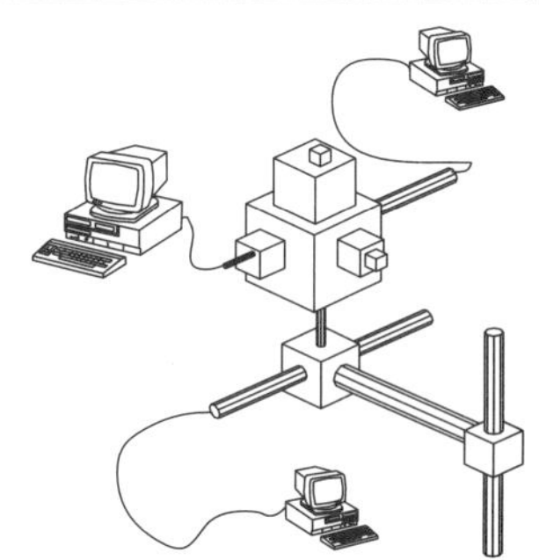

Introduction

In our consideration of network designs from the subnetting point of view we have looked at the allocation of IP addresses and subnet masks on a network-by-network basis. The reality of network design is that although these values are vitally important they are only a part of the whole network design process. So far we have seen that it is necessary to set up and configure our computers to use an IP address, a subnet mask and possibly various other components. These components are items like DNS server addresses, WINS server addresses, router addresses, NETBIOS node types and various other parameters that make up a modern network. What if we do not want to have to do this each time that another computer is added onto our system? Alternatively, perhaps we have a sales force that travels round the countryside going into each of our main offices to submit quotes, check price lists etc. In each of these cases they will need to connect to the local office network. Should we expect them to configure the IP component of their computer each time they log onto the network? The answer is almost certainly no. In situations like this DHCP (Dynamic Host Configuration Protocol) is the solution. This chapter does not cover the setting up and running of such a server but introduces the principles behind which the protocol works. On a medium-to-large network the presence of a correctly configured DHCP server can considerably reduce the administrative overhead with regards to IP address allocation.

History and Background

DHCP is a development of an earlier protocol called BOOTP (Boot Protocol). BOOTP was intended to be used by diskless workstations (computers without a hard disk drive) that would use BOOTP to connect to a main server and get all the necessary programs from it. BOOTP is still in use in some situations since it is useful for automatic downloading of programs and data, but it is now steadily being replaced by DHCP. The major difference between the two, in terms of day-to-day use, is that DHCP offers leases on its IP addresses whereas BOOTP does not. Servers using the two protocols can co-exist on the same network. In essence, a DHCP server contains a pool of valid IP addresses. These, together with the relevant subnet mask and any other information, are allocated to a computer as the client computer attaches to the network. Figure 8.1 illustrates this.

Figure 8.1 DHCP in action

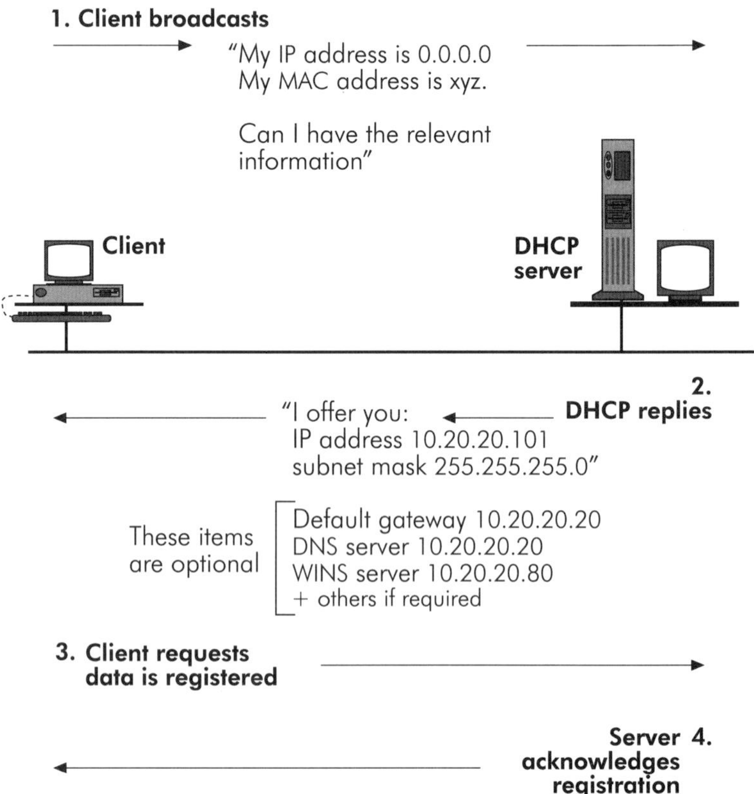
1. Client broadcasts
"My IP address is 0.0.0.0
My MAC address is xyz.
Can I have the relevant information"
Client
DHCP server
2. DHCP replies
"I offer you:
IP address 10.20.20.101
subnet mask 255.255.255.0"
These items are optional
Default gateway 10.20.20.20
DNS server 10.20.20.20
WINS server 10.20.20.80
+ others if required
3. Client requests data is registered
Server acknowledges registration 4.

How DHCP is Used

The DHCP server can be used to allocate this information on a permanent basis or on a leasehold basis. It is this latter use that is relevant for our "travelling salesman" example. Let us imagine that we have three offices organised on a geographical basis. We will use our East, West and North offices as examples. A salesman arrives at the East office to upload (transfer) some orders to the main server. These orders would then become part of the standard "ordering" system within the company. Before this, of course, the salesman must get onto the network.

The DHCP server in the East office offers our salesman's computer all of the relevant IP setup data but for a limited time of, say, one hour. After this if the salesman is no longer working on the system the DHCP server will reclaim the IP address and re-allocate it to the address pool. When the salesman travels round the country and visits the North office the same process is repeated and he or she is allocated an IP address relevant to that site.

In the above example the IP addresses are allocated for a finite period only. If the address is required for a longer period the salesman's computer will "renegotiate" with the server for a lease extension. In most cases this would be granted and the salesman allowed to continue with the connection. When the client eventually disconnects, the system will reclaim the IP address and return it to the relevant pool of IP addresses.

DHCP allows for the automatic allocation of IP addresses either for a limited period of time (leases) or as a permanent allocation. The sensible integration of DHCP into a network can simplify the allocation and setup of IP addresses and also assist in the configuration of DNS and WINS servers.

DHCP Address Allocation

How does the allocation of addresses occur? Figure 8.2 shows a network analysis trace from a client computer (set up to use DHCP) coming onto the network for the first time. In this illustration there are two computers on the network: a workstation (actually a Windows 95 "box") and an NT 4.0 server that is acting as the DHCP server. The machine names are WIN95WS and OFFICESERVER respectively.

Figure 8.2 Initial DHCP offer

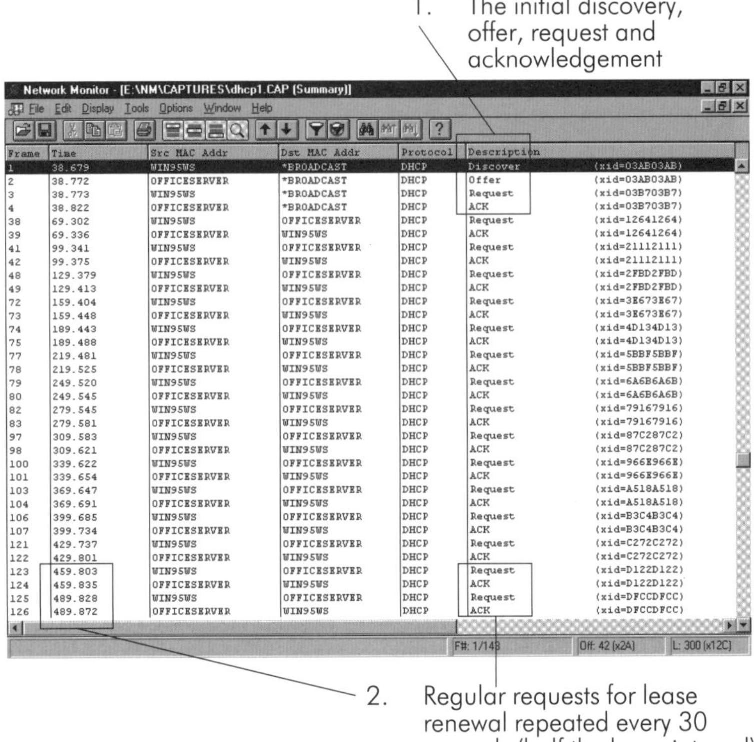

Frame	Time	Src MAC Addr	Dst MAC Addr	Protocol	Description
1	38.679	WIN95WS	*BROADCAST	DHCP	Discover (xid=03AB03AB)
2	38.772	OFFICESERVER	*BROADCAST	DHCP	Offer (xid=03AB03AB)
3	38.773	WIN95WS	*BROADCAST	DHCP	Request (xid=03B703B7)
4	38.822	OFFICESERVER	*BROADCAST	DHCP	ACK (xid=03B703B7)
38	69.302	WIN95WS	OFFICESERVER	DHCP	Request (xid=12641264)
39	69.336	OFFICESERVER	WIN95WS	DHCP	ACK (xid=12641264)
41	99.341	WIN95WS	OFFICESERVER	DHCP	Request (xid=21112111)
42	99.375	OFFICESERVER	WIN95WS	DHCP	ACK (xid=21112111)
48	129.379	WIN95WS	OFFICESERVER	DHCP	Request (xid=2FBD2FBD)
49	129.413	OFFICESERVER	WIN95WS	DHCP	ACK (xid=2FBD2FBD)
72	159.404	WIN95WS	OFFICESERVER	DHCP	Request (xid=3E673E67)
73	159.448	OFFICESERVER	WIN95WS	DHCP	ACK (xid=3E673E67)
74	189.443	WIN95WS	OFFICESERVER	DHCP	Request (xid=4D134D13)
75	189.488	OFFICESERVER	WIN95WS	DHCP	ACK (xid=4D134D13)
77	219.481	WIN95WS	OFFICESERVER	DHCP	Request (xid=5BBF5BBF)
78	219.525	OFFICESERVER	WIN95WS	DHCP	ACK (xid=5BBF5BBF)
79	249.520	WIN95WS	OFFICESERVER	DHCP	Request (xid=6A6B6A6B)
80	249.545	OFFICESERVER	WIN95WS	DHCP	ACK (xid=6A6B6A6B)
82	279.545	WIN95WS	OFFICESERVER	DHCP	Request (xid=79167916)
83	279.581	OFFICESERVER	WIN95WS	DHCP	ACK (xid=79167916)
97	309.583	WIN95WS	OFFICESERVER	DHCP	Request (xid=87C287C2)
98	309.621	OFFICESERVER	WIN95WS	DHCP	ACK (xid=87C287C2)
100	339.622	WIN95WS	OFFICESERVER	DHCP	Request (xid=966E966E)
101	339.654	OFFICESERVER	WIN95WS	DHCP	ACK (xid=966E966E)
103	369.647	WIN95WS	OFFICESERVER	DHCP	Request (xid=A518A518)
104	369.691	OFFICESERVER	WIN95WS	DHCP	ACK (xid=A518A518)
106	399.685	WIN95WS	OFFICESERVER	DHCP	Request (xid=B3C4B3C4)
107	399.734	OFFICESERVER	WIN95WS	DHCP	ACK (xid=B3C4B3C4)
121	429.737	WIN95WS	OFFICESERVER	DHCP	Request (xid=C272C272)
122	429.801	OFFICESERVER	WIN95WS	DHCP	ACK (xid=C272C272)
123	459.803	WIN95WS	OFFICESERVER	DHCP	Request (xid=D122D122)
124	459.835	OFFICESERVER	WIN95WS	DHCP	ACK (xid=D122D122)
125	489.828	WIN95WS	OFFICESERVER	DHCP	Request (xid=DFCCDFCC)
126	489.872	OFFICESERVER	WIN95WS	DHCP	ACK (xid=DFCCDFCC)

The DHCP server has a pool of addresses from 10.20.20.100 through to 10.20.20.150 and uses a 24-bit mask as standard. Figures 8.3 and 8.4 show the scope as it appears in the DHCP server manager dialog box. The stages in our process of assigning our client computer a DHCP address are as follows. All the stages can be followed through the network trace on Figure 8.2

1. The client machine broadcasts to any DHCP server that is listening. The broadcast requests an address allocation quoting the client's IP address as 0.0.0.0 (the discover packet).
2. All servers that "hear" the request respond with an offer of a suitable IP address. The client will usually accept the first response.

3. The client broadcasts a request to say "please may I have the IP address that you just offered". Since this is broadcast and contains a transaction ID from the originating DHCP server, all the other servers on the network, should there be any, will receive this and cancel any remaining offers that they may have made.
4. The originating DHCP server will then, almost certainly, acknowledge that the client can have the lease for the lease period and all relevant caches will be updated accordingly.

In our example the leases were allocated for a 1 minute period. On a real network this would be ridiculous since it would generate a vast amount of network traffic, but as an example it is valuable.

Once the lease has been granted the client retains this even after power off. When 50% of the lease has expired the client tries to renew the lease from the originating server. The server will usually agree to extend the lease for another lease period and will confirm this fact with the client.

If the server is unable to renew the lease the client will wait until 87.5% (7/8) of the lease has expired and then try to find another server that is capable of renewing. If this fails the lease is lost and the client can on longer connect to the network. The usual reason for this is that the address pool is too small for the number of computers on the network. The protocol is designed to minimise the allocation of existing IP addresses to other machines if at all possible. This reduces the need for cache updates and other "untimely" MAC and IP conflicts that would otherwise occur. Figures 8.3 and 8.4 illustrate the settings for the DHCP scope.

Figure 8.3

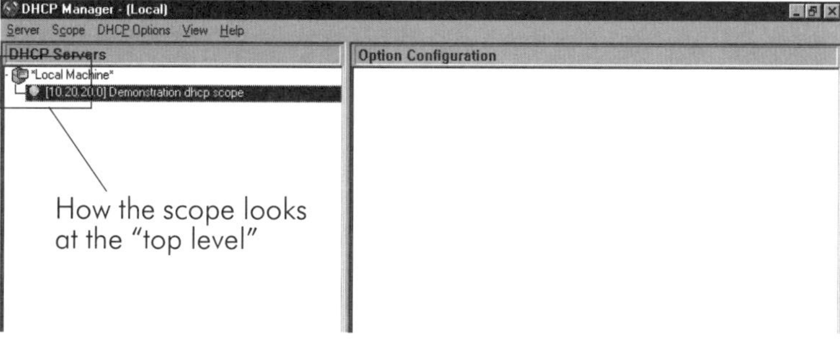

Figure 8.4

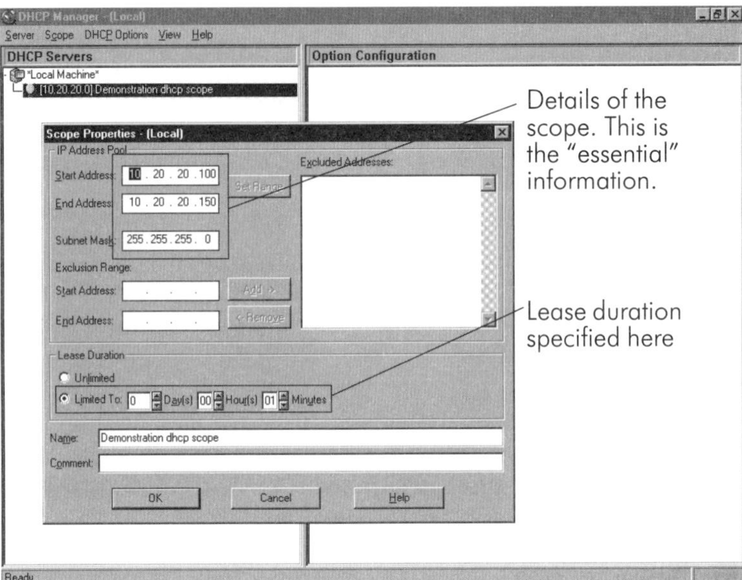

In our "travelling salesmen's" example one of our sales staff connects to the East office and gets a lease, together with whatever relevant information they require. This lease is for, say, one hour. After this period the client leaves the East office and drives to the North office. During this period the lease has expired on the client machine and is no longer valid. The original server has not received a request to renew the lease and so cancels it and returns it to the address pool. When the client connects to the North office network a lease is obtained from that DHCP server and the process continues. This ability to allocate addresses dynamically has made DHCP very popular in busy network environments.

DHCP on Multiple Subnets

In all of the above examples we have used one DHCP server on a single network. How can this be of use on a busy, complex network using many different subnets? With one important difference the principles are identical on the smaller network and the larger ones. This important difference is illustrated below.

Our problem is that the client computer initialises using a broadcast and that this will, by default, get stopped at any router between itself and the DHCP server. If we wish to access DHCP servers across subnets we have to overcome this limitation. Of equal importance is where we want to use two or more DHCP servers to build fault tolerance into our networks. Again the problem is that any intervening routers will intercept the broadcast data and stop it.

This type of situation is illustrated in Figure 8.5. Here we have a two-subnet network where a DHCP server has been set up on each subnet. Each server has 60% of the IP addresses for its own subnet and 40% of the addresses for the "remote" subnet. The actual percentages can be adjusted depending on the number of machines on each subnet and other factors such as how often machines are added and how many new addresses need to be allocated over a given period.

Say that one of the servers has failed. The problem that we face is twofold:

1. We have to get the client's broadcast data across the router to the DHCP server on the other subnet.
2. The remote DHCP server has to know which IP address pool to use to allocate the IP address for the "remote" subnet.

The answer to both of these issues is to configure the router to be able to act as a "BOOTP relay agent" (sometimes this is referred to as being RFC 1542 compliant). This is usually a trivial task for most modern routers but the majority that I have come across all seem to have this disabled by default.

When configured as a BOOTP relay agent the router acts as follows:

1. The router receives a DHCP broadcast "Discover" from the client computer.
2. The router inserts the IP address of the local interface into a pre-allocated field in the DHCP datagram. This field is the GIADDR (Gateway IP Address Field).
3. The router then forwards the broadcast onto the remote network.
4. The remote DHCP server picks up the datagram and uses the GIADDR entry to select the correct IP pool from which to allocate an address.

5. The offer is made to the client via the router and is usually acknowledged.
6. The usual sequence of "request and acknowledgement" is then entered into as a direct "machine to machine" IP sequence. Because of this it is essential that the default gateway is included as part of the DHCP offer made by the server. If this is not done the lease renewal will fail after the initial lease period has expired.

This sequence of events is shown in Figures 8.5 through 8.10. In Figure 8.7 we can see the data analysed by Microsoft's network monitor. This shows the GIADDR field containing the relevant router IP address. The network layout and the sequence of events producing the datagram of Figure 8.7 are shown in Figure 8.8.

Figure 8.5 DHCP setup for fault-tolerance

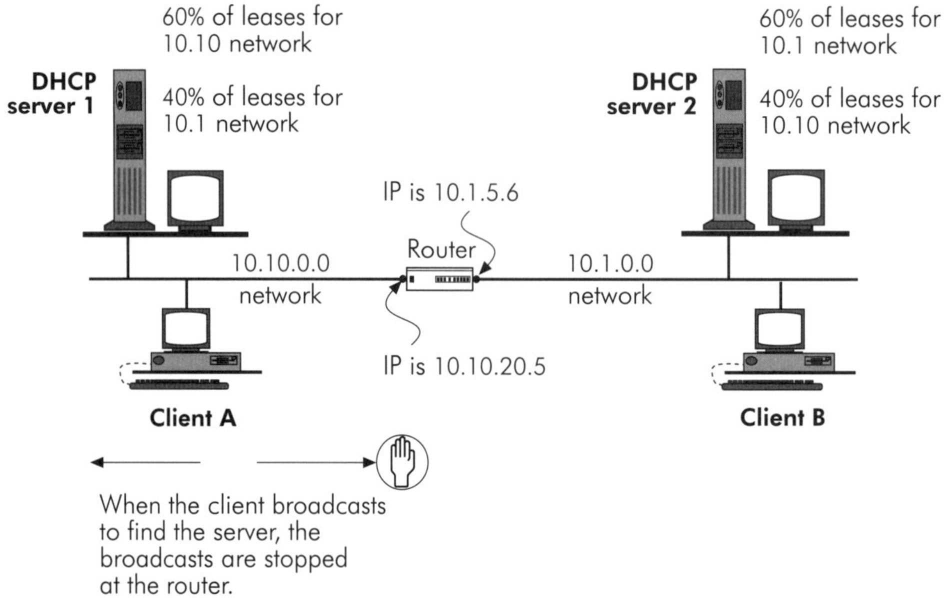

Figure 8.6 DHCP working with server failure

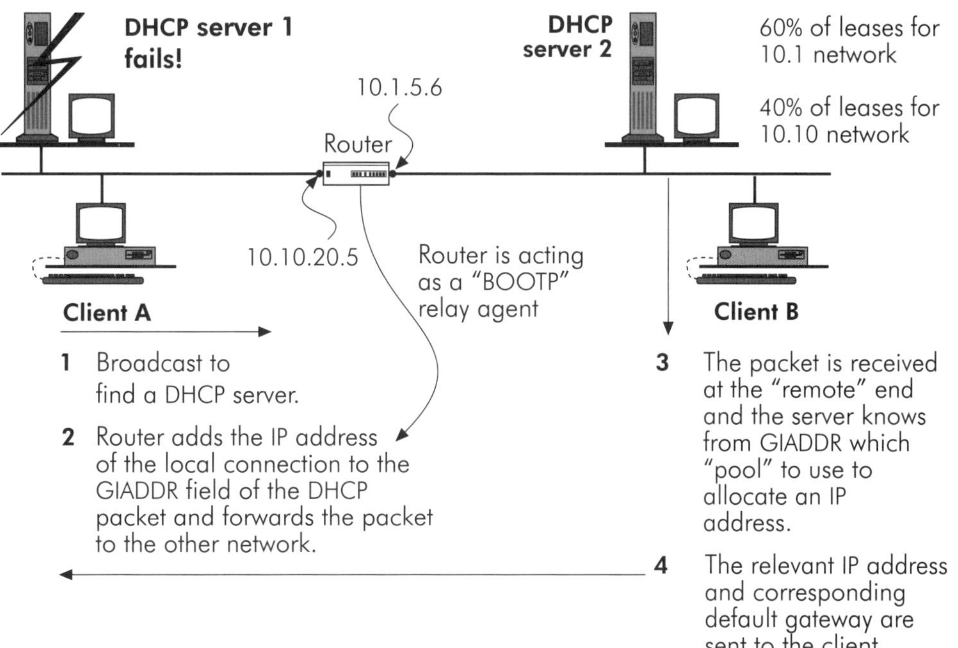

Figure 8.7 The GIADDR field (see Figure 8.8)

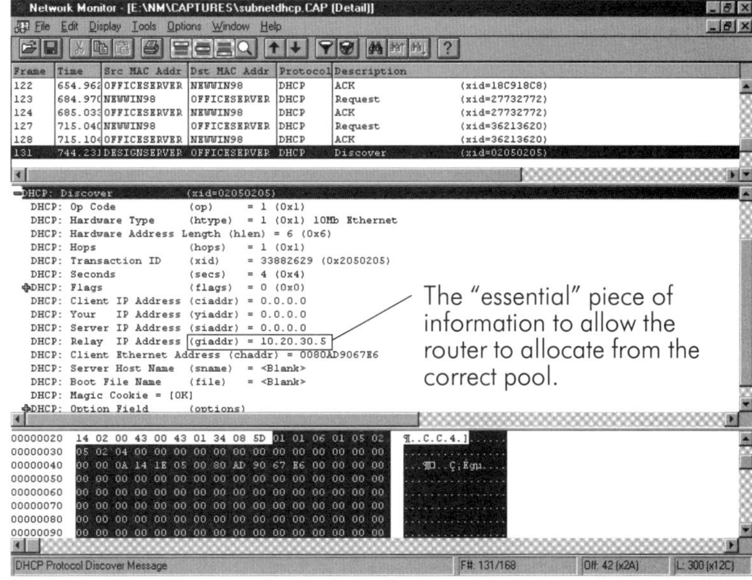

Figure 8.8 Sequence of events for a "cross router" DHCP request

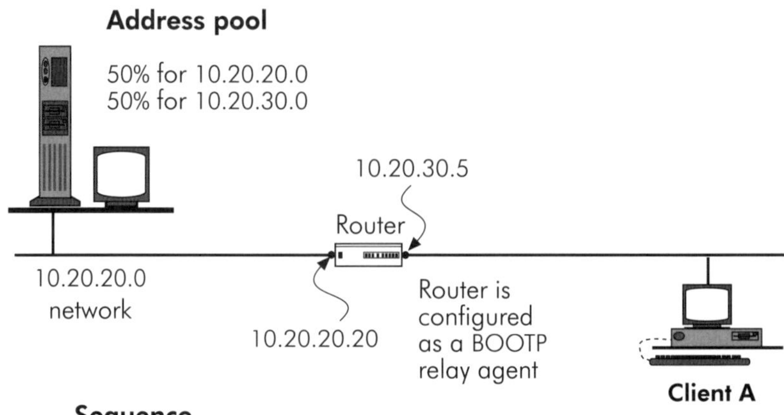

Sequence

1 **A** broadcasts with IP 0.0.0.0

2 Router inserts relevant IP address (10.20.30.5) into the GIADDR field then forwards the data (BOOTP relay)

3 The DHCP server receives the data and allocates the address 10.20.30.100 for client **A**

4 The IP setup data **must** contain the relevant default gateway address in order for the client and server to establish and maintain communication

Figures 8.9 and 8.10 show the continuation of the renewal and acknowledgement process. In these datagrams we can see that the GIADDR field is no longer used and that the communication is host to host using the IP addresses and the relevant default gateway. It is for this reason that the gateway address must be included in the original DHCP offer.

Figure 8.9

Once the IP address is assigned, the request and acknowledgement are carried out as normal – i.e., without reference to the BOOTP router.

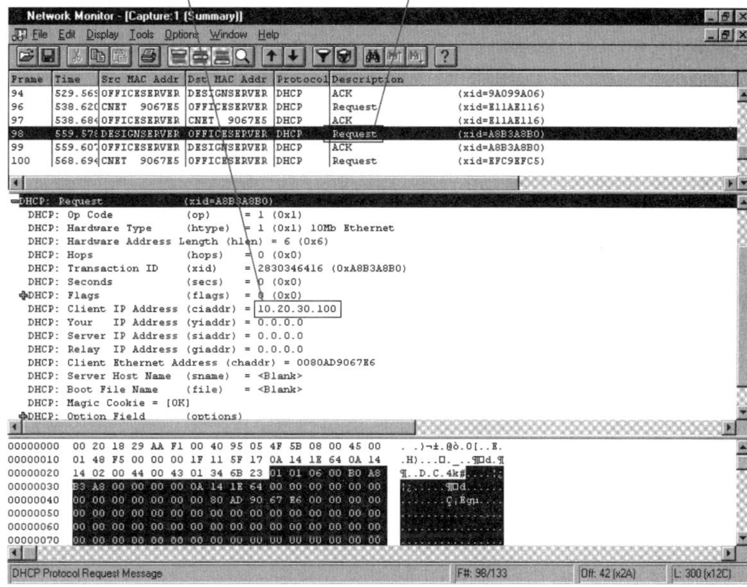

Figures 8.11 and 8.12 show how the active lease appears on the DHCP server and also illustrates how the "additional" information of the default gateway (router) is shown on the DHCP server.

In summary, DHCP can be used to automate the setting up of subnetted networks. It is also invaluable for the dynamic allocation of client IP addresses especially where the configuration of these changes over a relatively short period of time. If multiple DHCP servers are to be used for fault tolerance or performance considerations any routers between the clients and the DHCP servers *must* be configured to act as BOOTP relay agents otherwise they will not be visible from the remote clients.

Figure 8.10

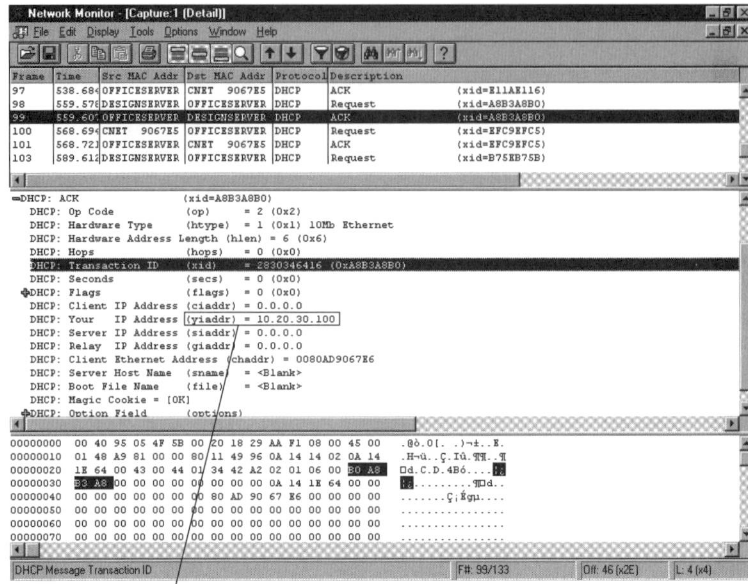

As in the previous figure, confirmation is sent by normal IP communication. The BOOTP feature is not used.

Figure 8.11

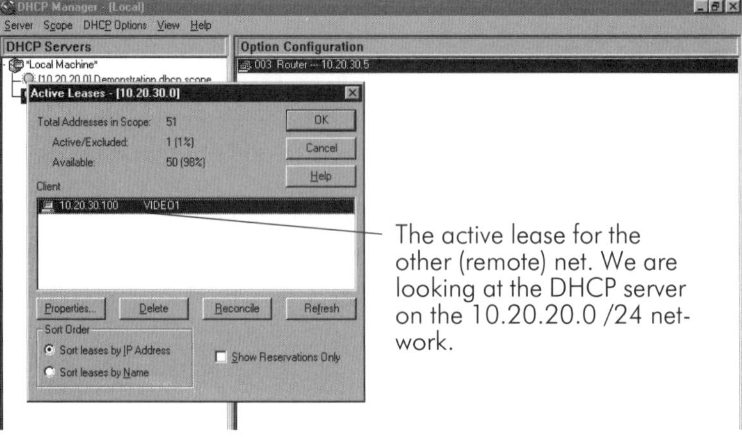

The active lease for the other (remote) net. We are looking at the DHCP server on the 10.20.20.0 /24 network.

Figure 8.12

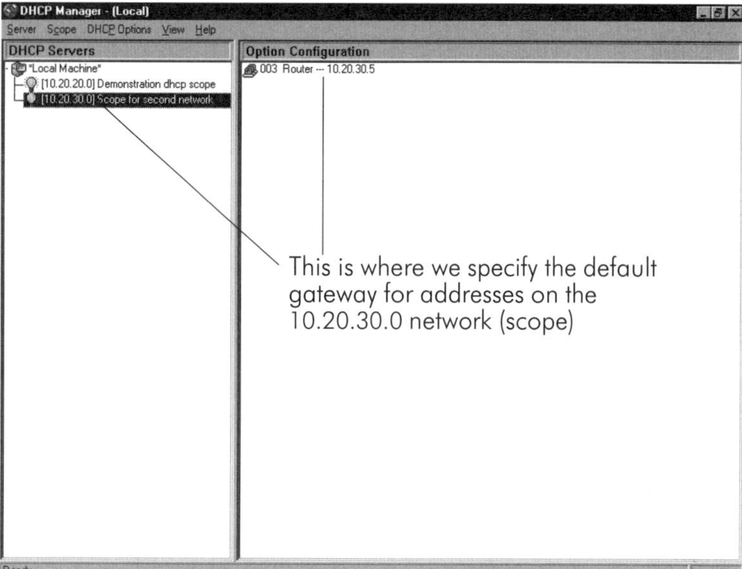
DHCP Manager - (Local)
Server Scope DHCP Options View Help
DHCP Servers
Local Machine
[10.20.20.0] Demonstration dhcp scope
[10.20.30.0] Scope for second network
Option Configuration
003 Router --- 10.20.30.5
Ready
This is where we specify the default gateway for addresses on the 10.20.30.0 network (scope)

9

Subnet Problems

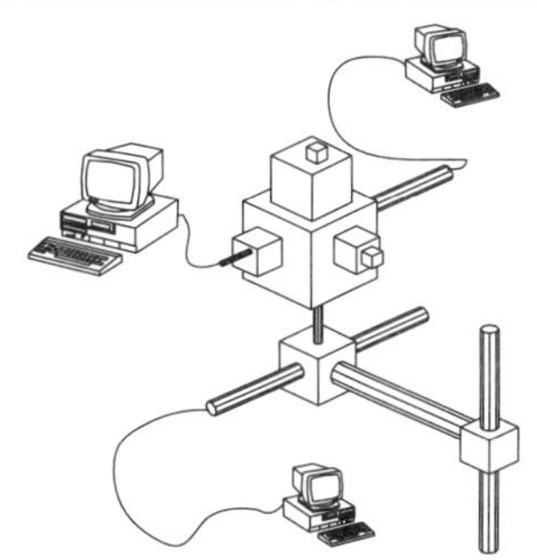

Problems, Problems ...

Throughout the last few years I have come across a wide variety of network designs. The majority of these have grown almost "organically". In the better cases the original network design was sound and there were the usual wiring diagrams and all the support information that a trained network designer would come to expect. Unfortunately, many networks have proven to be the training grounds of their designers. Quite often these designers have come from supposedly reputable "consultancy" organisations and the individuals concerned have left long before the problems arise.

Too often I have heard it said:

> "So-and-so really knew what they were doing but they left us after a year to go to ..."

as I am looking at a tangled mass of cabling, usually vanishing into a hole in the wall, a very variable range of subnet masks and a network with four or five protocols running on it! Today, one is often required to be able to retrospectively "un-engineer" the network while imposing some form of order onto it.

Figure 9.1 illustrates a "sanitised" version of one of these networks. Let us imagine that you have been brought in to "sort out" the network. I have not shown all of the servers, printers, modems etc. At this stage we are simply concerned with getting the "guts" of the system to work correctly. All of the machines on this network are able to run using TCP/IP. We will also assume that each of the networks represents a "functional" area of the organisation: so network 1 could be the sales area, network 2 the design department, network 3 finance and administration and so on.

Figure 9.1 The inconsistent network

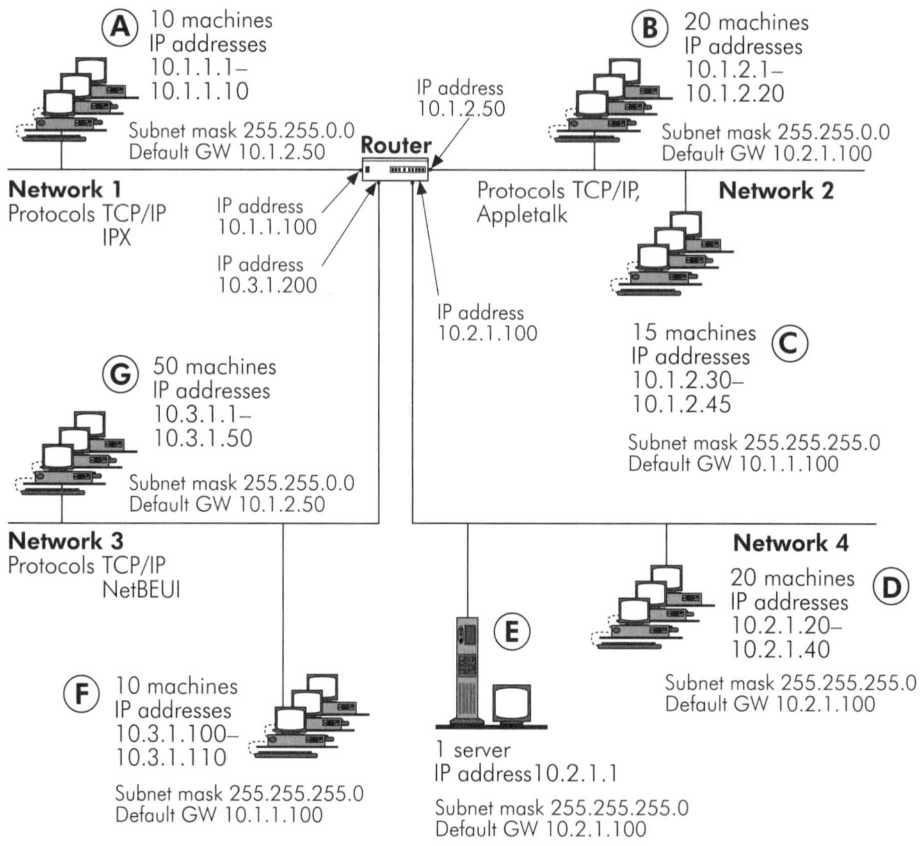

How should we approach this? My first step is to try and get a "feel" for what the original "designer" was trying to achieve. Clearly, some thought has gone into this. A non-assigned class A network address has been used and the company divided up into functional areas. These are good initial steps. At this stage we will assume that the cabling has been set up correctly.

What are the Major Problems?

1. The address allocation is reasonably satisfactory. It broadly follows the major groupings of machines within the organisation. The problem is with the allocation of subnet masks. These are inconsistent and therefore produce variable "network visibility" problems.
2. The allocation of default gateways is quite wrong; many are simply incorrect. Quite often I have seen default gateways pointing to the "wrong end" of the router causing numerous "network unreachable" messages. The default gateway has to point to the router end of the current network. So in network 1 (the 10.1.0.0 network using the current mask), the "far end" of this network that is attached to the router is 10.1.1.100. With the default gateway set to 10.1.2.50 (on another network) the machines so configured will get "network unreachable" messages almost all the time. Often this type of problem has been made worse by the designers trying to modify the local routing table on the host machine to overcome the deficiencies of the incorrect default gateway. We will not assume this is the case here.

What are the Minor Problems?

The many different protocols on each network will cause unnecessary broadcast traffic. I suggest they are all removed and that mapped drives are used using the IP address to locate the remote server. If full network browsing is required then a WINS (Windows Internet Naming Service) server will have to be added with the relevant LMHOSTS files pointing to the domain PDC. Unfortunately, a full discussion on WINS and setting up static and dynamic routing tables is outside the scope of this book.

Solutions

My feeling is that we should use a 24-bit subnet mask. Only by discussion with relevant organisation staff would we be able to determine if this will give a sufficient number of hosts on each of the subnets. At the moment with 60 machines maximum on network 3 this allocation seems reasonable. With a /24 mask and a class A address we get 2,097,152 networks each with 254 hosts on them. This seems a slight case of "overkill", a non-assigned class B or a series of non-assigned class C networks would have worked just as well.

Sticking to a non-assigned class A network with a /24 mask we are able to specify the networks as follows:

Network 1

Ⓐ	IP address ranges: 10.1.1.1 through 10.1.1.10	subnet: 255.255.255.0

Network 2

Ⓑ	IP address ranges: 10.1.2.1 through 10.1.2.20	subnet: 255.255.255.0
Ⓒ	IP address ranges: 10.1.2.30 through 10.1.2.45	subnet: 255.255.255.0

Network 3

Ⓖ	IP address ranges: 10.3.1.1 through 10.3.1.50	subnet: 255.255.255.0
Ⓕ	IP address ranges: 10.3.1.100 through 10.3.1.110	subnet: 255.255.255.0

Network 4

Ⓓ	IP address ranges: 10.2.1.20 through 10.2.1.40	subnet: 255.255.255.0
Ⓔ	IP address ranges: 10.2.1.1	subnet 255.255.255.0

The router ports all remain the same but the default gateways on each of the network hosts are as follows:

- **Network 1**: default gateway for all machines 10.1.1.100
- **Network 2**: default gateway for all machines 10.1.2.50
- **Network 3**: default gateway for all machines 10.3.1.200
- **Network 4**: default gateway for all machines 10.2.1.100

This gives a network layout shown in Figure 9.2.

Figure 9.2 The consistent network

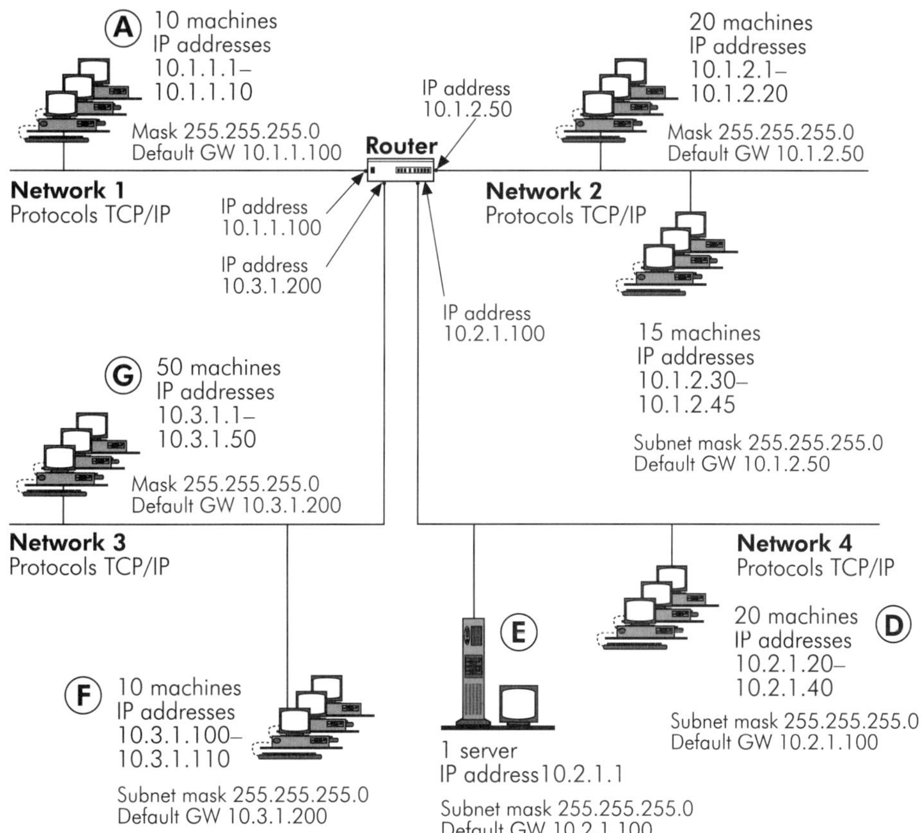

How could we reduce the problems of IP address, subnet mask allocation and default gateway for future additions to the network? I would suggest adding at least one DHCP server with scopes set up for each network and the default gateway set up for each scope. The main router must be checked for RFC 1542 compliance and if fault tolerance were required a second DHCP server should be added. If a second DHCP server is used the scopes in the two machines must not overlap.

This would give us a consistent expandable network with few future IP problems. A complete new network could be added (router permitting) by using, say, 10.1.4.0 as the network address. This would give us another 254 machines for a new department without affecting the existing design. Similarly, additional networks could be added as needs dictate.

10

General Network Designs

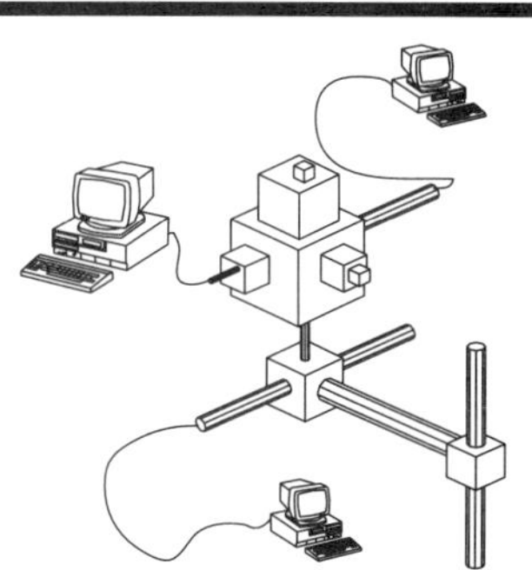

Network Layouts

When it comes to designing networks for specific organisations it is impossible to accurately specify individual layouts without clear reference to the local building designs and other immediate environmental factors. With wide area networks the decision to use microwave, ATM switches, X.25 or other means of connection often imposes restrictions on what the designer has to work with. Bearing in mind all of the above, this chapter covers the major IP related points that I consider are of importance to the modern designer of TCP/IP based networks. First let us remind ourselves what the non-assigned IP address classes are:

1. **Class A non-assigned** – 10.0.0.0

   This gives us either a single network with 16,777,214 hosts on it, or, by using subnets, a large variety of networks each with a smaller number of hosts on them.

2. **Class B non-assigned** – 172.16.0.0 through 172.31.255.255

   This gives us a number of networks (172.16 to 172.31) each with 65,534 hosts on them or, again using subnetting, a greater number of networks each with a smaller number of hosts.

3. **Class C non-assigned** – 192.168.0.0 through 192.168.255.255

   This gives us a number of networks (192.168.1 to 192.168.255) each with 254 hosts on them or, using subnetting, a greater number of networks each with a smaller number of hosts.

Ideally, we should choose our address class to suit our networking requirements. In practice, people seem to use the class A (10.0.0.0) address because it allows virtually "unlimited" expansion and is also more tolerant of rapidly expanding networks and of those whose layout is open to change.

The simplified designs of Figures 10.1 through 10.4 illustrate the way in which these address ranges could be used. With subnetting it is possible to produce a vast array of network layouts. Here I summarised the "bare bones" of some suitable networks.

Figure 10.1 Class A network subnetted with 16 bits

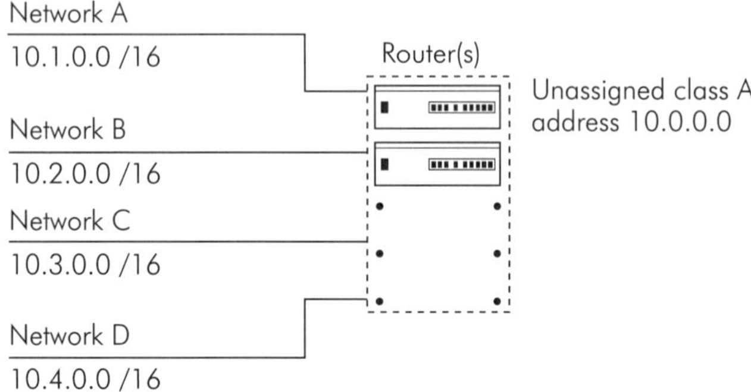

Figure 10.2 Class A network subnetted with 24 bits

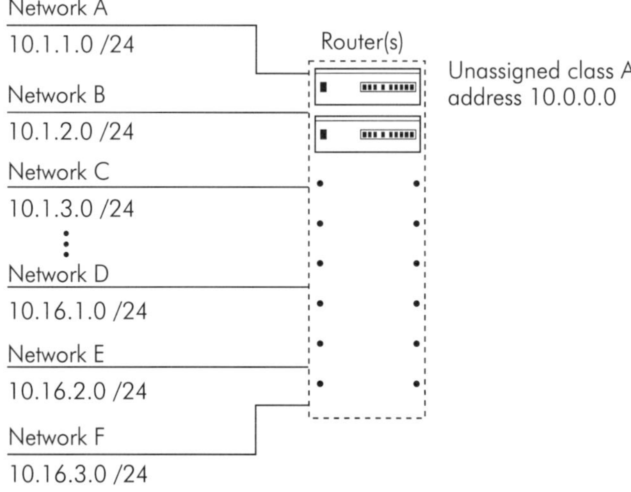

Figure 10.3 Class B networks subnetted with 24 bits

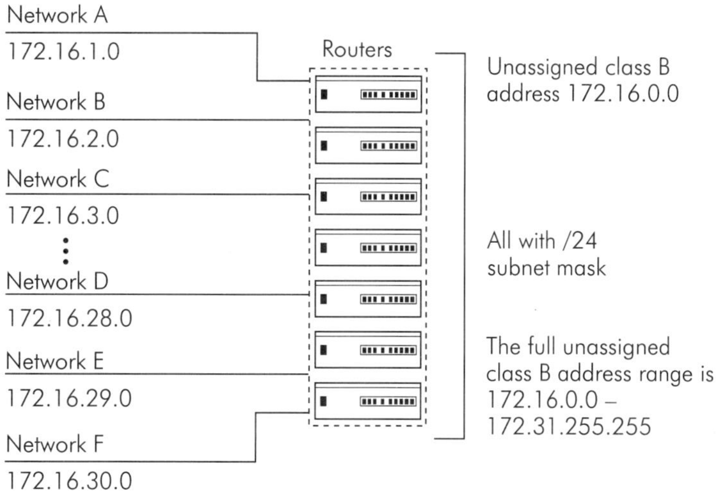

Figure 10.4 Aggregate, non-subnetted class C networks

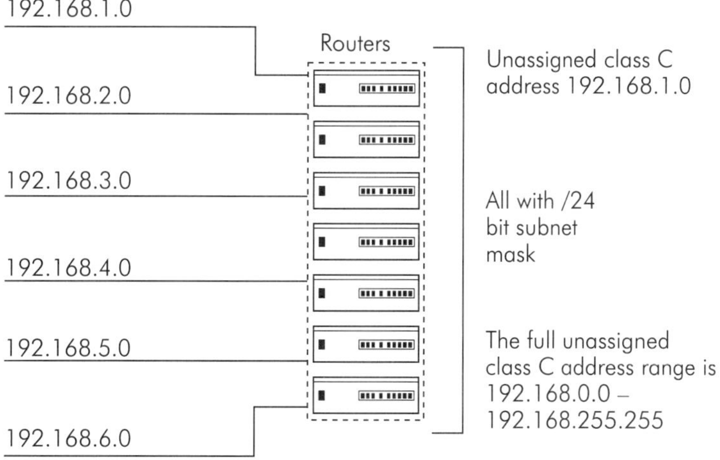

All of the above is ideal if we do not want our network to connect to the Internet – but what if we do? Are we denied access to the Internet by using the above designs? The answer is most definitely *no*. Figure 10.5 shows a simplified design using a proxy server. This proxy server has (on its external connection) a valid IP address, either assigned to us or obtained through an ISP (Internet Service Provider). The role of the proxy server is to translate our internal IP addresses to the external one and make the outside world see all traffic from the internal network as coming from the one valid IP source. This translation does not affect e-mail transmissions – only the movement of IP data across networks.

Clearly there are bandwidth considerations here and I would not suggest that the design of Figure 10.5 is suitable in all circumstances. All I am trying to show is that it is possible to extend the simplified designs in Figure 10.1 to a more sophisticated Internet-based connection.

Figure 10.5

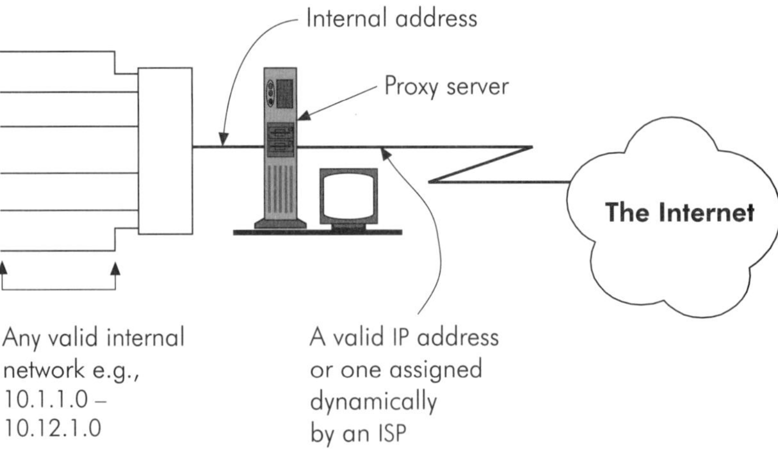

Finally, imagine that our organisation consisted of a number of geographically separate units. Could we expand the above model to accommodate this type of structure? Once again the answer is yes. Figure 10.6 shows how this could be structured.

Figure 10.6

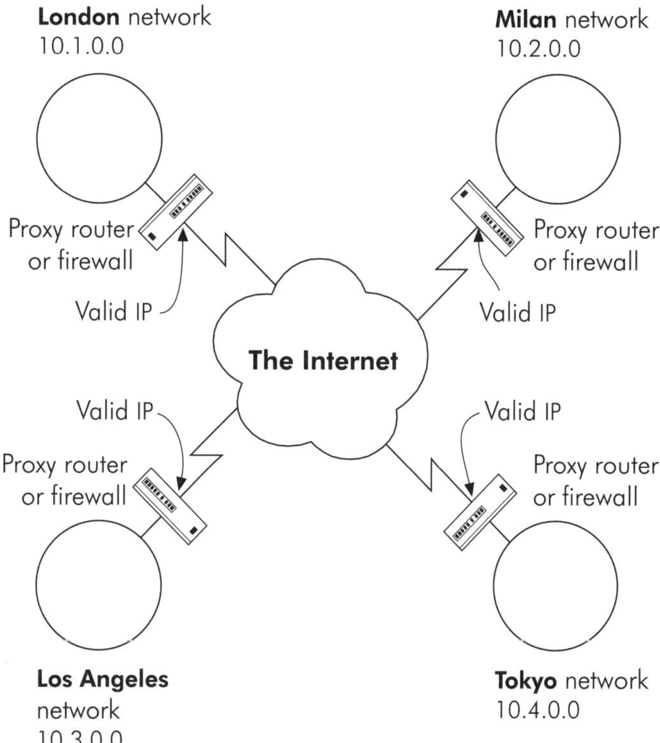

We use the non-assigned class A network and give each of our operational units one of the subnetted networks i.e., London has 10.1, Milan has 10.2, Los Angeles has 10.3 and so on. Within each of these units the network can be further subdivided by using the appropriate subnet mask. By utilising a suitable number of proxy servers and/or firewalls the corporation can maintain an Internet "presence" and can use the Internet to carry most of the corporate data around the world. Additional centres can be added to this design to increase the network size as required.

11

Logical Subnets

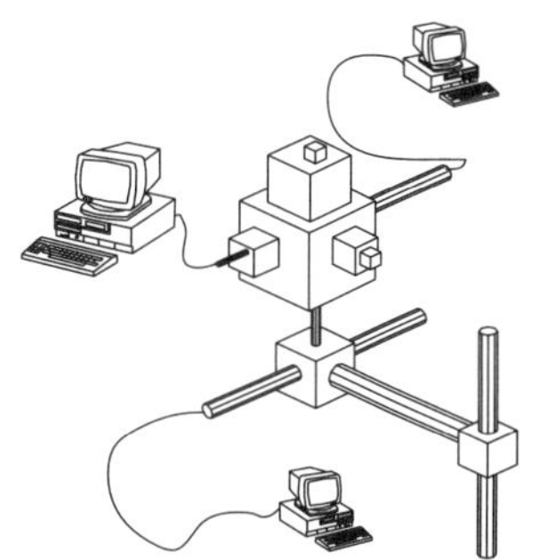

Introduction

In recent years the growth of the Internet, and with it the growth of the associated technologies, has left many companies facing considerable problems with regards to network growth and redesign. One of the ways in which Microsoft and other software companies have sought to address this problem is by allowing network cards to have more than one IP address assigned to them. By using this aspect of the technology it is possible to plan a network with sufficient regard to future expansion so that major restructuring of the IP addresses is minimised.

All of this is possible because of the way in which operating systems designers have "virtualised" the networking sub-systems of the various operating systems. In the following section we will look at Microsoft's implementation of its networking sub-system.

Some History

Before we go into detail with Microsoft's solution to the "flexible network software" problem let us look at how, historically, software was written. During the 1960s and 1970s all sorts of software tended to be written in large, single, blocks of code which completely covered all aspects of the particular program. These "monolithic" programs used to start at line 1 and progress to, say, line 10,000. There was very little functional separation of sections of code; consequently, if any part of the program had to be changed then the whole program would need re-editing, re-compiling and usually debugging before any simple change could be relied on.

Various authorities felt that as computer programs and systems were becoming more and more complex this situation could not continue. Their solution was to produce a "structured" model of how computer code should be produced, in a functional sense. By this I mean that the program should be divided into specific functional sections whose code should not overlap with regards to the tasks that each section performed. Data and results may well pass from one section to another but different parts of the code cannot directly interfere with each other.

If we consider how, a few years ago, a new graphics card would be added to a system we will see the problems inherent in such a non-structured approach. Until recently if we wanted to add a new graphics card to our computer the following steps would be necessary. (I am concentrating here on the software installation, not the actual fitting of the card into the PC).

- Firstly, we would have to attach the card into the computer. In most systems this would give us basic graphics output.
- Next, to make use of the improved features that our new card offers we would have to install the drivers for the operating system. This would improve the appearance of the output for the general system utilities but would be unlikely to improve any of the applications that we would want to use with the machine.
- Finally, and the most time-consuming part of the operation, we would have to patch each of our applications with the associated software patches. If the card manufacturer did not provide suitable patches for a particular piece of software then we would not be able to use all of the card's features when using that piece of software.

Similarly, because of the complexities of testing all card settings with all available software we would not be surprised if some resolutions did not work with particular applications. The above scenario is typical of the older monolithic code that was around in the early part of the personal computer's evolution.

When we consider the situation with regards to network cards the position is even worse. The early networking software was such an integral part of the operating system that setting up the network card required intimate knowledge of the operating system and the particular vagaries of the cards themselves. If you wished to change the networking protocol to communicate with a different server the system would have to be reconfigured (to reflect the new drivers and other software required for the connection) and then rebooted to load the new software onto the card. Should you wish to go back to the original configuration the process would have to be repeated to reflect the requirements of the new configuration. Changing the network card was likely to require substantial changes to the underlying software system.

Our monolithic software model proved too cumbersome and inflexible for the modern demands of networked computers. Clearly, some additional method of designing the software had to be found.

The Solution

A number of international organisations were addressing the problems associated with the older style of programming. One of the first to lay out their "modular" designs for networking software was the American Department of Defence in their TCP/IP model. This appeared in the early 1970s but was not widely taken up due to the specific nature of the protocol. The International Organisation for Standardisation (ISO) produced their now famous seven-layer-model in the mid-1970s and this has become the yardstick by which all other networking standards are judged. This model is referred to (confusingly) as the OSI (Open Systems Interconnection) model.

This model is a theoretical one and I do not think that any software manufacturer produces a system which is 100% compliant with this. Its importance lies in the way in which it allowed manufacturers to produce functionally separate blocks of code and thus allow flexible and reliable modules to be written.

Figure 11.1 illustrates both the older monolithic style and the seven-layer OSI model.

Figure 11.1 Monolithic and OSI structures

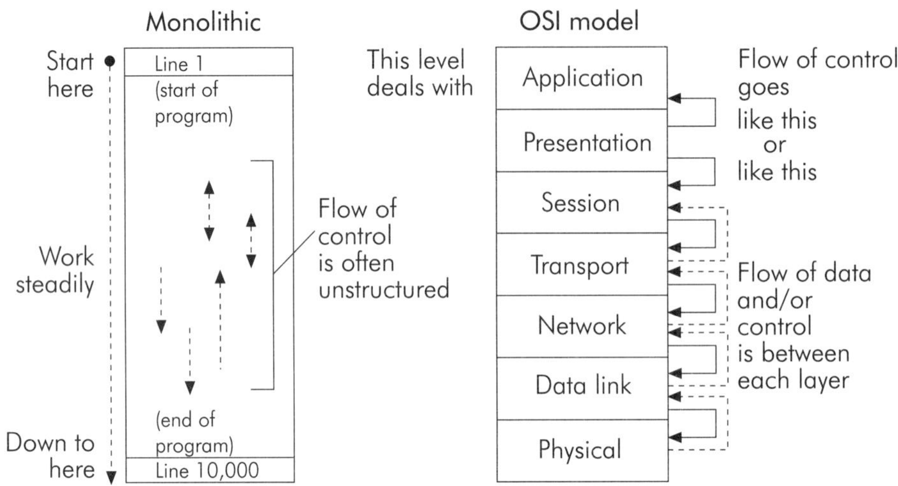

When looking at these two designs imagine that the way in which the systems function is like two large organisations. The Managing Director of one wishes to send a package of material to the Managing Director of the other. At the application level we have the Managing Director; below him, or her, (in a data transfer sense) we have the Personal Assistant or Office Manager, then the head of the internal post room, an outside courier service and then the courier van driver. In our monolithic model these functions would be mixed up throughout the program.

Let us look at how the data would be moved in both cases.

In the monolithic model the MD would pick up the data, run out of his or her office and down the stairs. Leaving the building they would hail a taxi and travel across town to their colleague's office. Identifying themselves to the doorman they would climb the stairs (or lift) and gain entry to their opposite number's office. Once inside the package would be delivered. Meanwhile back in their own office all manner of important decisions and other matters have been held up awaiting their return.

Not exactly an efficient way of working! But this is exactly how many of the older networking systems handled the movement of data across the network.

Figure 11.2 OSI layers and the corporate explanation

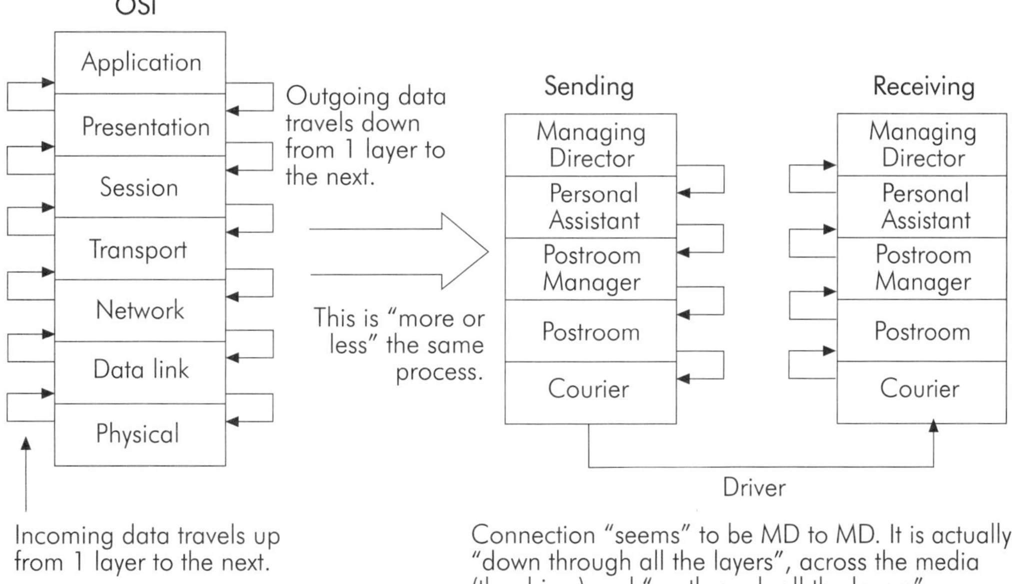

In the OSI model the data is prepared by the application (our MD). Once prepared it is handed down to the next layer (in a functional sense), the PA, who then calls the post room and the post room administrator collects the package and contacts the courier. The courier sends round the driver who signs for the data and proceeds to the recipient's office. Here the opposite sequence of events takes place and the package passes up the layers from courier, to post room, to PA, to MD.

Neither of the two MDs is interested in what courier service is used. They are simply interested in the successful delivery of the data to their opposite number. In the same sense the application software is not interested in whether we use Ethernet, Token Ring or ATM as our network type. Similarly, the application is not interested in whether we use fat cables, thin cables and so on. All the application wants to know is "Did the data get there?".

The overall effect is that communication seems to be occurring on a level-to-level basis. By this I mean that one MD will call the other MD to see if the package has been received. If there has been a delay the MD is unlikely to chase the couriers directly. He or she will contact their PA who will contact the post room supervisor who will then chase-up the couriers.

In the software version of this model there is no way in which the top layer (MD) can directly contact the lower layer (courier). Each layer has to communicate with the layer above and below it. The overall impression is that each layer communicates with its opposite number but in fact the data travels down through the layers and then up through the layers on the opposite side.

Figure 11.3 Virtual layers

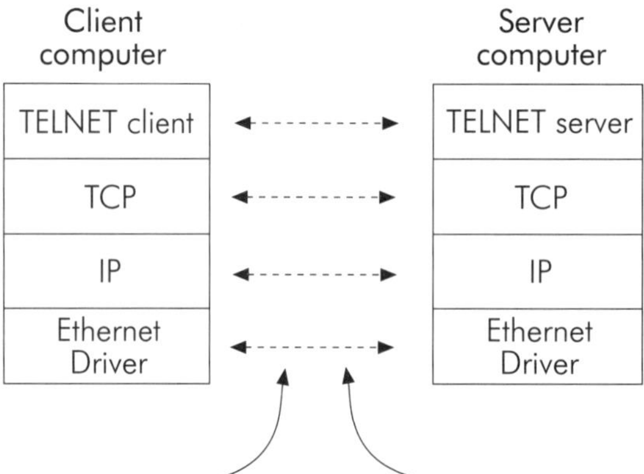

Figure 11.4 Actual path of the data

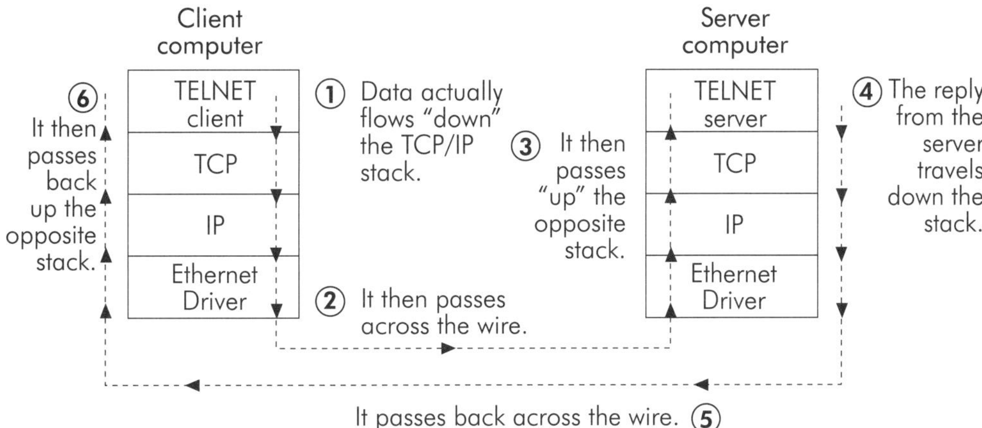

The Two Models

Our "layered" model means that the software developers have to produce code which is functionally separate and they have to enforce the rule that each layer of code can only talk to the layers above and below respectively. This means that if the code of a particular layer has to be changed, as long as it interfaces with its neighbouring layers in a consistent fashion none of the other layers will have to be changed. This "virtualises" the software and, in theory, makes it much more reliable.

The manufacturer of a new network card now needs to produce a software interface into the layer above and does not need to provide "patches" for each of the associated parts of the networking system. Figure 11.5 is a diagram of the virtual layers and the way a new card will fit into this.

The two models, OSI and DOD, serve the same functions. They virtualise the software into functional layers and enforce the independence of each of the layers. Although the layers are different they relate to each other in the following way.

Figure 11.5 The layered model and TCP/IP programs

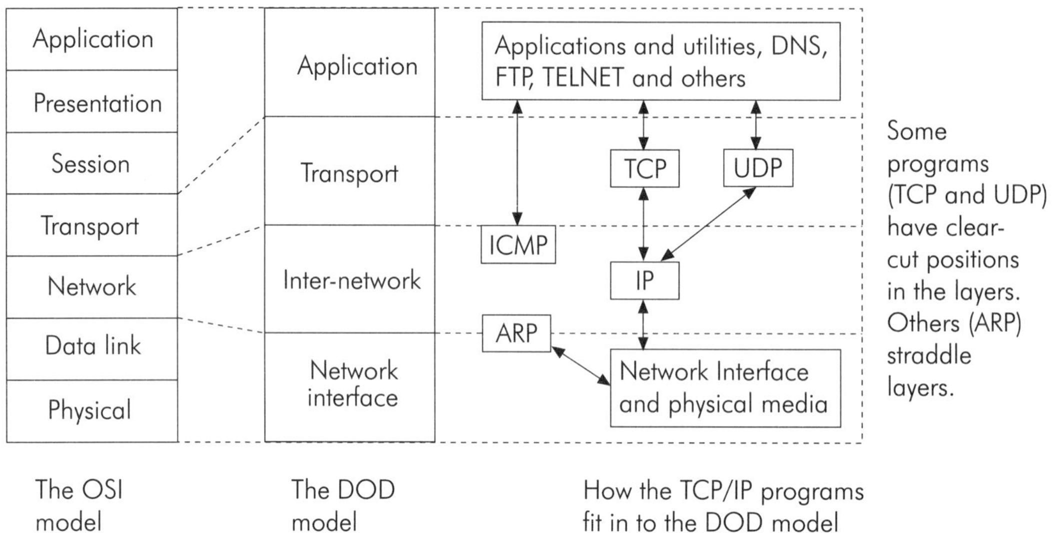

The Real World

Microsoft's implementation of the OSI model is illustrated in Figure 11.6. Although similar to the OSI model it has two important differences. These differences are brought about by the requirements of a software package that has to fit in with a "real world" operating system not just the demands of the International Committee that constructed the model.

The differences are the two "virtual" layers which separate the networking protocols from the applications and these protocols from the network cards. These are the *Transport Driver Interface* and *Network Device Interface Specification* respectively. They are usually referred to as TDI and NDIS. From here on this is how I will refer to them. Why are these layers so important? The answer lies in the fact that these layers hide the functioning of the protocols from the applications and of the hardware from the protocols. In this way a program can be written that, if it wants to connect to a network, will direct the various requests (open a file, copy the data, etc.) to the TDI layer and this will direct the calls to the relevant protocol. The application will therefore work whether the protocol that is used is IPX, TCP/IP or Appletalk and so on. The application does not need to be changed for each protocol since it talks directly to TDI and this handles the necessary interfacing with the underlying protocol.

Figure 11.6 The OSI model and Microsoft's implementation

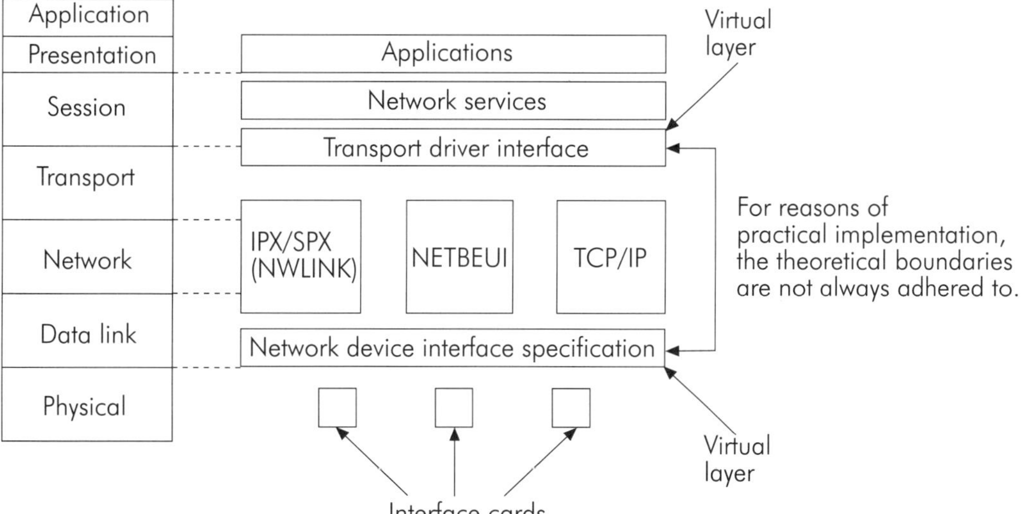

At the lower end of the networking system the protocols talk to NDIS and are completely unconcerned about the network card that is used. We could change from an SMC card to an NE2000 or a 3Com and all we would have to do is to load the software interface into NDIS and the applications above would all work. That Microsoft has made all this so simple and easy is a credit to the developers of this part of their operating system.

When this system was first produced I demonstrated to some very surprised clients that it was possible to have three protocols attached to one network card and seemingly "talking" to five different servers in what appeared to be concurrent sessions. These clients were used to complete reloads and reboots of their computers if they wanted to talk to two different servers. All of this is provided "free of charge" through the subtleties of the layered networking stack!

One of the additional benefits from this layered approach is that the IP address is bound (attached or loaded into the network card's memory) by means of the NDIS layer. This layer is able to support many protocols by switching them into and out of the associated card's memory. In a similar fashion it can support a number of IP addresses concurrently on one card. Microsoft states that you can attach over 1500 – yes, *one thousand five hundred* IP addresses on one card). I have not tested this claim but I can state that it works well with three or four IP addresses on one card. Why would you want to do such a thing? The major reason is to provide a cheap and efficient way of "future proofing" your network designs.

The Logical Network

At the start of this chapter I described how a network designer might want to produce a network that was as "future proof" as possible. Logical subnets provide us with just such a way of doing this.

Figure 11.7 The initial logical subnets

Stage 1

In this diagram, all computers use a subnet mask of /24. This means that computers on the finance "network" will be unable to contact computers on the sales and design "networks" and vice-versa. We could gain connectivity by modifying the routing tables (more later) or by entering multiple IP addresses onto each machine. In this way, the design computer 10.1.3.4 could also have IP addresses 10.1.2.90 and 10.1.1.90 and, therefore, be a host on each of the logical subnets. As the whole network becomes physically subdivided these multiple IP addresses will be removed.

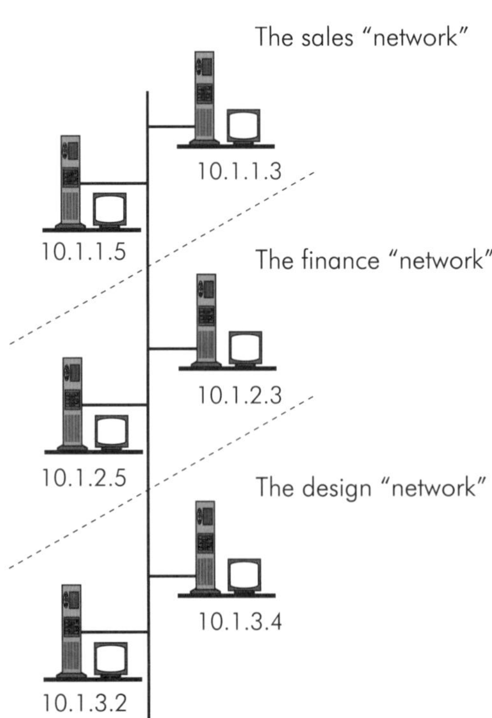

Let us imagine a small company that is just getting started on designing its networks. It is interested in saving money but wishes to retain as much flexibility as possible in the future expansion of its networks. One possible solution would be to design a network based on a simple one-hub model but to give the different computers their IP addresses based on the role that they will play in the final network model. This is illustrated in Figure 11.7 above.

Strictly speaking these three separate IP subnets all coexist on the same physical network. As the network grows more computers can be added to the systems until a point is reached whereby additional cabling can be added. Because the default gateways and other IP parameters are consistent there is no need for the complete redesign of the networking system as it grows.

Figures 11.8 and 11.9 illustrate the various stages in this process.

Figure 11.8 The second phase of the logical subnet

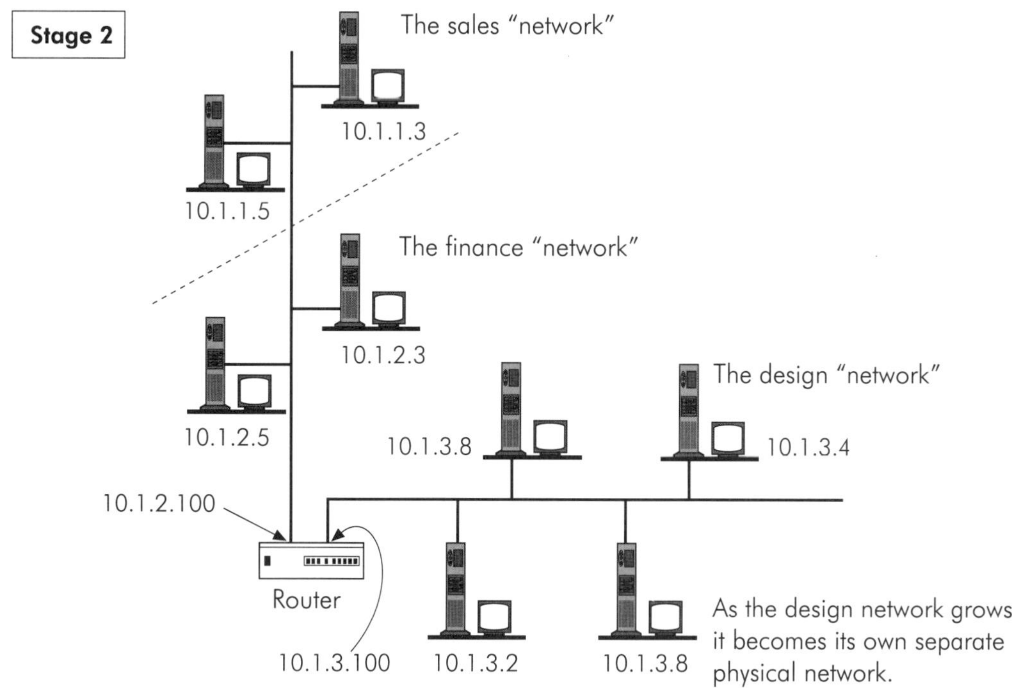

Figure 11.9 The final development of the logical subnet

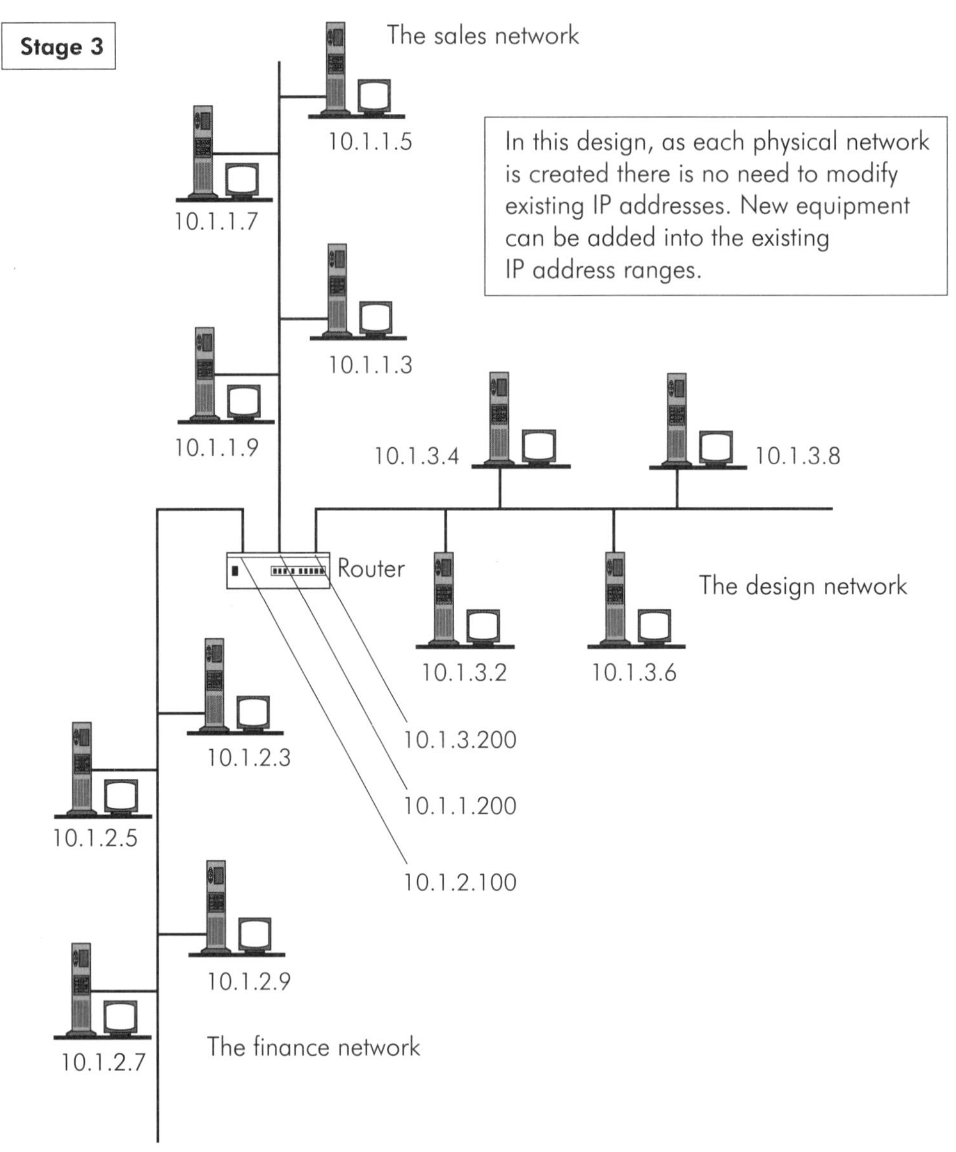

Adding Extra IP Addresses to a Network Card

So, just how can we go about adding an extra IP address to our network card? Figures 11.10, 11.11, 11.12 and 11.13 show how this can be done on a Windows NT system.

Figure 11.10 Setting multiple IP addresses (1)

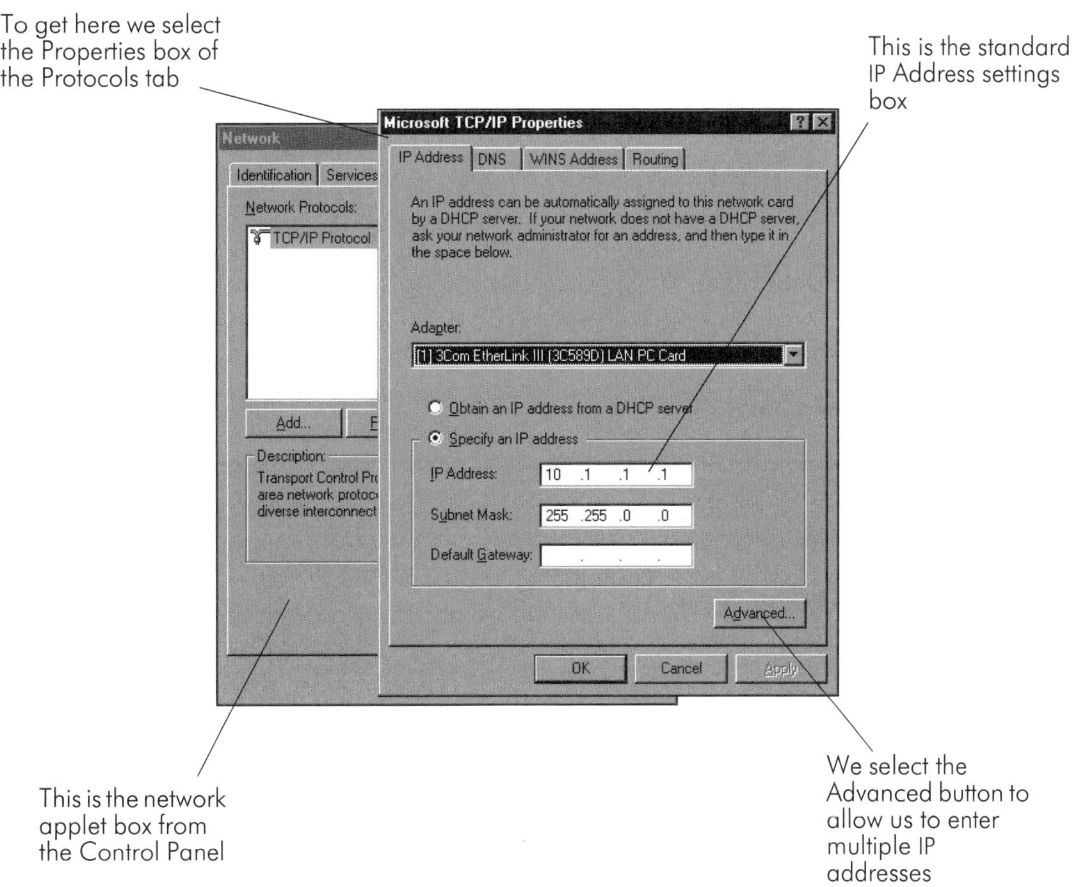

Figure 11.11 Setting multiple IP addresses (2)

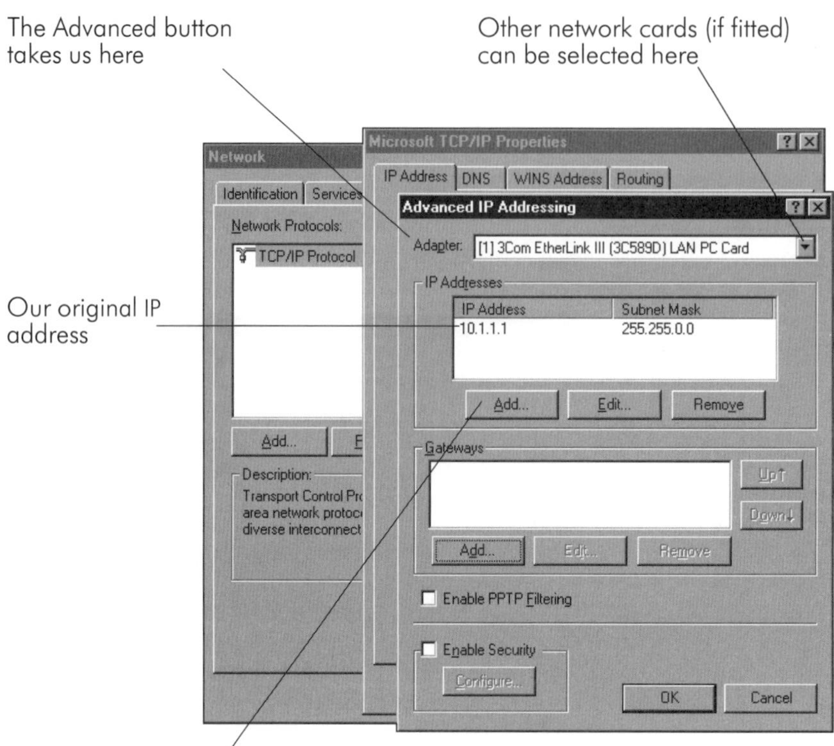

Figure 11.12 Setting multiple IP addresses (3)

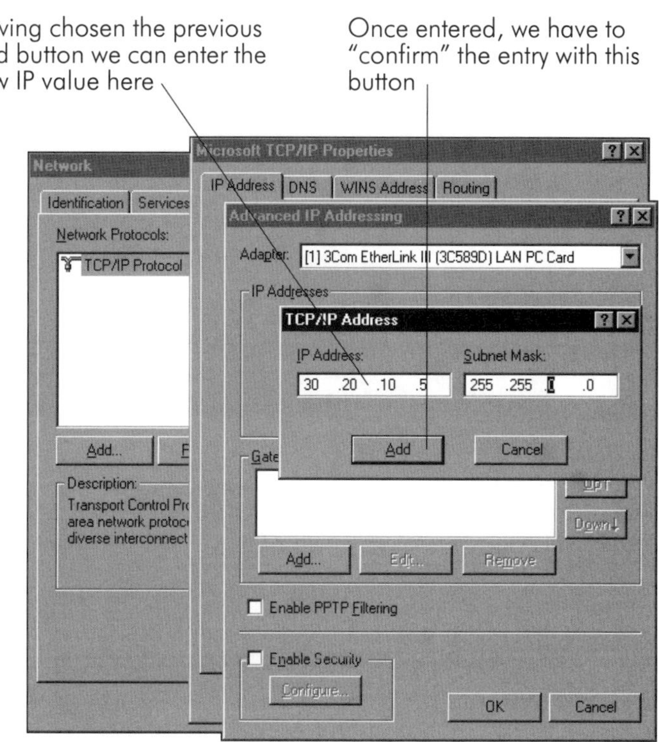

Figure 11.13 Setting multiple IP addresses (4)

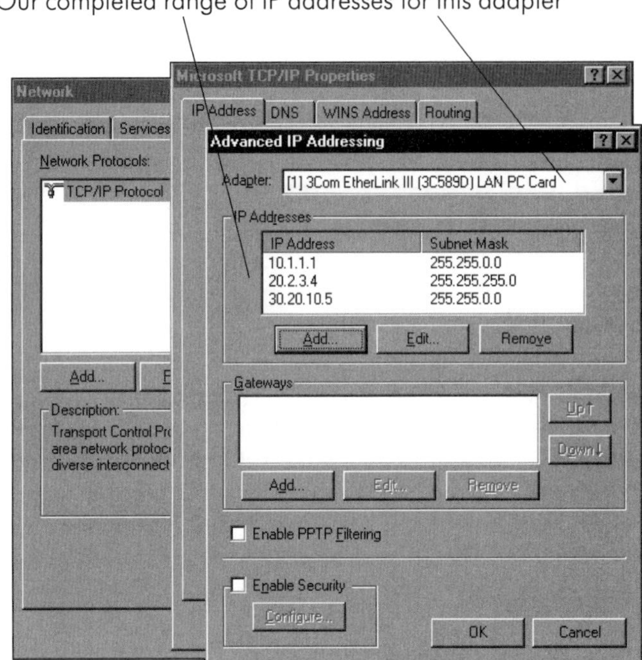

"Future Proofing" – a Further Example

One additional example will serve to illustrate this technique of "future proofing". Imagine a company that is planning to implement some form of intranet. As before, they wish to save money while allowing the possibility of future growth. One of their initial decisions is to provide a web server for each of the departments involved in the intranet project. These are the sales, finance and design departments. They set up their web server with three IP addresses. The web server has only one network card but they have attached three IP addresses to it in the same way as shown above. One of these addresses is assigned to the sales web server, one to the finance web server and the third to the design web server.

Figure 11.14 shows how the new server will fit into our network.

Figure 11.14 Multiple web servers and multiple IP addresses on 1 physical machine

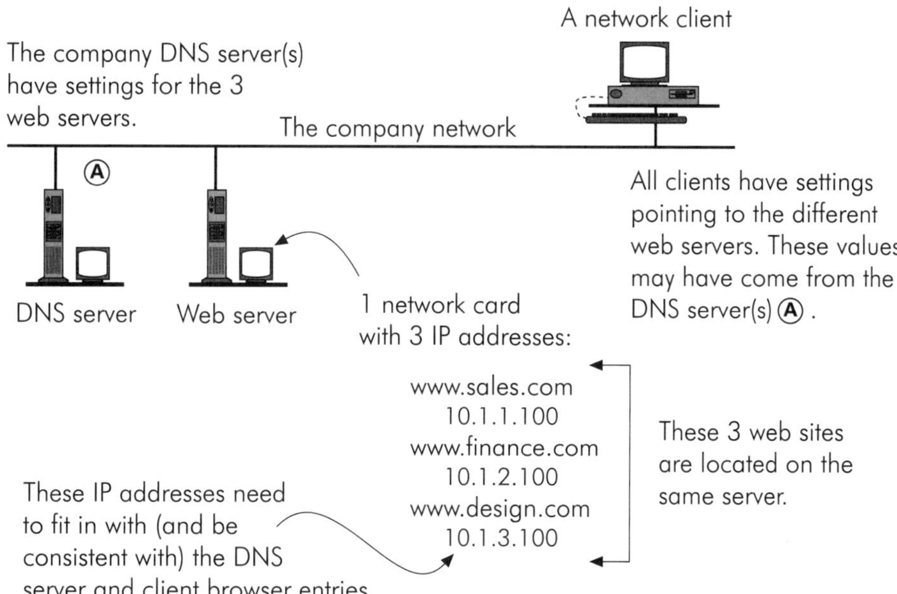

We will use the three network addresses 10.1.1.100, 10.1.2.100 and 10.1.3.100 for each of the web servers. These IP addresses will be set into our clients and the associated DNS servers. We will use the first for the sales web server, the second for the finance web server and the final address for the design web server. All of these "logical" IP addresses will be on the one physical web server. As our business grows the demands placed on the one, physical, web server will also grow. As it becomes slower and slower, as demand and throughput increase, we can simply remove each of the separate web sites and move them to a separate physical machine. The corresponding IP address will also move to the new machine. In this way the addresses that the clients use and that are entered into the DNS server will not have to be changed. All that our clients will notice is (hopefully) a faster and more reliable web service.

Figure 11.15 illustrates the principle of this.

Figure 11.15 The corporate web servers once they have moved to 3 separate servers

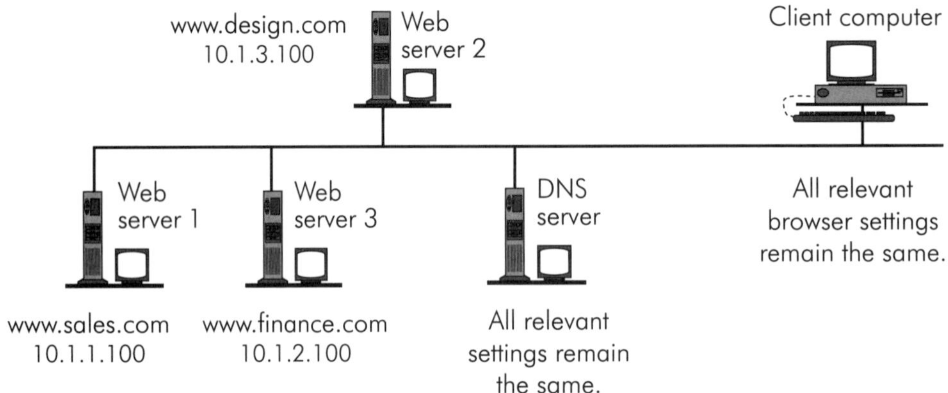

With a little careful forethought our design will allow us to grow and adapt to future changes in hardware requirements without a drastic restructuring of the underlying IP system. The nightmare scenario of having to update all of our client IP address references and having to modify all of the DNS entries associated with our web servers has also been removed.

All of this flexibility comes about by virtue of the implementation of the "virtual layers" concept introduced in both the DOD and OSI models of networking software.

12
Routing

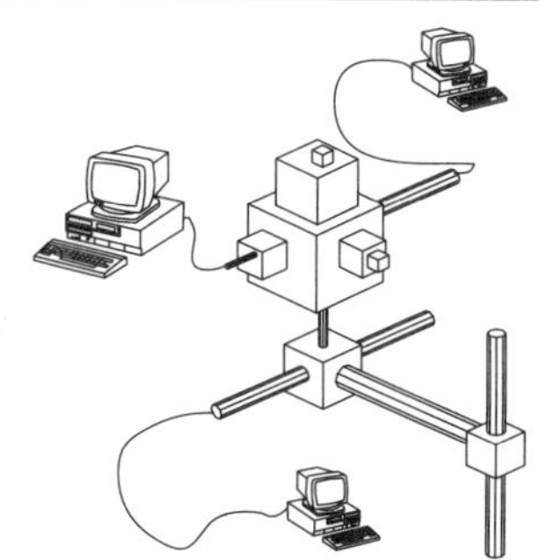

What are Routers and Routing Tables?

In the following discussions we talk about routers. By this we mean a machine that has more than one IP interface and can move data between these interfaces. The actual router could be a computer with two or more interface cards, a dedicated router or some more subtle entity dreamt up by the hardware industry.

One of the important aspects of designing networks based around subnets is: How can I get the data from point A to point B? In a simple network design this is relatively easy but as the network complexity increases the task becomes more and more subtle. In most complex networks there will be one or more routers combining together the various subnets which, together, make up the complete network.

Routers move data around networks based on decisions along the lines of: Where do I move this piece of data? These decisions are themselves based on tables of route information, similar in overall concept to bus routes through a city. If you want to get to the Cathedral go to the main station then to the post office and then you will see the Cathedral.

Let us look at a couple of examples. All of the following diagrams are taken from a Microsoft Windows network consisting of NT servers and Windows 98 and 95 clients. The NT servers are also acting as routers.

A Simple One-router Network

In Figure 12.1 Client 1 can reach the other network by setting the default gateway to address B (10.1.2.60). This gets any "non local" data to the router and the router forwards the data to the opposite side. Similarly, Client 2 can reach the opposite network by setting the default gateway to address C (10.20.30.60). In both cases the router receives incoming data and moves it to the opposite port as required.

Figure 12.1 A simple routed network

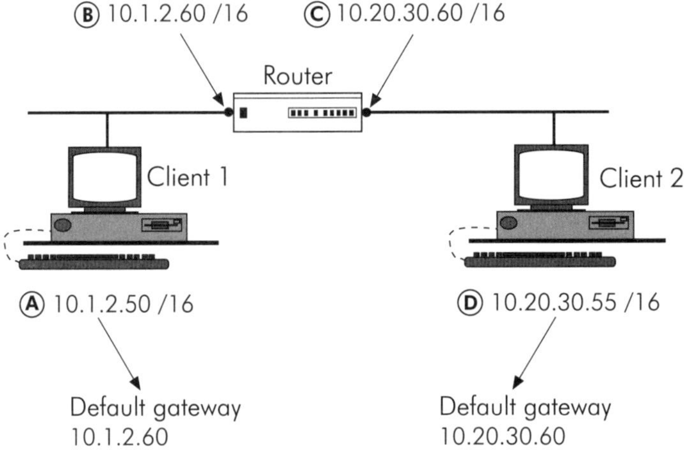

The function of the default gateway in this example is to move any data that the adjacency test decides is "non local" to the router. After this it is up to the router how it handles the data. Recall from Chapter 3 that the adjacency test is applied to the source and destination IP addresses to see if their network identifiers (NetIDs) are the same.

A Two-router Network

Figure 12.2 shows some of the problems on even a modest two-router network. Our previous expedient of setting the various client default gateways to the relevant interface on the router will no longer work.

There are too many router interfaces and setting one client's default to a particular router may not provide full network connectivity.

Figure 12.2 A more complex routed network

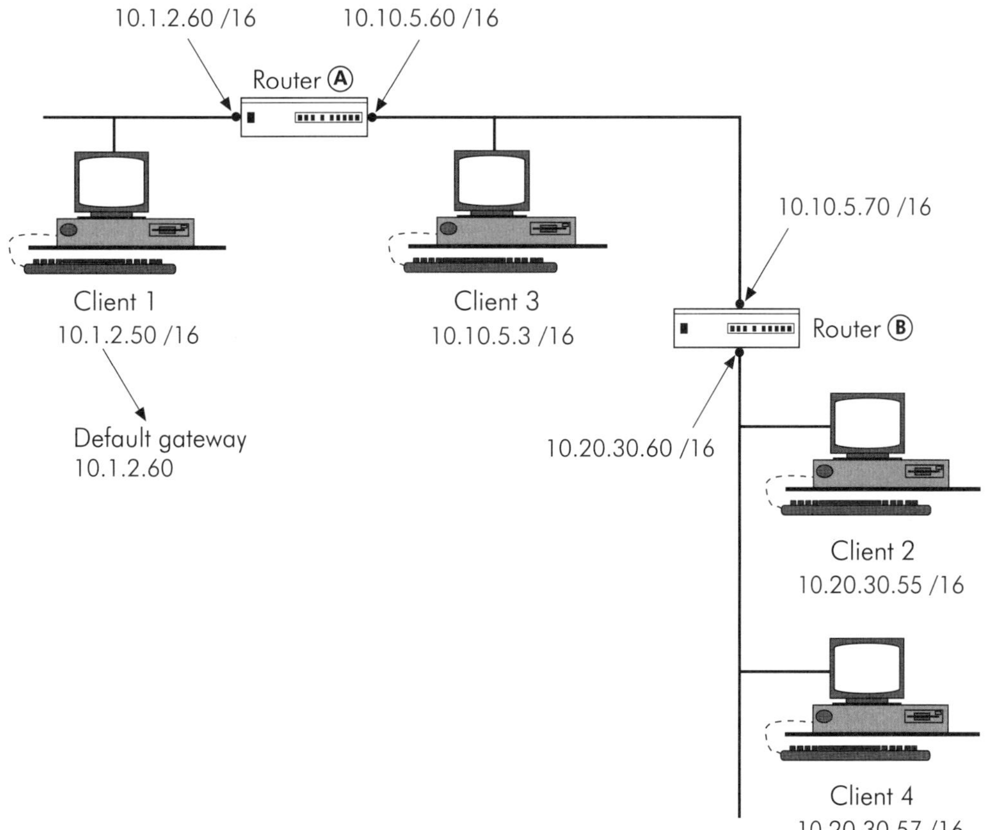

As an example consider Client 1 in Figure 12.2. Here we can set the client's default gateway to port 10.1.2.60 on Router A. This means that any data which cannot be sent to machines on the local network, using the MAC address, will be sent to the router.

Router A, at present, knows only about the two networks 10.1.0.0 and 10.10.0.0 (remember we are using a 16-bit mask here). Router A knows nothing whatsoever about network 10.20.0.0 so is unable to forward data to it.

We have two alternatives:

1. we can either modify the client's routing table to let it know about "far away" networks; or,
2. we can modify the routers' routing tables to let them know about the remote networks.

While the first option is suitable for very small networks it soon becomes very unwieldy where we have a number of routers and a number of networks connecting them.

The second option is the best and we are able to modify the internal routing tables of a router in two general ways:

1. *Manually add static routes*. This was how routers were originally configured and in some cases is still the best option.
2. *Have the routers automatically update their own tables*. This is the way that most routers now update their information. Although this makes for simpler network administration it also introduces additional problems such as security and network bandwidth consumption.

Summary of the Problem

With reference to Figure 12.2 we can see the potential problem. Although Client 1 has a default gateway to Router A there is no way, at present, of getting the data from Router A to Router B and so the far side of the network (from Client 1's perspective) is unreachable. We need to arrange a way for Client 1 to be able to reach Client 2 and Client 4 on the far side of the network.

Our solution was to modify the routing table. This can be done in one of two ways. The simplest way for smaller networks is to directly enter into the routing table the route paths that specify how the data is to be moved across the network. These paths are called *static routes*. Although, with proper care, it is possible to construct tables for quite large networks this way, it is impractical to construct larger networks using the same method. To cope with the needs of larger networks a more dynamic method of updating the tables has to be found. This, more automatic method, is referred to as *dynamic routing* and there are three common methods of doing this. These are RIP, RIP-2 and OSPF. We will restrict our discussion to RIP, the earliest of the dynamic routing algorithms. For a detailed discussion of the various pros-and-cons of the different methods you will have to refer to more detailed textbooks. My aim here is to cover the principles of routing as far as subnet design is concerned.

Static Entries

Before we discuss how static entries are added into routing tables let us look at the underlying principles on which routers base their decision making.

The flow chart that describes the process is shown in Figure 12.3 – note that it is a *generalised* flow chart. By this I mean that many routers may have a modified form of this routing algorithm designed to optimise some aspect of their decision making. This enables them to prioritise certain routes and generally to work in a more efficient way. The algorithm described forms the basis on which many routing systems are based and allows us to look at the general aspects of routing decisions.

As data enters the router the destination address (DA) of the data is examined. If the router or the host (remember that host computers can act as routers) has a direct connection that matches the DA of the incoming packet then the data is sent directly to it. On a busy router this might happen rarely but with a host computer the DA might well be one of its network cards. This is Decision 1 in the flow chart.

If there is no direct connection the routing table is checked to see if there is a host-specific route that matches the destination address of the incoming data. If there is a match the data is sent to the port (network card) specified in the routing table. This is Decision 2 in the flow chart.

The third Decision is checked if Decisions 1 and 2 fail. If this is the case the router checks to see if there is a network in the routing table that matches the network portion of the DA. If there is a match the data is sent out to the relevant port.

The final decision is reached if the previous three fail. This is Decision 4 in our diagram and here the router checks to see if it has a default route present. If it does then the data is sent out to this port and, hopefully, reaches its destination. If all of the above fail, a routing error is produced and an error message is returned to the source computer.

Figure 12.3 A generalised flow chart showing router logic

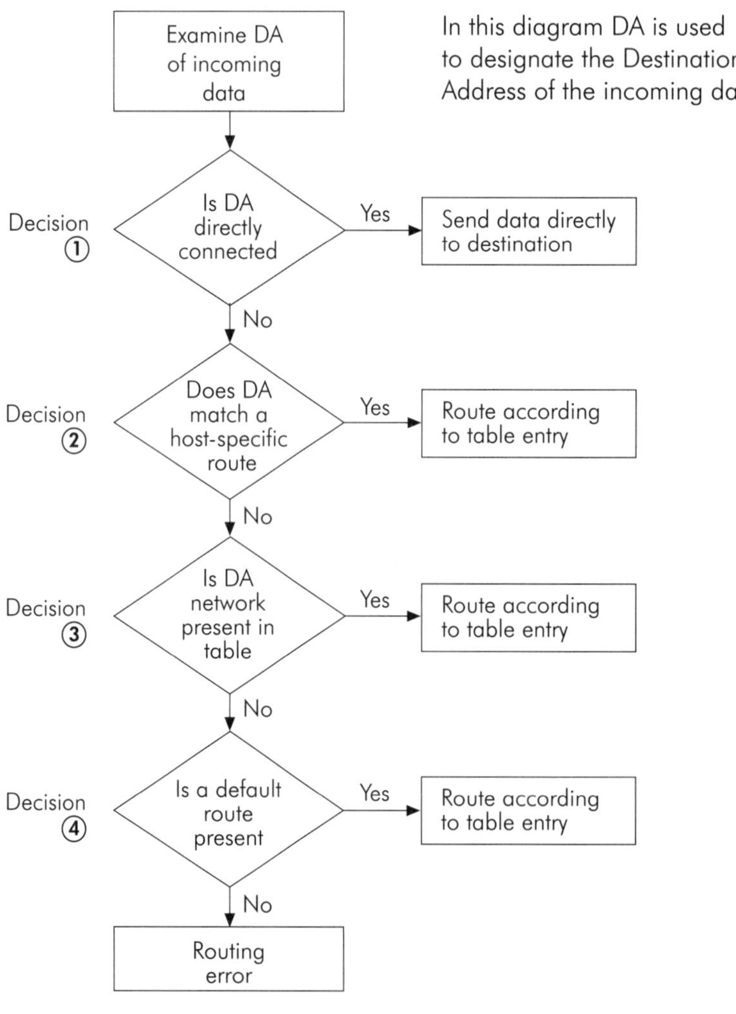

It is this order of events on early routers that caused some bad habits to spread. Due to the nature of routing the early systems that were used were often UNIX machines with multiple network cards fitted. Due to the processing overhead of the decision-making process and a desire to squeeze every ounce of performance out of systems it was considered better to enter host-specific routes into routing tables. Remember, here we are talking about static tables. This means that someone has to enter this data manually into the tables.

So with host-specific routes we get a faster routing table (decisions are usually made at the Decision 2 level in our flow chart). Using this method the cost to us is in the number of entries required to maintain this type of table.

With a four-subnet network containing 100 computers, a host-specific routing table would require 100 entries. If this four-subnet network had 1000 computers we would have to enter all 1000 machine addresses. Expand this to 5000 computers and each machine on the network would need an entry in the router. If we had two routers this data would have to be entered almost twice to maintain connectivity. Needless to say as networks grew in size and complexity the host-specific entries became a less and less popular way of building routing tables.

So what should we use? The answer is to use network-specific entries. On any but the largest networks the performance issue is not as pressing as it was. Now most routers produce fast data movement even if default routes are concerned. Using the network-specific entries makes no apparent difference in speed. With the above example even with 20,000 computers on a four-subnet network (I am *not* suggesting this is done!) you could route them using the four network entries alone. If the system used more routers you would only need to reproduce the four network entries on each router.

How do we build up a routing table using these static network entries? We will illustrate this by using the simple network illustrated in Figures 12.5 to 12.11.

The network to which these relate is shown in Figure 12.4. We can see in this diagram that the network consists of two routers and five subnets. In all cases the subnet mask is 255.255.255.0. Neither of our routers is configured apart from the IP addresses having been assigned to each network card. The first of the routing tables (Figure 12.5) comes from the design router.

Figure 12.4 The office network

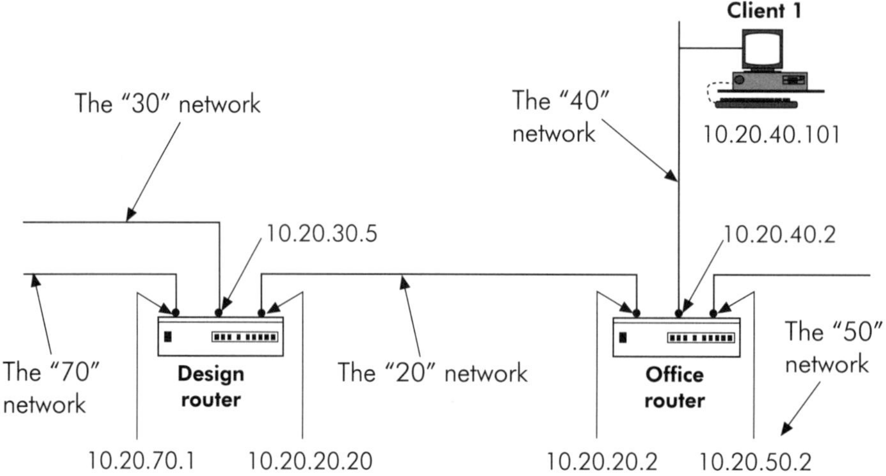

Interpreting the Routing Table

The machine from which this table comes is an NT computer with two network cards. One of these cards has two IP addresses assigned to it. As we saw in the last chapter this means that we are using logical subnets on this network. Figure 12.5 shows the routing table from the "design" router in Figure 12.4. By comparing Figures 12.4 and 12.5 we can start to make sense of this routing table.

The first two lines (10.20.20.0 and 10.20.20.20) deal with the network address of the card and the actual IP address of the card. Reading from left to right in the first line we can see that any data for network 10.20.20.0 with a subnet mask of 255.255.255.0 will be sent out on gateway 10.20.20.20 through interface 10.20.20.20 and in this case the metric is 1. The metric is a rough means of determining how "far away" the relevant network is. In this case the network in question is connected to the router and so the metric is calculated as 1. The algorithm used to calculate the metric varies between different implementations. Local networks (this means networks on the LAN) are usually calculated as a metric of 1. Some more sophisticated routers allow the metric to be used to prioritise routes. If two routes to the same destination exist, one with a metric of 1 and the other with a metric of 5 the route with a metric of 1 will be chosen in preference to the other.

Figure 12.5 Initial routing table from the "design" router

```
C:\>route print

Active Routes:

  Network Address          Netmask  Gateway Address        Interface  Metric
        10.20.20.0    255.255.255.0      10.20.20.20      10.20.20.20       1
       10.20.20.20  255.255.255.255        127.0.0.1        127.0.0.1       1
        10.20.30.0    255.255.255.0       10.20.30.5       10.20.30.5       1
        10.20.30.5  255.255.255.255        127.0.0.1        127.0.0.1       1
        10.20.70.0    255.255.255.0       10.20.70.1       10.20.30.5       1
        10.20.70.1  255.255.255.255        127.0.0.1        127.0.0.1       1
    10.255.255.255  255.255.255.255      10.20.20.20      10.20.20.20       1
         127.0.0.0        255.0.0.0        127.0.0.1        127.0.0.1       1
         224.0.0.0        224.0.0.0       10.20.30.5       10.20.30.5       1
         224.0.0.0        224.0.0.0      10.20.20.20      10.20.20.20       1
   255.255.255.255  255.255.255.255      10.20.20.20      10.20.20.20       1

C:\>
```

Network broadcast
General broadcast

Line 2 states how the explicit IP address of 10.20.20.20 is dealt with. The mask used here is a full /32 bit mask and this is interpreted as a host (computer or interface) IP address. The gateway and the interface values are 127.0.0.1. As stated earlier in the book this value is the loopback address and here means "this computer". Any data sent to 10.20.20.20 is intended for this computer and is dealt with accordingly. The other entries that have 127.0.0.1 as their gateway and/or interface addresses are also addresses on this machine.

Line 3 in the table states that any data for the 10.20.30.0 network using a /24 bit mask is to be sent through gateway 10.20.30.5 which is on interface 10.20.30.5. In our simple routing table most of the gateways are on the actual interface card. With a more sophisticated model this would not be the case. Again, the metric is 1 suggesting that the "30" network is connected to the router.

Line 4 deals with the explicit address 10.20.30.5 and is interpreted in the same way as above.

The next line details the 10.20.70.0 network; again, with a /24 bit mask. This is the first of our multiple address interfaces. In this line we can see that any data for the 10.20.70.0 network is to go out through the 10.20.70.1 gateway which is on the 10.20.30.5 interface. This allows us to assume that the 10.20.30.5 network card actually has two addresses on it. These are 10.20.30.5 and 10.20.70.1.

The 10.20.70.1 entry is an explicit one and is dealt with as before.

On line 7, 10.255.255.255 is a broadcast address on the 10.0.0.0 network. Any information for the 10.0.0.0 network is sent out through 10.20.20.20.

The next three lines deal with the 127.0.0.0 network (the loopback address) and the 224.0.0.0 entries are multicast addresses that would allow us to set up a multicast network for streaming video or streaming audio – should we have software to support this. These three entries (127,224,224) are added automatically. Not all routing systems will automatically add entries for multicast addresses.

The final entry is the general broadcast address. This differs from the network-specific broadcast address in that data containing a network-specific broadcast address will usually cross routers. Data containing the general broadcast address will not. This is, however, router dependant. Some older systems will not pass any broadcast data.

Adding Static Routes

Let us imagine that we are sitting at the machine that is acting as the design router. We wish to look at the routing table and so we type the command:

```
C:\>route print
```

The output is shown in the top part of Figure 12.6. This is the same data as in Figure 12.5.

Figure 12.6 Design routing table after static route added

```
C:\>route print

Active Routes:

  Network Address          Netmask  Gateway Address        Interface  Metric
       10.20.20.0    255.255.255.0      10.20.20.20      10.20.20.20       1
      10.20.20.20  255.255.255.255        127.0.0.1        127.0.0.1       1
       10.20.30.0    255.255.255.0       10.20.30.5       10.20.30.5       1
       10.20.30.5  255.255.255.255        127.0.0.1        127.0.0.1       1
       10.20.70.0    255.255.255.0       10.20.70.1       10.20.30.5       1
       10.20.70.1  255.255.255.255        127.0.0.1        127.0.0.1       1
   10.255.255.255  255.255.255.255      10.20.20.20      10.20.20.20       1
        127.0.0.0        255.0.0.0        127.0.0.1        127.0.0.1       1
        224.0.0.0        224.0.0.0       10.20.30.5       10.20.30.5       1
        224.0.0.0        224.0.0.0      10.20.20.20      10.20.20.20       1
  255.255.255.255  255.255.255.255      10.20.20.20      10.20.20.20       1

C:\>route add 10.20.40.0 mask 255.255.255.0 10.20.20.2

C:\>route print

Active Routes:

  Network Address          Netmask  Gateway Address        Interface  Metric
       10.20.20.0    255.255.255.0      10.20.20.20      10.20.20.20       1
      10.20.20.20  255.255.255.255        127.0.0.1        127.0.0.1       1
       10.20.30.0    255.255.255.0       10.20.30.5       10.20.30.5       1
       10.20.30.5  255.255.255.255        127.0.0.1        127.0.0.1       1
       10.20.40.0    255.255.255.0       10.20.20.2      10.20.20.20       1
       10.20.70.0    255.255.255.0       10.20.70.1       10.20.30.5       1
       10.20.70.1  255.255.255.255        127.0.0.1        127.0.0.1       1
   10.255.255.255  255.255.255.255      10.20.20.20      10.20.20.20       1
        127.0.0.0        255.0.0.0        127.0.0.1        127.0.0.1       1
        224.0.0.0        224.0.0.0       10.20.30.5       10.20.30.5       1
        224.0.0.0        224.0.0.0      10.20.20.20      10.20.20.20       1
  255.255.255.255  255.255.255.255      10.20.20.20      10.20.20.20       1

C:\>
```

The static route we wish to add

Go through this interface to get here

Looking back at Figure 12.4 we can see that there is no way in which the design router knows about network 10.20.40.0. Since the routers have not been configured to automatically share data we will have to enter an explicit entry for this route. What do we want to tell the router? The information that we wish to convey is as follows:

"Any data for the 10.20.40.0 network must be delivered to the 'office' router."

Assuming that the office router is set up correctly then this will deal with the data according to its own routing table.

How can we deliver data to this router? We do so by getting the data to the 10.20.20.2 port on the office router. Can we reach the 10.20.20.2 port? The answer to this is "yes" because the 10.20.20.2 port is on the 10.20.20.0 network and we are directly connected to this through our own port 10.20.20.20. In other words we have the connectivity to reach the receiving end of the connection. In a more complex routing example, if we were unable to get to the "far end" we may well have to add an intermediate routing entry to give us the necessary connectivity.

To reach the 10.20.40.0 network we add the following entry to our routing table.

```
route add 10.20.40.0 mask 255.255.255.0  10.20.20.2
```

This states that to get data to the 10.20.40.0 network using a /24 bit mask we have to deliver the data to the 10.20.20.2 port on the 10.20.20.0 network.

In most `route add` commands there is an additional optional entry that goes at the end of the line above. This is the metric command and this could be used to specify the metric to the route in question. We will leave all entries as the default metric since our network is a simple one and none of our routing algorithms make use of this information.

The lower section of Figure 12.6 shows the design router's routing table after the above line has been added. There should be no surprises here. The entry in the routing table states that to get to network 10.20.40.0 using a /24 bit mask we get data to gateway 10.20.20.2 (the entry point from our router into the next router) using interface 10.20.20.20. This is what we would expect from our earlier discussions.

The lower part of Figure 12.7 shows a successful ping from our router to a host on the 10.20.40.0 network. Remember that this host and its associated router will also have to be able to reach our router. If the computer at address 10.20.40.101 cannot "see" its own router it will be unable to reply. In this simple test the computer on 10.20.40.101 has the relevant information set up.

Figure 12.7 Adding a route to the design router

```
        10.20.70.0    255.255.255.0      10.20.70.1      10.20.30.5      1
        10.20.70.1  255.255.255.255      127.0.0.1        127.0.0.1      1
    10.255.255.255  255.255.255.255    10.20.20.20      10.20.20.20      1
         127.0.0.0        255.0.0.0      127.0.0.1        127.0.0.1      1
         224.0.0.0        224.0.0.0     10.20.30.5       10.20.30.5      1
         224.0.0.0        224.0.0.0    10.20.20.20      10.20.20.20      1
   255.255.255.255  255.255.255.255    10.20.20.20      10.20.20.20      1

C:\>route add 10.20.40.0 mask 255.255.255.0 10.20.20.2

C:\>route print

Active Routes:

   Network Address          Netmask  Gateway Address       Interface  Metric
        10.20.20.0    255.255.255.0    10.20.20.20      10.20.20.20      1
       10.20.20.20  255.255.255.255      127.0.0.1        127.0.0.1      1
        10.20.30.0    255.255.255.0     10.20.30.5       10.20.30.5      1
        10.20.30.5  255.255.255.255      127.0.0.1        127.0.0.1      1
        10.20.40.0    255.255.255.0     10.20.20.2      10.20.20.20      1
        10.20.70.0    255.255.255.0     10.20.70.1       10.20.30.5      1
        10.20.70.1  255.255.255.255      127.0.0.1        127.0.0.1      1
    10.255.255.255  255.255.255.255    10.20.20.20      10.20.20.20      1
         127.0.0.0        255.0.0.0      127.0.0.1        127.0.0.1      1
         224.0.0.0        224.0.0.0     10.20.30.5       10.20.30.5      1
         224.0.0.0        224.0.0.0    10.20.20.20      10.20.20.20      1
   255.255.255.255  255.255.255.255    10.20.20.20      10.20.20.20      1

C:\>ping 10.20.40.101

Pinging 10.20.40.101 with 32 bytes of data:

Reply from 10.20.40.101: bytes=32 time<10ms TTL=127
Reply from 10.20.40.101: bytes=32 time<10ms TTL=127
Reply from 10.20.40.101: bytes=32 time<10ms TTL=127
Reply from 10.20.40.101: bytes=32 time<10ms TTL=127

C:\>
```

The client knows how to get back to 10.20.20.20

Figure 12.8 shows us adding another static route on the design router. This one allows us to get to the "50" network. We do this by adding the line:

```
route add 10.20.50.0 mask 255.255.255.0 10.20.20.2
```

The ping testing this connection follows this command and the final routing table for the design router is at the bottom of Figure 12.8. The new route appears in the table in the same way as before.

Figure 12.8 The final design routing table

```
Pinging 10.20.40.101 with 32 bytes of data:

Reply from 10.20.40.101: bytes=32 time<10ms TTL=127
Reply from 10.20.40.101: bytes=32 time<10ms TTL=127
Reply from 10.20.40.101: bytes=32 time<10ms TTL=127
Reply from 10.20.40.101: bytes=32 time<10ms TTL=127

C:\>route add 10.20.50.0 mask 255.255.255.0 10.20.20.2

C:\>ping 10.20.50.2

Pinging 10.20.50.2 with 32 bytes of data:

Reply from 10.20.50.2: bytes=32 time<10ms TTL=128
Reply from 10.20.50.2: bytes=32 time<10ms TTL=128
Reply from 10.20.50.2: bytes=32 time<10ms TTL=128
Reply from 10.20.50.2: bytes=32 time<10ms TTL=128

C:\>route print

Active Routes:

  Network Address          Netmask  Gateway Address        Interface  Metric
       10.20.20.0    255.255.255.0      10.20.20.20      10.20.20.20       1
      10.20.20.20  255.255.255.255        127.0.0.1        127.0.0.1       1
       10.20.30.0    255.255.255.0       10.20.30.5       10.20.30.5       1
       10.20.30.5  255.255.255.255        127.0.0.1        127.0.0.1       1
       10.20.40.0    255.255.255.0       10.20.20.2      10.20.20.20       1
       10.20.50.0    255.255.255.0       10.20.20.2      10.20.20.20       1
       10.20.70.0    255.255.255.0       10.20.70.1       10.20.30.5       1
       10.20.70.1  255.255.255.255        127.0.0.1        127.0.0.1       1
   10.255.255.255  255.255.255.255      10.20.20.20      10.20.20.20       1
        127.0.0.0        255.0.0.0        127.0.0.1        127.0.0.1       1
        224.0.0.0        224.0.0.0       10.20.30.5       10.20.30.5       1
        224.0.0.0        224.0.0.0      10.20.20.20      10.20.20.20       1
  255.255.255.255  255.255.255.255      10.20.20.20      10.20.20.20       1

C:\>
```

Connectivity Problems

Now that we have sorted out the design router we have to turn our attention to the office router. Figure 12.9 shows its routing table. We can see that very little differs from the design-server's table. The one major difference is that there is an entry for a default route. This is a little strange in a simple router configuration and hints at the fact that this computer is acting as more than a straightforward router. In fact it is a local DNS server with a connection to an external (forwarder) DNS server and also it acts a proxy server for the internal network. The way in which it reaches the "outside" world is through an ISDN router connected at 10.20.40.5.

Figure 12.9 The office router

```
C:\>route print
Active Routes:

  Network Address          Netmask  Gateway Address        Interface  Metric
          0.0.0.0          0.0.0.0       10.20.40.5       10.20.40.2       1
       10.20.20.0    255.255.255.0       10.20.20.2       10.20.20.2       1
       10.20.20.2  255.255.255.255        127.0.0.1        127.0.0.1       1
       10.20.40.0    255.255.255.0       10.20.40.2       10.20.40.2       1
       10.20.40.2  255.255.255.255        127.0.0.1        127.0.0.1       1
       10.20.50.0    255.255.255.0       10.20.50.2       10.20.40.2       1
       10.20.50.2  255.255.255.255        127.0.0.1        127.0.0.1       1
   10.255.255.255  255.255.255.255       10.20.20.2       10.20.20.2       1
        127.0.0.0        255.0.0.0        127.0.0.1        127.0.0.1       1
        224.0.0.0        224.0.0.0       10.20.20.2       10.20.20.2       1
  255.255.255.255  255.255.255.255       10.20.20.2       10.20.20.2       1

C:\>
```

The entry for this default route is shown on the first line 0.0.0.0 with the somewhat strange mask of 0.0.0.0. What this says is that anything which the office router does not know how to handle gets sent to the ISDN router on port 10.20.40.5 which is reached through interface 10.20.40.2.

By looking back to Figure 12.4 we can see the problem. For a connection to work, both sides of the connection must know how to reach each other. Imagine a computer on the 10.20.30.0 network. If data is sent from the "30" network to the office router it will arrive at the relevant port on office since we have configured the design router. Now the office router tries to reply to the computer on the "30" network. What does it do? It interrogates its routing table and finds no entry for 10.20.30.0. Under these circumstances it will resort to the default route and the ISDN router will be contacted. This will dial up the service provider, establish a connection and contact the remote DNS server. This will return a negative reply and the connection will fail. All of this will have been charged at the standard telephone rates!

If the ISDN router was switched off (as it was when we were testing the network!) there is no entry for the "30" network and the default route produces no response and so the connection fails. This is illustrated in Figure 12.10 where we try to ping the design router port of 10.20.30.5 from the office router.

Figure 12.10 Failed ping from office to design

No entry here

For this network

```
C:\>route print

Active Routes:

  Network Address          Netmask  Gateway Address        Interface  Metric
          0.0.0.0          0.0.0.0      10.20.40.5       10.20.40.2       1
       10.20.20.0    255.255.255.0      10.20.20.2       10.20.20.2       1
       10.20.20.2  255.255.255.255       127.0.0.1        127.0.0.1       1
       10.20.40.0    255.255.255.0      10.20.40.2       10.20.40.2       1
       10.20.40.2  255.255.255.255       127.0.0.1        127.0.0.1       1
       10.20.50.0    255.255.255.0      10.20.50.2       10.20.40.2       1
       10.20.50.2  255.255.255.255       127.0.0.1        127.0.0.1       1
   10.255.255.255  255.255.255.255      10.20.20.2       10.20.20.2       1
        127.0.0.0        255.0.0.0       127.0.0.1        127.0.0.1       1
        224.0.0.0        224.0.0.0      10.20.20.2       10.20.20.2       1
  255.255.255.255  255.255.255.255      10.20.20.2       10.20.20.2       1

C:\>ping 10.20.30.5

Pinging 10.20.30.5 with 32 bytes of data:

Request timed out.
Request timed out.
Request timed out.
Request timed out.

C:\>
```

What we need to do is to tell the office router how to reach network 10.20.30.0. We do this by the table entry shown in Figure 12.11. This entry tells the office router that to get to the 10.20.30.0 network it has to deliver the data to the 10.20.20.20 port and that to do this it must send data out through the 10.20.20.2 interface.

Figure 12.11 Route entry for office server

```
C:\>route print

Active Routes:

  Network Address          Netmask  Gateway Address        Interface  Metric
          0.0.0.0          0.0.0.0      10.20.40.5       10.20.40.2       1
       10.20.20.0    255.255.255.0      10.20.20.2       10.20.20.2       1
       10.20.20.2  255.255.255.255       127.0.0.1        127.0.0.1       1
       10.20.40.0    255.255.255.0      10.20.40.2       10.20.40.2       1
       10.20.40.2  255.255.255.255       127.0.0.1        127.0.0.1       1
       10.20.50.0    255.255.255.0      10.20.50.2       10.20.40.2       1
       10.20.50.2  255.255.255.255       127.0.0.1        127.0.0.1       1
   10.255.255.255  255.255.255.255      10.20.20.2       10.20.20.2       1
        127.0.0.0        255.0.0.0       127.0.0.1        127.0.0.1       1
        224.0.0.0        224.0.0.0      10.20.20.2       10.20.20.2       1
  255.255.255.255  255.255.255.255      10.20.20.2       10.20.20.2       1

C:\>ping 10.20.30.5

Pinging 10.20.30.5 with 32 bytes of data:

Request timed out.
Request timed out.
Request timed out.
Request timed out.

C:\>route add 10.20.30.0 mask 255.255.255.0 10.20.20.20

C:\>ping 10.20.30.5

Pinging 10.20.30.5 with 32 bytes of data:

Reply from 10.20.30.5: bytes=32 time<10ms TTL=128
Reply from 10.20.30.5: bytes=32 time<10ms TTL=128
Reply from 10.20.30.5: bytes=32 time<10ms TTL=128
Reply from 10.20.30.5: bytes=32 time<10ms TTL=128

C:\>
```

The command is:

```
route add 10.20.30.0 mask 255.255.255.0 10.20.20.20
```

Once this is done the ping succeeds. Both sides now know how to reach each other.

For full network connectivity we have to add a similar route for the "70" network and make sure that the clients on all networks know how to get to their respective default gateways. Figure 12.12 shows the last entry (for network 10.20.70.0) and a test ping to 10.20.70.1. This ping works so we have bi-directional connectivity between the office router and port 10.20.70.1.

Figure 12.12 Final entries for office router

```
Request timed out.
Request timed out.
Request timed out.

C:\>route add 10.20.30.0 mask 255.255.255.0 10.20.20.20

C:\>ping 10.20.30.5

Pinging 10.20.30.5 with 32 bytes of data:

Reply from 10.20.30.5: bytes=32 time<10ms TTL=128
Reply from 10.20.30.5: bytes=32 time<10ms TTL=128
Reply from 10.20.30.5: bytes=32 time<10ms TTL=128
Reply from 10.20.30.5: bytes=32 time<10ms TTL=128

C:\>route add 10.20.70.0 mask 255.255.255.0 10.20.20.20

C:\>ping 10.20.70.1

Pinging 10.20.70.1 with 32 bytes of data:

Reply from 10.20.70.1: bytes=32 time<10ms TTL=128
Reply from 10.20.70.1: bytes=32 time<10ms TTL=128
Reply from 10.20.70.1: bytes=32 time<10ms TTL=128
Reply from 10.20.70.1: bytes=32 time<10ms TTL=128

C:\>route print

Active Routes:

  Network Address          Netmask  Gateway Address        Interface  Metric
          0.0.0.0          0.0.0.0       10.20.40.5       10.20.40.2       1
       10.20.20.0    255.255.255.0       10.20.20.2       10.20.20.2       1
       10.20.20.2  255.255.255.255        127.0.0.1        127.0.0.1       1
       10.20.30.0    255.255.255.0      10.20.20.20       10.20.20.2       1
       10.20.40.0    255.255.255.0       10.20.40.2       10.20.40.2       1
       10.20.40.2  255.255.255.255        127.0.0.1        127.0.0.1       1
       10.20.50.0    255.255.255.0       10.20.50.2       10.20.40.2       1
       10.20.50.2  255.255.255.255        127.0.0.1        127.0.0.1       1
       10.20.70.0    255.255.255.0      10.20.20.20       10.20.20.2       1
   10.255.255.255  255.255.255.255       10.20.20.2       10.20.20.2       1
        127.0.0.0        255.0.0.0        127.0.0.1        127.0.0.1       1
        224.0.0.0        224.0.0.0       10.20.20.2       10.20.20.2       1
  255.255.255.255  255.255.255.255       10.20.20.2       10.20.20.2       1

C:\>
```

The final part of Figure 12.12 shows the routing table for the office router after all relevant network routes have been added.

To guarantee connectivity across the network all of the client computers must be set up to reach their respective default gateways, once these routers are correctly configured. For the client's tables a more complex but rather more efficient method of working would be to have explicit network entries in the routing tables of the various client computers. Usually most people settle for the simpler solution of having default gateways on their clients.

Dynamic Routing

All of the above can be used to create quite complex networks. It doesn't take too much imagination to see that even with a modest network, perhaps of a few hundred machines, maintaining the relevant routing tables can be a complex task.

If you wish to save yourself the effort of entering and maintaining static routing tables it is necessary to implement some form of *dynamic* routing.

With dynamic routing the routers themselves talk to each other and advertise the networks they are connected to. Using this information they then update their routing tables accordingly.

There are two major types of dynamic routing algorithm found in "standard" computer systems. Other, proprietary, algorithms exist but these are usually associated with specialist pieces of equipment.

These two algorithms are RIP (Routing Information Protocol) and OSPF (Open Shortest Path First). OSPF is by far the more sophisticated algorithm. It is efficient, relatively fast, relatively secure and is not, at the time of writing, implemented as standard on Microsoft-based systems.

RIP was the original dynamic routing protocol. It is now generally considered slow, inefficient, not fault-tolerant and it transfers data by broadcasts. My experience is that it is quite suitable for the smaller network. I have successfully implemented systems of a few hundred computers and 5 to 10 routers using RIP. On smaller intranets the limitations of RIP do not manifest themselves too often.

As such, and because it is supplied as standard on NT 4.0, I think it is quite suitable for smaller networked systems. A later version of RIP called RIP-2 deals with many of the shortcomings of RIP. If RIP-2 is available on your system it should be used in place of RIP. All of the following discussion applies both to RIP and RIP-2.

We will use RIP to illustrate the benefits of dynamic routing. Should you decide to implement dynamic routing on a network system I would strongly suggest that you analyse the data requirements and the network traffic implications before any decision is made as to which dynamic routing algorithm to use.

Setting up RIP on NT

Before we can utilise the benefits of RIP on our simple network we have to install the software on our NT machine. Figure 12.13 shows how this is done. In the Network applet of the Control Panel we select the Services tab and then the Add button. This opens up the dialog shown in Figure 12.13. We can now select the RIP for IP Protocol service and choose OK. The service is then installed. A separate version of RIP for IPX is also provided, should we require it.

Figure 12.13 Adding the RIP service

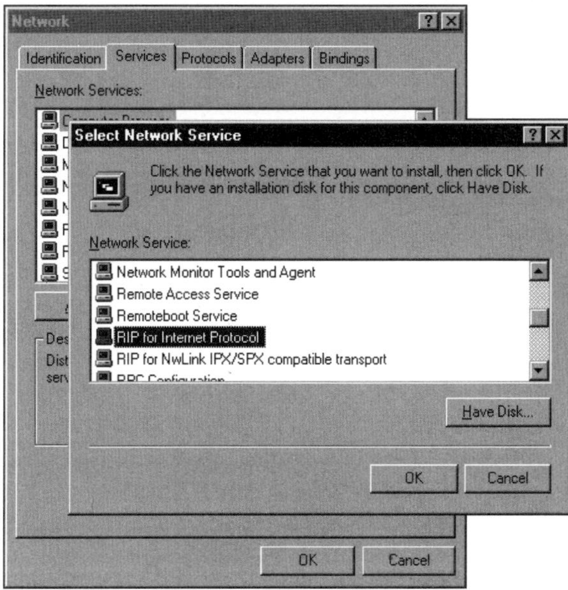

Once installed we have to start the RIP service. Figure 12.14 shows how this is done. We select the Services applet in Control Panel and then drill down to the RIP for IP service. After clicking on this to select it we click the Start button on the right of the dialog box. This opens the dialog shown in Figure 12.14 and the service starts.

Figure 12.14 Manually starting RIP

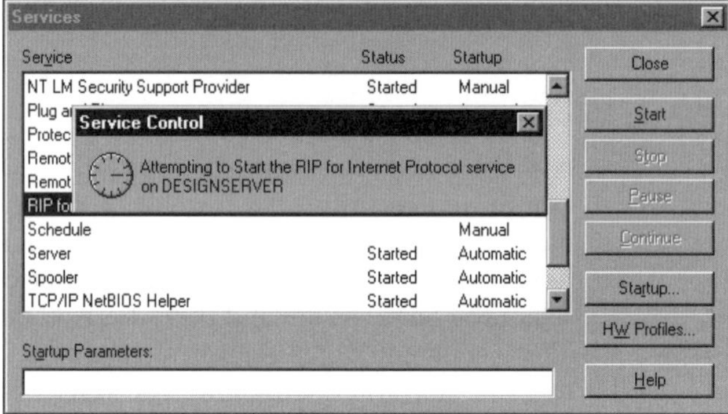

Since RIP is going to be a key part of our networking strategy it is important that it starts automatically when the computer restarts. We have to configure this using the same dialog box presented in Figure 12.14.

Figure 12.15 shows this. Here we have selected RIP for IP and then chosen the Startup button on the right of the dialog box. This presents us with the dialog box shown in Figure 12.15, from which we can select the type of startup required. The selection of Automatic means that the RIP service will commence automatically whenever the server restarts.

Figure 12.15 Configuring the RIP service to start automatically

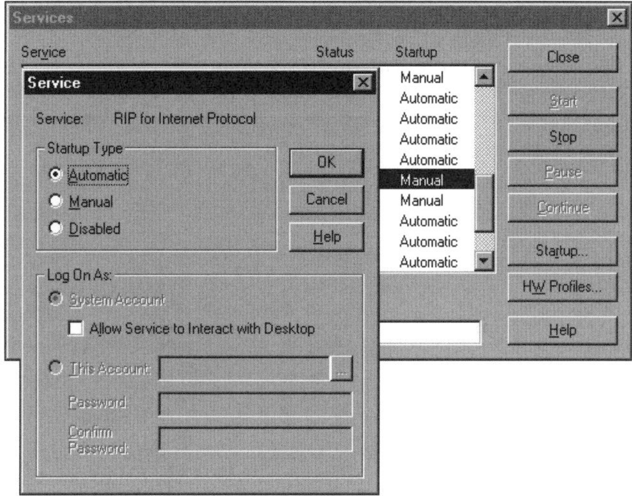

Dynamic Table Updates

Once RIP has been installed and started on both the routers, the two computers update information and share their routing tables regularly. Figure 12.16 shows the design router's table immediately after RIP has been started.

Figure 12.16 Initial design routing table after RIP protocol has started

```
Microsoft(R) Windows NT(TM)
(C) Copyright 1985-1996 Microsoft Corp.

C:\>route print

Active Routes:

  Network Address          Netmask  Gateway Address        Interface  Metric
        10.20.20.0    255.255.255.0      10.20.20.20      10.20.20.20       1
       10.20.20.20  255.255.255.255        127.0.0.1        127.0.0.1       1
        10.20.30.0    255.255.255.0       10.20.30.5       10.20.30.5       1
        10.20.30.5  255.255.255.255        127.0.0.1        127.0.0.1       1
        10.20.70.0    255.255.255.0       10.20.70.1       10.20.30.5       1
        10.20.70.1  255.255.255.255        127.0.0.1        127.0.0.1       1
    10.255.255.255  255.255.255.255      10.20.20.20      10.20.20.20       1
         127.0.0.0        255.0.0.0        127.0.0.1        127.0.0.1       1
         224.0.0.0        224.0.0.0       10.20.30.5       10.20.30.5       1
         224.0.0.0        224.0.0.0      10.20.20.20      10.20.20.20       1
   255.255.255.255  255.255.255.255      10.20.20.20      10.20.20.20       1

C:\>
```

There is nothing different to our previous initial table in Figure 12.5. In other words, the routers have not yet exchanged information. After a couple of minutes the two routing tables (for the design and office routers) are as shown in Figures 12.17 and 12.18.

Figure 12.17 Dynamic table for the design router

```
Microsoft(R) Windows NT(TM)
(C) Copyright 1985-1996 Microsoft Corp.

C:\>route print

Active Routes:

  Network Address          Netmask  Gateway Address        Interface  Metric
       10.20.20.0    255.255.255.0      10.20.20.20      10.20.20.20       1
      10.20.20.20  255.255.255.255        127.0.0.1        127.0.0.1       1
       10.20.30.0    255.255.255.0       10.20.30.5       10.20.30.5       1
       10.20.30.5  255.255.255.255        127.0.0.1        127.0.0.1       1
       10.20.40.0    255.255.255.0       10.20.20.2      10.20.20.20       3
       10.20.50.0    255.255.255.0       10.20.20.2      10.20.20.20       3
       10.20.70.0    255.255.255.0       10.20.70.1       10.20.30.5       1
       10.20.70.1  255.255.255.255        127.0.0.1        127.0.0.1       1
   10.255.255.255  255.255.255.255      10.20.20.20      10.20.20.20       1
        127.0.0.0        255.0.0.0        127.0.0.1        127.0.0.1       1
        224.0.0.0        224.0.0.0       10.20.30.5       10.20.30.5       1
        224.0.0.0        224.0.0.0      10.20.20.20      10.20.20.20       1
  255.255.255.255  255.255.255.255      10.20.20.20      10.20.20.20       1

C:\>
```

Figure 12.18 Dynamic table for the office router

```
Microsoft(R) Windows NT(TM)
(C) Copyright 1985-1996 Microsoft Corp.

C:\>route print

Active Routes:

  Network Address          Netmask  Gateway Address        Interface  Metric
          0.0.0.0          0.0.0.0       10.20.40.5       10.20.40.2       1
       10.20.20.0    255.255.255.0       10.20.20.2       10.20.20.2       1
       10.20.20.2  255.255.255.255        127.0.0.1        127.0.0.1       1
       10.20.30.0    255.255.255.0      10.20.20.20       10.20.20.2       3
       10.20.40.0    255.255.255.0       10.20.40.2       10.20.40.2       1
       10.20.40.2  255.255.255.255        127.0.0.1        127.0.0.1       1
       10.20.50.0    255.255.255.0       10.20.50.2       10.20.40.2       1
       10.20.50.2  255.255.255.255        127.0.0.1        127.0.0.1       1
       10.20.70.0    255.255.255.0      10.20.20.20       10.20.20.2       3
   10.255.255.255  255.255.255.255       10.20.20.2       10.20.20.2       1
        127.0.0.0        255.0.0.0        127.0.0.1        127.0.0.1       1
        224.0.0.0        224.0.0.0       10.20.20.2       10.20.20.2       1
  255.255.255.255  255.255.255.255       10.20.20.2       10.20.20.2       1

C:\>
```

These updated tables have been produced automatically with no static entries and they look very similar to our manually updated tables. Since the routers exchange information every couple of minutes (by default) any changes to the network design will be conveyed across the network and the associated routing tables updated in a short period of time.

The metric values for the remote networks are different from our static entries and these reflect the fact that the RIP algorithm calculates its metrics differently to our simple assumptions. To understand what is happening in this metric calculation let us consider the situation in the office router. This is the router table shown in Figure 12.18. The metrics to the "30" and the "70" networks are calculated as 3. This calculation is as follows: all of the networks that the office router is directly connected to have a metric of 1. To get to the "30" network the router has to go across 1 other network (10.20.20.0) and then beyond the "far" router to network 10.20.30.0. This represents two additional jumps and so the metric increases to 3. The same applies to the metric for the "70" network.

Apart from the metric differences the rest of the information on the routing tables is identical to that on the tables produced from our static entries. The benefits of dynamic routing are that network changes are communicated to the routers within a few minutes and that no static entries need to be added to retain network connectivity.

In the examples above we have used the standard RIP installation that comes with NT4.0. In addition to this Microsoft has produced an excellent implementation of a software router. This is called RRAS (Routing and Remote Access Server) and is available for download (free of charge) from:

`http://www.microsoft.com/msdownload/`

This server includes RIP, RIP-2 (an improved RIP), OSPF and a very comprehensive management interface. It allows you to turn all those "low-powered pentium" machines into low-cost routers. For cost-effective small network routing it is an excellent solution.

Appendix A
Useful RFCs

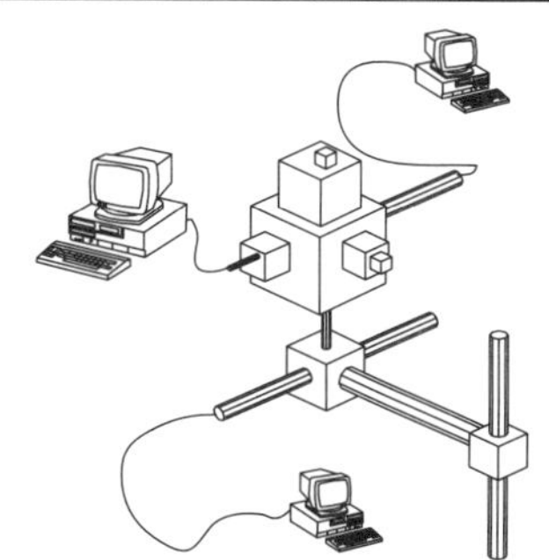

RFCs dealing with subnets

- 0917 *Internet subnets*. This covers the original "basics" of subnet design.
- 0922 *Broadcasting Internet datagrams in the presence of subnets*. This is a discussion of broadcast issues with subnets.

CIDR

- 1467 *Status of CIDR Deployment in the Internet*. Discussion about the role of CIDR in subnet design.
- 1518 *An Architecture for IP Address Allocation with CIDR*. A long paper comprehensively discussing the details of CIDR.
- 1519 *Classless Inter-Domain Routing (CIDR)*. Discusses address assignment and the implications to a CIDR-based network.
- 1817 *CIDR and Classful Routing*. A discussion of the implication of CIDR to routing issues.

DHCP

- 1533 *DHCP Options and BOOTP Vendor Extensions*. Discusses the various options under DHCP and BOOTP.
- 1534 *Interoperation Between DHCP and BOOTP*. Covers what it says!
- 2132 *DHCP Options and BOOTP Vendor Extensions*. Updates on the DHCP options.
- 2241 *DHCP Options for Novell Directory Services*. An update of DHCP options for Novell based systems.
- 2489 *Procedure for Defining New DHCP Options*. A discussion of new DHCP options.

All obtained from HyperRFC at `www.csl.sony.co.ip/rfc/`

Appendix B
The InterNIC Web Site

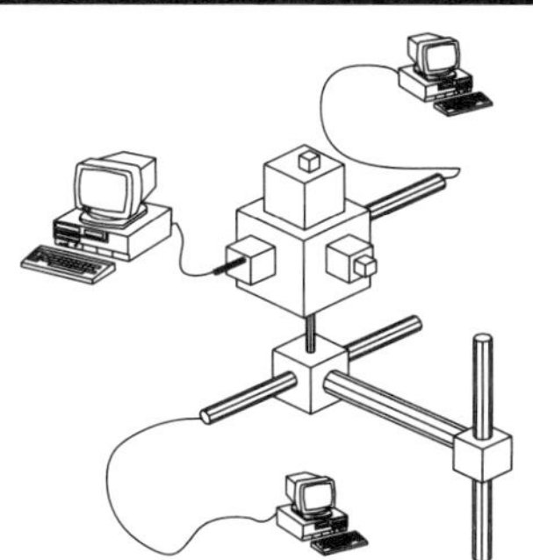

Registering your domain name and other IP matters. Do it from InterNIC at `http://www.internic.net`

The next two diagrams show screen shots from the initial Internic page. These illustrate the initial stages in gaining domain registration and some additional information.

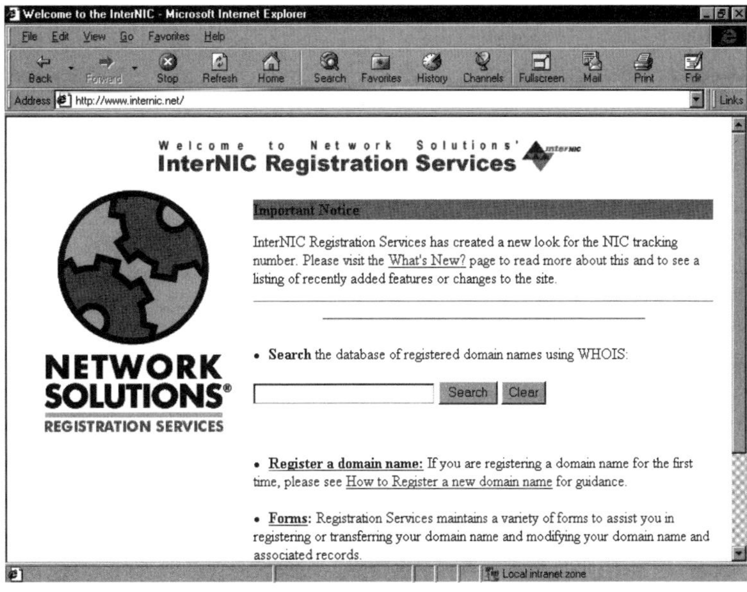

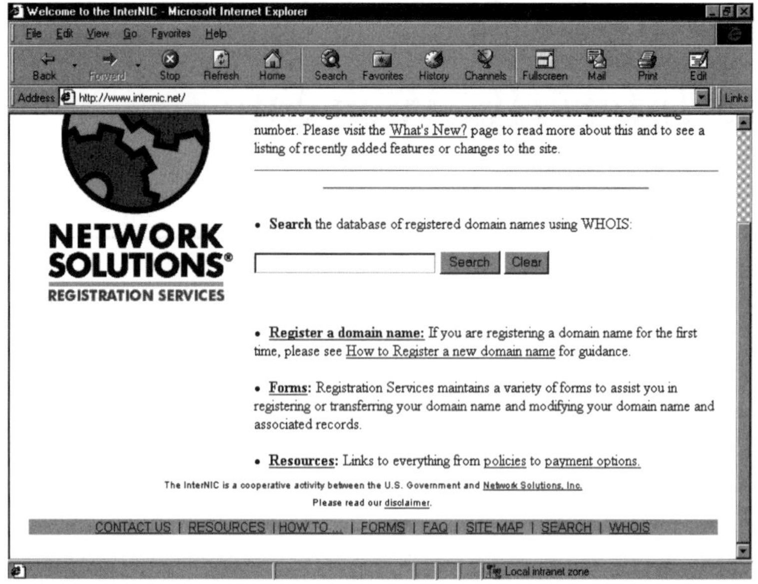
Welcome to the InterNIC - Microsoft Internet Explorer
File Edit View Go Favorites Help
Back Forward Stop Refresh Home Search Favorites History Channels Fullscreen Mail Print Edit
Address http://www.internic.net/
Links
number. Please visit the What's New? page to read more about this and to see a listing of recently added features or changes to the site.
NETWORK SOLUTIONS®
REGISTRATION SERVICES
• Search the database of registered domain names using WHOIS:
Search Clear
• Register a domain name: If you are registering a domain name for the first time, please see How to Register a new domain name for guidance.
• Forms: Registration Services maintains a variety of forms to assist you in registering or transferring your domain name and modifying your domain name and associated records.
• Resources: Links to everything from policies to payment options.
The InterNIC is a cooperative activity between the U.S. Government and Network Solutions, Inc.
Please read our disclaimer.
CONTACT US | RESOURCES | HOW TO ... | FORMS | FAQ | SITE MAP | SEARCH | WHOIS
Local intranet zone

Appendix C
Some Sample Questions on Subnets

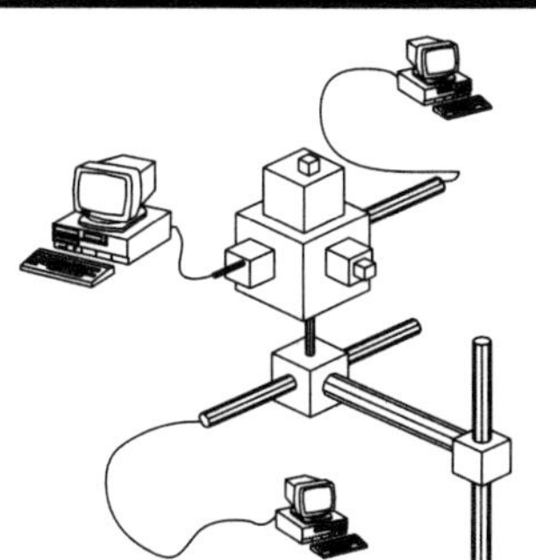

The correct answers are marked with an asterisk (*). For a more extensive range of questions and a list of practice examinations covering MCSE, CISCO and CNE examinations contact

`http://www.bfq.com`

and fill in the registration forms.

1. You have been assigned a network identifier of 195.5.2.0. Which subnet mask will give you the maximum hosts per subnet?

   A. 255.248.0.0
   B.* 255.255.255.0
   C. 255.255.248.0
   D. 255.255.255.192

2. In the example above what is the maximum number of machines that could be put on the above subnet?

   A. 255
   B. 256
   C.* 254
   D. 248

3. In question 1., how many networks would be available using the subnet mask for the maximum number of hosts?

   A. 2
   B. 255
   C. 0
   D.* 1

4. Assuming a default subnet mask, what is the network identifier of 133.13.30.1.

   A. 133.13.30.1
   B. 133.0.0.0
   C. 255.255.30.1
   D.* 133.13.0.0

5. You have a class B network address and have 25 sites and expect to grow to 45 in the next few years. Which of the following subnet masks will provide sufficient subnets with the maximum number of hosts on each?

   A.* 255.255.252.0
   B. 255.255.192.0
   C. 255.255.254.0
   D. 255.255.128.0

6. Assuming an IP address of 129.212.131.254, what would be the class and the default subnet mask for that class?

   A. Class C, 255.255.255.0
   B. Class A, 255.255.255.0
   C. Class A, 255.0.0.0
   D.* Class B, 255.255.0.0

7. From the list below select the valid hosts on a network of 147.14.12.0 with a subnet mask of 255.255.255.0.

   A. 147.14.12.255
   B.* 147.14.12.30
   C. 147.14.12.0
   D.* 147.14.12.60

8. Irrespective of the number of hosts on each subnet, which of the following subnet masks will give you exactly 30 legal subnets should the mask be used to subnet the associated network?

   A.* 255.255.248.0
   B. 255.255.255.0
   C.* 255.248.0.0
   D. 255.255.255.248

9. Assuming a default subnet mask for this IP address, what is the network identifier of 194.250.25.1?

   A. 194.250.0.0
   B.* 194.250.25.0
   C. 194.0.0.0
   D. 194.255.255.0

10. You are given an address of 218.134.154.0 and you need 5 subnets with at least 20 hosts per network ID. Which subnet mask could be used?

    A.* 255.255.255.224
    B.* 255.255.255.240
    C. 255.255.0.0
    D. 255.255.255.192

Appendix D
RFC 1518

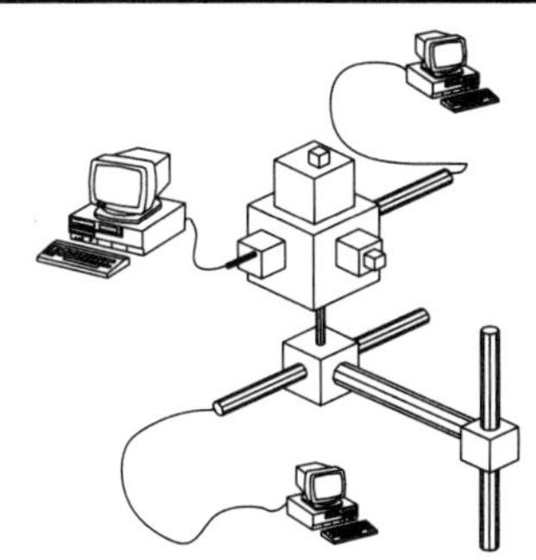

Preface to Appendix D

When teaching my classes many students have expressed an interest in "seeing" one or two RFCs without wanting to go to the trouble of locating and downloading them. I include the following RFC for two reasons:

1. Because it allows the interested reader to see the detail into which the RFC goes when covering the topic of classless routing. The various arguments in favour of one approach over another are covered. As such, it is a good example of a "standard" RFC.
2. For the reader who does not want to bother with locating and downloading any RFCs it allows them to see what the RFC format and structure is like.

An Architecture for IP Address Allocation with CIDR

Y. Rekhter *T.J. Watson Research Center, IBM Corp.*
T. Li *cisco Systems*
September 1993

Status of this Memo

This RFC specifies an Internet standards track protocol for the Internet community, and requests discussion and suggestions for improvements. Please refer to the current edition of the "Internet Official Protocol Standards" for the standardization state and status of this protocol. Distribution of this memo is unlimited.

1. Introduction

This paper provides an architecture and a plan for allocating IP addresses in the Internet. This architecture and the plan are intended to play an important role in steering the Internet towards the Address Assignment and Aggregating Strategy outlined in [1].

The IP address space is a scarce shared resource that must be managed for the good of the community. The managers of this resource are acting as its custodians. They have a responsibility to the community to manage it for the common good.

2. Scope

The global Internet can be modeled as a collection of hosts interconnected via transmission and switching facilities. Control over the collection of hosts and the transmission and switching facilities that compose the networking resources of the global Internet is not homogeneous, but is distributed among multiple administrative authorities. Resources under control of a single administration form a domain. For the rest of this paper, "domain" and "routing domain" will be used interchangeably. Domains that share their resources with other domains are called network service providers (or just providers). Domains that utilize other domain's resources are called network service subscribers (or just subscribers). A given domain may act as a provider and a subscriber simultaneously.

There are two aspects of interest when discussing IP address allocation within the Internet. The first is the set of administrative requirements for obtaining and allocating IP addresses; the second is the technical aspect of such assignments, having largely to do with routing, both within a routing domain (intra-domain routing) and between routing domains (inter-domain routing). This paper focuses on the technical issues.

In the current Internet many routing domains (such as corporate and campus networks) attach to transit networks (such as regionals) in only one or a small number of carefully controlled access points. The former act as subscribers, while the latter act as providers.

The architecture and recommendations provided in this paper are intended for immediate deployment. This paper specifically does not address long-term research issues, such as complex policy-based routing requirements.

Addressing solutions which require substantial changes or constraints on the current topology are not considered.

The architecture and recommendations in this paper are oriented primarily toward the large-scale division of IP address allocation in the Internet. Topics covered include:

- Benefits of encoding some topological information in IP addresses to significantly reduce routing protocol overhead;
- The anticipated need for additional levels of hierarchy in Internet addressing to support network growth;
- The recommended mapping between Internet topological entities (i.e., service providers, and service subscribers) and IP addressing and routing components;
- The recommended division of IP address assignment among service providers (e.g., backbones, regionals), and service subscribers (e.g., sites);
- Allocation of the IP addresses by the Internet Registry;
- Choice of the high-order portion of the IP addresses in leaf routing domains that are connected to more than one service provider (e.g., backbone or a regional network).

It is noted that there are other aspects of IP address allocation, both technical and administrative, that are not covered in this paper.

Topics not covered or mentioned only superficially include:

- Identification of specific administrative domains in the Internet;
- Policy or mechanisms for making registered information known to third parties (such as the entity to which a specific IP address or a portion of the IP address space has been allocated);
- How a routing domain (especially a site) should organize its internal topology or allocate portions of its IP address space; the relationship between topology and addresses is discussed, but the method of deciding on a particular topology or internal addressing plan is not; and,
- Procedures for assigning host IP addresses.

3. Background

Some background information is provided in this section that is helpful in understanding the issues involved in IP address allocation. A brief discussion of IP routing is provided.

IP partitions the routing problem into three parts:

- routing exchanges between end systems and routers (ARP),
- routing exchanges between routers in the same routing domain (interior routing), and,
- routing among routing domains (exterior routing).

4. IP Addresses and Routing

For the purposes of this paper, an IP prefix is an IP address and some indication of the leftmost contiguous significant bits within this address. Throughout this paper IP address prefixes will be expressed as <IP-address IP-mask> tuples, such that a bitwise logical AND operation on the IP-address and IP-mask components of a tuple yields the sequence of leftmost contiguous significant bits that form the IP address prefix. For example a tuple with the value <193.1.0.0 255.255.0.0> denotes an IP address prefix with 16 leftmost contiguous significant bits.

When determining an administrative policy for IP address assignment, it is important to understand the technical consequences. The objective behind the use of hierarchical routing is to achieve some level of routing data abstraction, or summarization, to reduce the cpu, memory, and transmission bandwidth consumed in support of routing.

While the notion of routing data abstraction may be applied to various types of routing information, this paper focuses on one particular type, namely reachability information. Reachability information describes the set of reachable destinations. Abstraction of reachability information dictates that IP addresses be assigned according to topological routing structures. However, administrative assignment falls along organizational or political boundaries. These may not be congruent to topological boundaries and therefore the requirements of the two may collide. It is necessary to find a balance between these two needs.

Routing data abstraction occurs at the boundary between hierarchically arranged topological routing structures. An element lower in the hierarchy reports summary routing information to its parent(s).

At routing domain boundaries, IP address information is exchanged (statically or dynamically) with other routing domains. If IP addresses within a routing domain are all drawn from non-contiguous IP address spaces (allowing no abstraction), then the boundary information consists of an enumerated list of all the IP addresses.

Alternatively, should the routing domain draw IP addresses for all the hosts within the domain from a single IP address prefix, boundary routing information can be summarized into the single IP address prefix. This permits substantial data reduction and allows better scaling (as compared to the uncoordinated addressing discussed in the previous paragraph).

If routing domains are interconnected in a more-or-less random (i.e., non-hierarchical) scheme, it is quite likely that no further abstraction of routing data can occur. Since routing domains would have no defined hierarchical relationship, administrators would not be able to assign IP addresses within the domains out of some common prefix for the purpose of data abstraction. The result would be flat inter-domain routing; all routing domains would need explicit knowledge of all other routing domains that they route to. This can work well in small and medium sized internets. However, this does not scale to very large internets. For example, we expect growth in the future to an Internet which has tens or hundreds of thousands of routing domains in North America alone. This requires a greater degree of the reachability information abstraction beyond that which can be achieved at the "routing domain" level.

In the Internet, however, it should be possible to significantly constrain the volume and the complexity of routing information by taking advantage of the existing hierarchical interconnectivity, as discussed in Section 5. Thus, there is the opportunity for a group of routing domains each to be assigned an address prefix from a shorter prefix assigned to another routing domain whose function is to interconnect the group of routing domains. Each member of the group of routing domains now has its (somewhat longer) prefix, from which it assigns its addresses.

The most straightforward case of this occurs when there is a set of routing domains which are all attached to a single service provider domain (e.g., regional network), and which use that provider for all external (inter-domain) traffic. A small prefix may be given to the provider, which then gives slightly longer prefixes (based on the provider's prefix) to each of the routing domains that it interconnects. This allows the provider, when informing other routing domains of the addresses that it can reach, to abbreviate the reachability information for a large number of routing domains as a single prefix. This approach therefore can allow a great deal of hierarchical abbreviation of routing information, and thereby can greatly improve the scalability of inter-domain routing.

Clearly, this approach is recursive and can be carried through several iterations. Routing domains at any "level" in the hierarchy may use their prefix as the basis for subsequent suballocations, assuming that the IP addresses remain within the overall length and structure constraints.

At this point, we observe that the number of nodes at each lower level of a hierarchy tends to grow exponentially. Thus the greatest gains in the reachability information abstraction (for the benefit of all higher levels of the hierarchy) occur when the reachability information aggregation occurs near the leaves of the hierarchy; the gains drop significantly at each higher level. Therefore, the law of diminishing returns suggests that at some point data abstraction ceases to produce significant benefits. Determination of the point at which data abstraction ceases to be of benefit requires a careful consideration of the number of routing domains that are expected to occur at each level of the hierarchy (over a given period of time), compared to the number of routing domains and address prefixes that can conveniently and efficiently be handled via dynamic inter-domain routing protocols.

4.1 Efficiency versus Decentralized Control

If the Internet plans to support a decentralized address administration [4], then there is a balance that must be sought between the requirements on IP addresses for efficient routing and the need for decentralized address administration. A proposal described in [3] offers an example of how these two needs might be met.

The IP address prefix <198.0.0.0 254.0.0.0> provides for administrative decentralization. This prefix identifies part of the IP address space allocated for North America. The lower order part of that prefix allows allocation of IP addresses along topological boundaries in support of increased data abstraction. Clients within North America use parts of the IP address space that is underneath the IP address space of their service providers. Within a routing domain addresses for subnetworks and hosts are allocated from the unique IP prefix assigned to the domain.

5. IP Address Administration and Routing in the Internet

The basic Internet routing components are service providers (e.g., backbones, regional networks), and service subscribers (e.g., sites or campuses). These components are arranged hierarchically for the most part. A natural mapping from these components to IP routing components is that providers and subscribers act as routing domains.

Alternatively, a subscriber (e.g., a site) may choose to operate as a part of a domain formed by a service provider. We assume that some, if not most, sites will prefer to operate as part of their provider's routing domain. Such sites can exchange routing information with their provider via interior routing protocol route leaking or via an exterior routing protocol. For the purposes of this discussion, the choice is not significant. The site is still allocated a prefix from the provider's address space, and the provider will advertise its own prefix into inter-domain routing.

Given such a mapping, where should address administration and allocation be performed to satisfy both administrative decentralization and data abstraction? The following possibilities are considered:

- at some part within a routing domain,
- at the leaf routing domain,
- at the transit routing domain (TRD), and
- at the continental boundaries.

A point within a routing domain corresponds to a subnetwork. If a domain is composed of multiple subnetworks, they are interconnected via routers. Leaf routing domains correspond to sites, where the primary purpose is to provide intra-domain routing services. Transit routing domains are deployed to carry transit (i.e., inter-domain) traffic; backbones and providers are TRDs.

The greatest burden in transmitting and operating on routing information is at the top of the routing hierarchy, where routing information tends to accumulate. In the Internet, for example, providers must manage the set of network numbers for all networks reachable through the provider. Traffic destined for other providers is generally routed to the backbones (which act as providers as well). The backbones, however, must be cognizant of the network numbers for all attached providers and their associated networks.

In general, the advantage of abstracting routing information at a given level of the routing hierarchy is greater at the higher levels of the hierarchy. There is relatively little direct benefit to the administration that performs the abstraction, since it must maintain routing information individually on each attached topological routing structure.

For example, suppose that a given site is trying to decide whether to obtain an IP address prefix directly from the IP address space allocated for North America, or from the IP address space allocated to its service provider. If considering only their own self-interest, the site itself and the attached provider have little reason to choose one approach or the other. The site must use one prefix or another; the source of the prefix has little effect on routing efficiency within the site. The provider must maintain information about each attached site in order to route, regardless of any commonality in the prefixes of the sites.

However, there is a difference when the provider distributes routing information to other providers (e.g., backbones or TRDs). In the first case, the provider cannot aggregate the site's address into its own prefix; the address must be explicitly listed in routing exchanges, resulting in an additional burden to other providers which must exchange and maintain this information.

In the second case, each other provider (e.g., backbone or TRD) sees a single address prefix for the provider, which encompasses the new site. This avoids the exchange of additional routing information to identify the new site's address prefix. Thus, the advantages primarily accrue to other providers which maintain routing information about this site and provider.

One might apply a supplier/consumer model to this problem: the higher level (e.g., a backbone) is a supplier of routing services, while the lower level (e.g., a TRD) is the consumer of these services. The price charged for services is based upon the cost of providing them. The overhead of managing a large table of addresses for routing to an attached topological entity contributes to this cost.

The Internet, however, is not a market economy. Rather, efficient operation is based on cooperation. The recommendations discussed below describe simple and tractable ways of managing the IP address space that benefit the entire community.

5.1 Administration of IP addresses within a domain

If individual subnetworks take their IP addresses from a myriad of unrelated IP address spaces, there will be effectively no data abstraction beyond what is built into existing intra-domain routing protocols. For example, assume that within a routing domain uses three independent prefixes assigned from three different IP address spaces associated with three different attached providers.

This has a negative effect on inter-domain routing, particularly on those other domains which need to maintain routes to this domain. There is no common prefix that can be used to represent these IP addresses and therefore no summarization can take place at the routing domain boundary. When addresses are advertised by this routing domain to other routing domains, an enumerated list of the three individual prefixes must be used.

This situation is roughly analogous to the present dissemination of routing information in the Internet, where each domain may have non-contiguous network numbers assigned to it. The result of allowing subnetworks within a routing domain to take their IP addresses from unrelated IP address spaces is flat routing at the A/B/C class network level. The number of IP prefixes that leaf routing domains would advertise is on the order of the number of attached network numbers; the number of prefixes a provider's routing domain would advertise is approximately the number of network numbers attached to the client leaf routing domains; and for a backbone this would be summed across all attached providers. This situation is just barely acceptable in the current Internet, and as the Internet grows this will quickly become intractable. A greater degree of hierarchical information reduction is necessary to allow continued growth in the Internet.

5.2 Administration at the Leaf Routing Domain

As mentioned previously, the greatest degree of data abstraction comes at the lowest levels of the hierarchy. Providing each leaf routing domain (that is, site) with a prefix from its provider's prefix results in the biggest single increase in abstraction. From outside the leaf routing domain, the set of all addresses reachable in the domain can then be represented by a single prefix. Further, all destinations reachable within the provider's prefix can be represented by a single prefix.

For example, consider a single campus which is a leaf routing domain which would currently require 4 different IP networks. Under the new allocation scheme, they might instead be given a single prefix which provides the same number of destination addresses. Further, since the prefix is a subset of the provider's prefix, they impose no additional burden on the higher levels of the routing hierarchy.

There is a close relationship between subnetworks and routing domains implicit in the fact that they operate a common routing protocol and are under the control of a single administration. The routing domain administration subdivides the domain into subnetworks. The routing domain represents the only path between a subnetwork and the rest of the internetwork. It is reasonable that this relationship also extend to include a common IP addressing space. Thus, the subnetworks within the leaf routing domain should take their IP addresses from the prefix assigned to the leaf routing domain.

5.3 Administration at the Transit Routing Domain

Two kinds of transit routing domains are considered, direct providers and indirect providers. Most of the subscribers of a direct provider are domains that act solely as service subscribers (they carry no transit traffic). Most of the subscribers of an indirect provider are domains that, themselves, act as service providers. In present terminology a backbone is an indirect provider, while a TRD is a direct provider. Each case is discussed separately below.

5.3.1 Direct Service Providers

It is interesting to consider whether direct service providers' routing domains should use their IP address space for assigning IP addresses from a unique prefix to the leaf routing domains that they serve. The benefits derived from data abstraction are greater than in the case of leaf routing domains, and the additional degree of data abstraction provided by this may be necessary in the short term.

As an illustration consider an example of a direct provider that serves 100 clients. If each client takes its addresses from 4 independent address spaces then the total number of entries that are needed to handle routing to these clients is 400 (100 clients times 4 providers). If each client takes its addresses from a single address space then the total number of entries would be only 100. Finally, if all the clients take their addresses from the same address space then the total number of entries would be only 1.

We expect that in the near term the number of routing domains in the Internet will grow to the point that it will be infeasible to route on the basis of a flat field of routing domains. It will therefore be essential to provide a greater degree of information abstraction.

Direct providers may give part of their address space (prefixes) to leaf domains, based on an address prefix given to the provider. This results in direct providers advertising to backbones a small fraction of the number of address prefixes that would be necessary if they enumerated the individual prefixes of the leaf routing domains. This represents a significant savings given the expected scale of global internetworking.

Are leaf routing domains willing to accept prefixes derived from the direct providers? In the supplier/consumer model, the direct provider is offering connectivity as the service, priced according to its costs of operation. This includes the "price" of obtaining service from one or more indirect providers (e.g., backbones). In general, indirect providers will want to handle as few address prefixes as possible to keep costs low. In the Internet environment, which does not operate as a typical marketplace, leaf routing domains must be sensitive to the resource constraints of the providers (both direct and indirect). The efficiencies gained in inter-domain routing clearly warrant the adoption of IP address prefixes derived from the IP address space of the providers.

The mechanics of this scenario are straightforward. Each direct provider is given a unique small set of IP address prefixes, from which its attached leaf routing domains can allocates slightly longer IP address prefixes. For example assume that NIST is a leaf routing domain whose inter-domain link is via SURANet. If SURANet is assigned an unique IP address prefix <198.1.0.0 255.255.0.0>, NIST could use a unique IP prefix of <198.1.0.0 255.255.240.0>.

If a direct service provider is connected to another provider(s) (either direct or indirect) via multiple attachment points, then in certain cases it may be advantageous to the direct provider to exert a certain degree of control over the coupling between the attachment points and flow of the traffic destined to a particular subscriber. Such control can be facilitated by first partitioning all the subscribers into groups, such that traffic destined to all the subscribers within a group should flow through a particular attachment point. Once the partitioning is done, the address space of the provider is subdivided along the group boundaries. A leaf routing domain that is willing to accept prefixes derived from its direct provider gets a prefix from the provider's address space subdivision associated with the group the domain belongs to. Note that the advertisement by the direct provider of the routing information associated with each subdivision must be done with care to ensure that such an advertisement would not result in a global distribution of separate reachability information associated with each subdivision, unless such distribution is warranted for some other purposes (e.g., supporting certain aspects of policy-based routing).

5.3.2 Indirect Providers (Backbones)

There does not appear to be a strong case for direct providers to take their address spaces from the IP space of an indirect provider (e.g., backbone). The benefit in routing data abstraction is relatively small. The number of direct providers today is in the tens and an order of magnitude increase would not cause an undue burden on the backbones. Also, it may be expected that as time goes by there will be increased direct interconnection of the direct providers, leaf routing domains directly attached to the backbones, and international links directly attached to the providers. Under these circumstances, the distinction between direct and indirect providers may become blurred.

An additional factor that discourages allocation of IP addresses from a backbone prefix is that the backbones and their attached providers are perceived as being independent. Providers may take their long-haul service from one or more backbones, or may switch backbones should a more cost-effective service be provided elsewhere. Having IP addresses derived from a backbone is inconsistent with the nature of the relationship.

5.4 Multi-homed Routing Domains

The discussions in Section 5.3 suggest methods for allocating IP addresses based on direct or indirect provider connectivity. This allows a great deal of information reduction to be achieved for those routing domains which are attached to a single TRD. In particular, such routing domains may select their IP addresses from a space delegated to them by the direct provider. This allows the provider, when announcing the addresses that it can reach to other providers, to use a single address prefix to describe a large number of IP addresses corresponding to multiple routing domains.

However, there are additional considerations for routing domains which are attached to multiple providers. Such "multi-homed" routing domains may, for example, consist of single-site campuses and companies which are attached to multiple backbones, large organizations which are attached to different providers at different locations in the same country, or multi-national organizations which are attached to backbones in a variety of countries worldwide. There are a number of possible ways to deal with these multi-homed routing domains.

One possible solution is for each multi-homed organization to obtain its IP address space independently from the providers to which it is attached. This allows each multi-homed organization to base its IP assignments on a single prefix, and to thereby summarize the set of all IP addresses reachable within that organization via a single prefix. The disadvantage of this approach is that since the IP address for that organization has no relationship to the addresses of any particular TRD, the TRDs to which this organization is attached will need to advertise the prefix for this organization to other providers. Other providers (potentially worldwide) will need to maintain an explicit entry for that organization in their routing tables.

For example, suppose that a very large North American company "Mega Big International Incorporated" (MBII) has a fully interconnected internal network and is assigned a single prefix as part of the North American prefix. It is likely that outside of North America, a single entry may be maintained in routing tables for all North American destinations. However, within North America, every provider will need to maintain a separate address entry for MBII. If MBII is in fact an international corporation, then it may be necessary for every provider worldwide to maintain a separate entry for MBII (including backbones to which MBII is not attached). Clearly this may be acceptable if there are a small number of such multi-homed routing domains, but would place an unacceptable load on routers within backbones if all organizations were to choose such address assignments. This solution may not scale to internets where there are many hundreds of thousands of multi-homed organizations.

A second possible approach would be for multi-homed organizations to be assigned a separate IP address space for each connection to a TRD, and to assign a single prefix to some subset of its domain(s) based on the closest interconnection point. For example, if MBII had connections to two providers in the U.S. (one east coast, and one west coast), as well as three connections to national backbones in Europe, and one in the far east, then MBII may make use of six different address prefixes. Each part of MBII would be assigned a single address prefix based on the nearest connection.

For purposes of external routing of traffic from outside MBII to a destination inside of MBII, this approach works similarly to treating MBII as six separate organizations. For purposes of internal routing, or for routing traffic from inside of MBII to a destination outside of MBII, this approach works the same as the first solution.

If we assume that incoming traffic (coming from outside of MBII, with a destination within MBII) is always to enter via the nearest point to the destination, then each TRD which has a connection to MBII needs to announce to other TRDs the ability to reach only those parts of MBII whose address is taken from its own address space. This implies that no additional routing information needs to be exchanged between TRDs, resulting in a smaller load on the inter-domain routing tables maintained by TRDs when compared to the first solution. This solution therefore scales better to extremely large internets containing very large numbers of multi- homed organizations.

One problem with the second solution is that backup routes to multi-homed organizations are not automatically maintained. With the first solution, each TRD, in announcing the ability to reach MBII, specifies that it is able to reach all of the hosts within MBII. With the second solution, each TRD announces that it can reach all of the hosts based on its own address prefix, which only includes some of the hosts within MBII. If the connection between MBII and one particular TRD were severed, then the hosts within MBII with addresses based on that TRD would become unreachable via inter-domain routing. The impact of this problem can be reduced somewhat by maintenance of additional information within routing tables, but this reduces the scaling advantage of the second approach.

The second solution also requires that when external connectivity changes, internal addresses also change.

Also note that this and the previous approach will tend to cause packets to take different routes. With the first approach, packets from outside of MBII destined for within MBII will tend to enter via the point which is closest to the source (which will therefore tend to maximize the load on the networks internal to MBII). With the second solution, packets from outside destined for within MBII will tend to enter via the point which is closest to the destination (which will tend to minimize the load on the networks within MBII, and maximize the load on the TRDs).

These solutions also have different effects on policies. For example, suppose that country "X" has a law that traffic from a source within country X to a destination within country X must at all times stay entirely within the country. With the first solution, it is not possible to determine from the destination address whether or not the destination is within the country. With the second solution, a separate address may be assigned to those hosts which are within country X, thereby allowing routing policies to be followed. Similarly, suppose that "Little Small Company" (LSC) has a policy that its packets may never be sent to a destination that is within MBII. With either solution, the routers within LSC may be configured to discard any traffic that has a destination within MBII's address space. However, with the first solution this requires one entry; with the second it requires many entries and may be impossible as a practical matter.

There are other possible solutions as well. A third approach is to assign each multi-homed organization a single address prefix, based on one of its connections to a TRD. Other TRDs to which the multi-homed organization are attached maintain a routing table entry for the organization, but are extremely selective in terms of which other TRDs are told of this route. This approach will produce a single "default" routing entry which all TRDs will know how to reach (since presumably all TRDs will maintain routes to each other), while providing more direct routing in some cases.

There is at least one situation in which this third approach is particularly appropriate. Suppose that a special interest group of organizations have deployed their own backbone. For example, lets suppose that the U.S. National Widget Manufacturers and Researchers have set up a U.S.-wide backbone, which is used by corporations who manufacture widgets, and certain universities which are known for their widget research efforts. We can expect that the various organizations which are in the widget group will run their internal networks as separate routing domains, and most of them will also be attached to other TRDs (since most of the organizations involved in widget manufacture and research will also be involved in other activities). We can therefore expect that many or most of the organizations in the widget group are dual-homed, with one attachment for widget-associated communications and the other attachment for other types of communications. Let's also assume that the total number of organizations involved in the widget group is small enough that it is reasonable to maintain a routing table containing one entry per organization, but that they are distributed throughout a larger internet with many millions of (mostly not widget-associated) routing domains.

With the third approach, each multi-homed organization in the widget group would make use of an address assignment based on its other attachment(s) to TRDs (the attachments not associated with the widget group). The widget backbone would need to maintain routes to the routing domains associated with the various member organizations. Similarly, all members of the widget group would need to maintain a table of routes to the other members via the widget backbone. However, since the widget backbone does not inform other general worldwide TRDs of what addresses it can reach (since the backbone is not intended for use by other outside organizations), the relatively large set of routing prefixes needs to be maintained only in a limited number of places. The addresses assigned to the various organizations which are members of the widget group would provide a "default route" via each members other attachments to TRDs, while allowing communications within the widget group to use the preferred path.

A fourth solution involves assignment of a particular address prefix for routing domains which are attached to precisely two (or more) specific routing domains. For example, suppose that there are two providers "SouthNorthNet" and "NorthSouthNet" which have a very large number of customers in common (i.e., there are a large number of routing domains which are attached to both). Rather than getting two address prefixes these organizations could obtain three prefixes. Those routing domains which are attached to NorthSouthNet but not attached to SouthNorthNet obtain an address assignment based on one of the prefixes. Those routing domains which are attached to SouthNorthNet but not to NorthSouthNet would obtain an address based on the second prefix. Finally, those routing domains which are multi-homed to both of these networks would obtain an address based on the third prefix. Each of these two TRDs would then advertise two prefixes to other TRDs, one prefix for leaf routing domains attached to it only, and one prefix for leaf routing domains attached to both.

This fourth solution is likely to be important when use of public data networks becomes more common. In particular, it is likely that at some point in the future a substantial percentage of all routing domains will be attached to public data networks. In this case, nearly all government-sponsored networks (such as some current regionals) may have a set of customers which overlaps substantially with the public networks.

There are therefore a number of possible solutions to the problem of assigning IP addresses to multi-homed routing domains. Each of these solutions has very different advantages and disadvantages. Each solution places a different real (i.e., financial) cost on the multi-homed organizations, and on the TRDs (including those to which the multi-homed organizations are not attached).

In addition, most of the solutions described also highlight the need for each TRD to develop policy on whether and under what conditions to accept addresses that are not based on its own address prefix, and how such non-local addresses will be treated. For example, a somewhat conservative policy might be that non- local IP address prefixes will be accepted from any attached leaf routing domain, but not advertised to other TRDs. In a less conservative policy, a TRD might accept such non-local prefixes and agree to exchange them with a defined set of other TRDs (this set could be an *a priori* group of TRDs that have something in common such as geographical location, or the result of an agreement specific to the requesting leaf routing domain). Various policies involve real costs to TRDs, which may be reflected in those policies.

5.5 Private Links

The discussion up to this point concentrates on the relationship between IP addresses and routing between various routing domains over transit routing domains, where each transit routing domain interconnects a large number of routing domains and offers a more-or-less public service.

However, there may also exist a number of links which interconnect two routing domains in such a way, that usage of these links may be limited to carrying traffic only between the two routing domains. We'll refer to such links as "private".

For example, let's suppose that the XYZ corporation does a lot of business with MBII. In this case, XYZ and MBII may contract with a carrier to provide a private link between the two corporations, where this link may only be used for packets whose source is within one of the two corporations, and whose destination is within the other of the two corporations. Finally, suppose that the point-to-point link is connected between a single router (router X) within XYZ corporation and a single router (router M) within MBII. It is therefore necessary to configure router X to know which addresses can be reached over this link (specifically, all addresses reachable in MBII). Similarly, it is necessary to configure router M to know which addresses can be reached over this link (specifically, all addresses reachable in XYZ Corporation).

The important observation to be made here is that the additional connectivity due to such private links may be ignored for the purpose of IP address allocation, and do not pose a problem for routing. This is because the routing information associated with such connectivity is not propagated throughout the Internet, and therefore does not need to be collapsed into a TRD's prefix.

In our example, let's suppose that the XYZ corporation has a single connection to a regional, and has therefore uses the IP address space from the space given to that regional. Similarly, let's suppose that MBII, as an international corporation with connections to six different providers, has chosen the second solution from Section 5.4, and therefore has obtained six different address allocations. In this case, all addresses reachable in the XYZ Corporation can be described by a single address prefix (implying that router M only needs to be configured with a single address prefix to represent the addresses reachable over this link). All addresses reachable in MBII can be described by six address prefixes (implying that router X needs to be configured with six address prefixes to represent the addresses reachable over the link).

In some cases, such private links may be permitted to forward traffic for a small number of other routing domains, such as closely affiliated organizations. This will increase the configuration requirements slightly. However, provided that the number of organizations using the link is relatively small, then this still does not represent a significant problem.

Note that the relationship between routing and IP addressing described in other sections of this paper is concerned with problems in scaling caused by large, essentially public transit routing domains which interconnect a large number of routing domains. However, for the purpose of IP address allocation, private links which interconnect only a small number of private routing domains do not pose a problem, and may be ignored. For example, this implies that a single leaf routing domain which has a single connection to a "public" backbone, plus a number of private links to other leaf routing domains, can be treated as if it were single-homed to the backbone for the purpose of IP address allocation. We expect that this is also another way of dealing with multi-homed domains.

5.6 Zero-Homed Routing Domains

Currently, a very large number of organizations have internal communications networks which are not connected to any service providers. Such organizations may, however, have a number of private links that they use for communications with other organizations. Such organizations do not participate in global routing, but are satisfied with reachability to those organizations with which they have established private links. These are referred to as zero-homed routing domains.

Zero-homed routing domains can be considered as the degenerate case of routing domains with private links, as discussed in the previous section, and do not pose a problem for inter-domain routing. As above, the routing information exchanged across the private links sees very limited distribution, usually only to the routing domain at the other end of the link. Thus, there are no address abstraction requirements beyond those inherent in the address prefixes exchanged across the private link.

However, it is important that zero-homed routing domains use valid globally unique IP addresses. Suppose that the zero-homed routing domain is connected through a private link to a routing domain. Further, this routing domain participates in an internet that subscribes to the global IP addressing plan. This domain must be able to distinguish between the zero-homed routing domain's IP addresses and any other IP addresses that it may need to route to. The only way this can be guaranteed is if the zero-homed routing domain uses globally unique IP addresses.

5.7 Continental aggregation

Another level of hierarchy may also be used in this addressing scheme to further reduce the amount of routing information necessary for inter-continental routing. Continental aggregation is useful because continental boundaries provide natural barriers to topological connection and administrative boundaries. Thus, it presents a natural boundary for another level of aggregation of inter-domain routing information. To make use of this, it is necessary that each continent be assigned an appropriate subset of the address space. Providers (both direct and indirect) within that continent would allocate their addresses from this space. Note that there are numerous exceptions to this, in which a service provider (either direct or indirect) spans a continental division. These exceptions can be handled similarly to multi- homed routing domains, as discussed above.

Note that, in contrast to the case of providers, the aggregation of continental routing information may not be done on the continent to which the prefix is allocated. The cost of inter- continental links (and especially trans-oceanic links) is very high. If aggregation is performed on the "near" side of the link, then routing information about unreachable destinations within that continent can only reside on that continent. Alternatively, if continental aggregation is done on the "far" side of an inter- continental link, the "far" end can perform the aggregation and inject it into continental routing. This means that destinations which are part of the continental aggregation, but for which there is not a corresponding more specific prefix can be rejected before leaving the continent on which they originated.

For example, suppose that Europe is assigned a prefix of <194.0.0.0 254.0.0.0>, such that European routing also contains the longer prefixes <194.1.0.0 255.255.0.0> and <194.2.0.0 255.255.0.0>. All of the longer European prefixes may be advertised across a trans-Atlantic link to North America. The router in North America would then aggregate these routes, and only advertise the prefix <194.0.0.0 255.0.0.0> into North American routing. Packets which are destined for 194.1.1.1 would traverse North American routing, but would encounter the North American router which performed the European aggregation. If the prefix <194.1.0.0 255.255.0.0> is unreachable, the router would drop the packet and send an ICMP Unreachable without using the trans-Atlantic link.

5.8 Transition Issues

Allocation of IP addresses based on connectivity to TRDs is important to allow scaling of inter-domain routing to an internet containing millions of routing domains. However, such address allocation based on topology implies that in order to maximize the efficiency in routing gained by such allocation, certain changes in topology may suggest a change of address.

Note that an address change need not happen immediately. A domain which has changed service providers may still advertise its prefix through its new service provider. Since upper levels in the routing hierarchy will perform routing based on the longest prefix, reachability is preserved, although the aggregation and scalability of the routing information has greatly diminished. Thus, a domain which does change its topology should change addresses as soon as convenient. The timing and mechanics of such changes must be the result of agreements between the old service provider, the new provider, and the domain.

This need to allow for change in addresses is a natural, inevitable consequence of routing data abstraction. The basic notion of routing data abstraction is that there is some correspondence between the address and where a system (i.e., a routing domain, subnetwork, or end system) is located. Thus if the system moves, in some cases the address will have to change. If it were possible to change the connectivity between routing domains without changing the addresses, then it would clearly be necessary to keep track of the location of that routing domain on an individual basis.

In the short term, due to the rapid growth and increased commercialization of the Internet, it is possible that the topology may be relatively volatile. This implies that planning for address transition is very important. Fortunately, there are a number of steps which can be taken to help ease the effort required for address transition. A complete description of address transition issues is outside of the scope of this paper. However, a very brief outline of some transition issues is contained in this section.

Also note that the possible requirement to transition addresses based on changes in topology imply that it is valuable to anticipate the future topology changes before finalizing a plan for address allocation. For example, in the case of a routing domain which is initially single-homed, but which is expecting to become multi-homed in the future, it may be advantageous to assign IP addresses based on the anticipated future topology.

In general, it will not be practical to transition the IP addresses assigned to a routing domain in an instantaneous "change the address at midnight" manner. Instead, a gradual transition is required in which both the old and the new addresses will remain valid for a limited period of time. During the transition period, both the old and new addresses are accepted by the end systems in the routing domain, and both old and new addresses must result in correct routing of packets to the destination.

During the transition period, it is important that packets using the old address be forwarded correctly, even when the topology has changed. This is facilitated by the use of "longest match" inter-domain routing.

For example, suppose that the XYZ Corporation was previously connected only to the NorthSouthNet regional. The XYZ Corporation therefore went off to the NorthSouthNet administration and got an IP address prefix assignment based on the IP address prefix value assigned to the NorthSouthNet regional. However, for a variety of reasons, the XYZ Corporation decided to terminate its association with the NorthSouthNet, and instead connect directly to the NewCommercialNet public data network. Thus the XYZ Corporation now has a new address assignment under the IP address prefix assigned to the NewCommercialNet. The old address for the XYZ Corporation would seem to imply that traffic for the XYZ Corporation should be routed to the NorthSouthNet, which no longer has any direct connection with XYZ Corporation.

If the old TRD (NorthSouthNet) and the new TRD (NewCommercialNet) are adjacent and cooperative, then this transition is easy to accomplish. In this case, packets routed to the XYZ Corporation using the old address assignment could be routed to the NorthSouthNet, which would directly forward them to the NewCommercialNet, which would in turn forward them to XYZ Corporation. In this case only NorthSouthNet and NewCommercialNet need be aware of the fact that the old address refers to a destination which is no longer directly attached to NorthSouthNet.

If the old TRD and the new TRD are not adjacent, then the situation is a bit more complex, but there are still several possible ways to forward traffic correctly.

If the old TRD and the new TRD are themselves connected by other cooperative transit routing domains, then these intermediate domains may agree to forward traffic for XYZ correctly. For example, suppose that NorthSouthNet and NewCommercialNet are not directly connected, but that they are both directly connected to the BBNet backbone. In this case, all three of NorthSouthNet, NewCommercialNet, and the BBNet backbone would need to maintain a special entry for XYZ corporation so that traffic to XYZ using the old address allocation would be forwarded via NewCommercialNet. However, other routing domains would not need to be aware of the new location for XYZ Corporation.

Suppose that the old TRD and the new TRD are separated by a noncooperative routing domain, or by a long path of routing domains. In this case, the old TRD could encapsulate traffic to XYZ Corporation in order to deliver such packets to the correct backbone.

Also, those locations which do a significant amount of business with XYZ Corporation could have a specific entry in their routing tables added to ensure optimal routing of packets to XYZ. For example, suppose that another commercial backbone "OldCommercialNet" has a large number of customers which exchange traffic with XYZ Corporation, and that this third TRD is directly connected to both NorthSouthNet and NewCommercialNet. In this case OldCommercialNet will continue to have a single entry in its routing tables for other traffic destined for NorthSouthNet, but may choose to add one additional (more specific) entry to ensure that packets sent to XYZ Corporation's old address are routed correctly.

Whichever method is used to ease address transition, the goal is that knowledge relating XYZ to its old address that is held throughout the global internet would eventually be replaced with the new information. It is reasonable to expect this to take weeks or months and will be accomplished through the distributed directory system. Discussion of the directory, along with other address transition techniques such as automatically informing the source of a changed address, are outside the scope of this paper.

Another significant transition difficulty is the establishment of appropriate addressing authorities. In order not to delay the deployment of this addressing scheme, if no authority has been created at an appropriate level, a higher level authority may allocated addresses instead of the lower level authority. For example, suppose that the continental authority has been allocated a portion of the address space and that the service providers present on that continent are clear, but have not yet established their addressing authority. The continental authority may foresee (possibly with information from the provider) that the provider will eventually create an authority. The continental authority may then act on behalf of that provider until the provider is prepared to assume its addressing authority duties.

Finally, it is important to emphasize, that a change of addresses due to changes in topology is not mandated by this document. The continental level addressing hierarchy, as discussed in Section 5.7, is intended to handle the aggregation of reachability information in the cases where addresses do not directly reflect the connectivity between providers and subscribers.

5.9 Interaction with Policy Routing

We assume that any inter-domain routing protocol will have difficulty trying to aggregate multiple destinations with dissimilar policies. At the same time, the ability to aggregate routing information while not violating routing policies is essential. Therefore, we suggest that address allocation authorities attempt to allocate addresses so that aggregates of destinations with similar policies can be easily formed.

6. Recommendations

We anticipate that the current exponential growth of the Internet will continue or accelerate for the foreseeable future. In addition, we anticipate a rapid internationalization of the Internet. The ability of routing to scale is dependent upon the use of data abstraction based on hierarchical IP addresses. As CIDR [1] is introduced in the Internet, it is therefore essential to choose a hierarchical structure for IP addresses with great care.

It is in the best interests of the internetworking community that the cost of operations be kept to a minimum where possible. In the case of IP address allocation, this again means that routing data abstraction must be encouraged.

In order for data abstraction to be possible, the assignment of IP addresses must be accomplished in a manner which is consistent with the actual physical topology of the Internet. For example, in those cases where organizational and administrative boundaries are not related to actual network topology, address assignment based on such organization boundaries is not recommended.

The intra-domain routing protocols allow for information abstraction to be maintained within a domain. For zero-homed and single-homed routing domains (which are expected to remain zero- homed or single-homed), we recommend that the IP addresses assigned within a single routing domain use a single address prefix assigned to that domain. Specifically, this allows the set of all IP addresses reachable within a single domain to be fully described via a single prefix.

We anticipate that the total number of routing domains existing on a worldwide Internet to be great enough that additional levels of hierarchical data abstraction beyond the routing domain level will be necessary.

In most cases, network topology will have a close relationship with national boundaries. For example, the degree of network connectivity will often be greater within a single country than between countries. It is therefore appropriate to make specific recommendations based on national boundaries, with the understanding that there may be specific situations where these general recommendations need to be modified.

6.1 Recommendations for an address allocation plan

We anticipate that public interconnectivity between private routing domains will be provided by a diverse set of TRDs, including (but not necessarily limited to):

- backbone networks (Alternet, ANSnet, CIX, EBone, PSI, SprintLink);
- a number of regional or national networks; and,
- a number of commercial Public Data Networks.

These networks will not be interconnected in a strictly hierarchical manner (for example, there is expected to be direct connectivity between regionals, and all of these types of networks may have direct international connections). However, the total number of such TRDs is expected to remain (for the foreseeable future) small enough to allow addressing of this set of TRDs via a flat address space. These TRDs will be used to interconnect a wide variety of routing domains, each of which may comprise a single corporation, part of a corporation, a university campus, a government agency, or other organizational unit.

In addition, some private corporations may be expected to make use of dedicated private TRDs for communication within their own corporation.

We anticipate that the great majority of routing domains will be attached to only one of the TRDs. This will permit hierarchical address aggregation based on TRD. We therefore strongly recommend that addresses be assigned hierarchically, based on address prefixes assigned to individual TRDs.

To support continental aggregation of routes, we recommend that all addresses for TRDs which are wholly within a continent be taken from the continental prefix.

For the proposed address allocation scheme, this implies that portions of IP address space should be assigned to each TRD (explicitly including the backbones and regionals). For those leaf routing domains which are connected to a single TRD, they should be assigned a prefix value from the address space assigned to that TRD.

For routing domains which are not attached to any publically available TRD, there is not the same urgent need for hierarchical address abbreviation. We do not, therefore, make any additional recommendations for such "isolated" routing domains. Where such domains are connected to other domains by private point-to-point links, and where such links are used solely for routing between the two domains that they interconnect, again no additional technical problems relating to address abbreviation is caused by such a link, and no specific additional recommendations are necessary.

Further, in order to allow aggregation of IP addresses at national and continental boundaries into as few prefixes as possible, we further recommend that IP addresses allocated to routing domains should be assigned based on each routing domain's connectivity to national and continental Internet backbones.

6.2 Recommendations for Multi-Homed Routing Domains

There are several possible ways that these multi-homed routing domains may be handled, as described in Section 5.4. Each of these methods vary with respect to the amount of information that must be maintained for inter-domain routing and also with respect to the inter-domain routes. In addition, the organization that will bear the brunt of this cost varies with the possible solutions. For example, the solutions vary with respect to:

- resources used within routers within the TRDs;
- administrative cost on TRD personnel; and,
- difficulty of configuration of policy-based inter-domain routing information within leaf routing domains.

Also, the solution used may affect the actual routes which packets follow, and may effect the availability of backup routes when the primary route fails.

For these reasons it is not possible to mandate a single solution for all situations. Rather, economic considerations will require a variety of solutions for different routing domains, service providers, and backbones.

6.3 Recommendations for the Administration of IP addresses

A companion document [3] provides recommendations for the administrations of IP addresses.

7. Acknowledgments

The authors would like to acknowledge the substantial contributions made by the authors of RFC 1237 [2], Richard Colella, Ella Gardner, and Ross Callon. The significant concepts (and a large portion of the text) in this document are taken directly from their work.

The authors would like to acknowledge the substantial contributions made by the members of the following two groups, the Federal Engineering Planning Group (FEPG) and the International Engineering Planning Group (IEPG). This document also reflects many concepts expressed at the IETF Addressing BOF which took place in Cambridge, MA in July 1992.

We would also like to thank Peter Ford (Los Alamos National Laboratory), Elise Gerich (MERIT), Steve Kent (BBN), Barry Leiner (ADS), Jon Postel (ISI), Bernhard Stockman (NORDUNET/SUNET), Claudio Topolcic (CNRI), and Kannan Varadhan (OARnet) for their review and constructive comments.

8. References

[1] Fuller, V., Li, T., Yu, J., and K. Varadhan, "Supernetting: an Address Assignment and Aggregation Strategy", RFC 1338, BARRNet, cicso, Merit, OARnet, June 1992.

[2] Colella, R., Gardner, E, and R. Callon, "Guidelines for OSI NSAP Allocation in the Internet", RFC 1237, JuNIST, Mitre, DEC, July 1991.

[3] Gerich, E., "Guidelines for Management of IP Address Space", RFC 1466, Merit, May 1993.

[4] Cerf, V., "IAB Recommended Policy on Distributing Internet Identifier Assignment and IAB Recommended Policy Change to Internet "Connected Status", RFC 1174, CNRI, August 1990.

9. Security Considerations

Security issues are not discussed in this memo.

10. Authors' Addresses

Yakov Rekhter
T.J. Watson Research Center, IBM Corporation
P.O. Box 218
Yorktown Heights, NY 10598

Phone: (914) 945-3896
E-mail: yakov@watson.ibm.com

Tony Li
cisco Systems, Inc.
1525 O'Brien Drive
Menlo Park, CA 94025

E-mail: tli@cisco.com

Index

Symbols

A—C

D—G

H—L

M—O

P—S

T—Z